e-service

e-service

24 ways to
keep your
customers
—when the
competition is
just a
<u>click</u> away

Ron Zemke   Tom Connellan

AMACOM
American Management Association
New York • Atlanta • Boston • Chicago • Kansas City • San Francisco • Washington, D.C.
Brussels • Mexico City • Tokyo • Toronto

Special discounts on bulk quantities of AMACOM books are available to corporations, professional associations, and other organizations. For details, contact Special Sales Department, AMACOM, a division of American Management Association, 1601 Broadway, New York, NY 10019
Tel.: 212-903-8316.   Fax: 212-903-8083.
Web Site: www.amacombooks.org

This publication is designed to provide accurate and authoritative information in regard to the subject matter covered. It is sold with the understanding that the publisher is not engaged in rendering legal, accounting, or other professional service. If legal advice or other expert assistance is required, the services of a competent professional person should be sought.

Library of Congress Cataloging-in-Publication Data

Zemke, Ron.
    E-service : 24 ways to keep your customers when the competition is just a click away / Ron Zemke, Tom Connellan.
        p. cm.
    ISBN 0-8144-0606-8
    1. Customer loyalty.   2. Internet marketing.   I. Connellan, Thomas K., 1942-   II. Title.

    HF5415.525 .Z46 2000
    658.8'12—dc21

                                                    00-057607

Printing number

10 9 8 7 6 5 4 3 2 1

CONTENTS

Acknowledgments vii

Chapter 1   Remember the Klondike 1

Chapter 2   Know Your Competition—Your Real Competition . .19

Chapter 3   Hockey-Stick Loyalty 35

Chapter 4   The Anatomy of Customer-Pleasing E-Service:
             Seven Principles, Twenty-Four Keys 51

Chapter 5   Practice Easy-to-Do-Business-With Thinking . . .57
             Key 1: Master the ETDBW Design Basics 60
             Key 2: Start ETDBW below the Line of Visibility 71
             Key 3: Make Your Systems Employee- and
                    Customer-Friendly .72

Chapter 6   Design for Distinction 95
             Key 4: Put Your Personality into Every Touchpoint . .97
             Key 5: Make Emotion Part of the Memory 101
             Key 6: Build in—and on—Security, Speed, and Easy
                    Navigation 104
             Key 7: Communicate Trust through Design 106
             Key 8: Build Trust from the First Click 110
             Key 9: Think Hyperlog—Not Cyberstore 113

Chapter 7   Personalize the E-Experience 117
             Key 10: Win Their Trust First—Ask for Info Later . . .129
             Key 11: Personalized E-Mail to Build Trust and
                     Credibility 132

Key 12: Market Live CSRs as Access to Experts Who
Can Do More than Answer Questions 140
Key 13: Create Community to Add Value 146

Chapter 8   Deliver End-to-End Service 149
Key 14: Focus on Fast, Efficient Fulfillment 158
Key 15: Take the Paper out of the System 166

Chapter 9   Encourage Human Contact 181
Key 16: Make Human Contact Easy, Ample,
and Varied 183
Key 17: Understand and Manage Contact
Expectations 190
Key 18: Hire People Who Do Text and Voice Well ...197
Key 19: Peg E-Service Standards to Web and
Customer Time 201

Chapter 10   Make Recovery a Point of Pride 217
Key 20: Master Service Recovery Basics 220
Key 21: Define Recovery from the Customer's
Point of View 228

Chapter 11   Build a Retention Strategy (or, out with the
Teflon, in with the Velcro) 241
Key 22: Practice Retention Planning 242
Key 23: Make the First Three Visits Memorable 246
Key 24: Use Incentives to Increase Spending 249

Chapter 12   A Seven-Lesson Crash Course in E-Service
Improvement 263

Chapter 13   The Future of the Net: Take These Predictions
to the Bank 291

Chapter 14   Browser's Guide 305

Notes 317

Additional Resources 323

Index 327

About the Authors 339

ACKNOWLEDGMENTS

Some version of the line, "this book is the product of many hands and minds" graces the acknowledgments page of just about every book we've ever read. We don't know how true that may actually be for those other books, but for this one, it is true in spades and aces.

The research, writing, and building of this book, is without fear of overstatement, a fantastic act of team work!

From the people at AMACOM who threw away the time-tested guidelines and asked, "When does it need to be in the marketplace?" instead of declaring, "This is how long it takes to bring a book to market," to the people at Maryland Composition who made the production process a high-speed interactive delight, to the researchers at Selah! Inc., the mystery shoppers at Shop 'n Chek who dared to plow new ground, and the analytical geniuses at ParaMetrica, Inc.—we are indebted. Spectacular!

"We" aren't just the two names on the cover. "We" is a five-person team who wrangled and fussed over every sentence, word, paragraph, and idea in this book as if they were precious human newborns, composed of Tom and Ron; Sarah Fister Gale and Dave Zielinski, two overachieving, tech-savvy journalist/writers of immense talent; and Jill Applegate who not only coordinated the research and writing, but strung the text together in a single package, surfed the Web tirelessly looking for exceptional sites, secondary sources, cases, and data. Not to mention being ground zero for all the communication it took to pull things together and keep them running smoothly.

All that said, we need to thank some other very specific players and acknowledge their contributions. There's Lindsay Willis of Selah! Inc., who made/makes our focus groups rich resources. April Vitale of Shop 'n Chek, who put together and managed a championship of professional mystery shoppers. Dr. Jeff McLeod of ParaMetrica, Inc., who made the loyalty/profitability metrics a reality. Ellen Kadin of AMACOM who championed our requests for speed and took our delays and machinations in stride without losing a single kidney. Helen Powers of Maryland Composition was flawless in interpreting what we were trying to do with every graph and image—regardless of how vaguely we expressed it.

And we absolutely must mention the generosity of John Goodman of e-Satisfy.com, Lauren Basham of SOCAP, Gene Camera of BizRate, and Jean Kong of Forrester Research in allowing us to see and report on their cutting-edge e-commerce research.

Others who put energy into this book—either directly or indirectly—include our partner Chip Bell, Allyson Campa, Edward Dubrawski, Jamie Rapperport, Penne Allen, Lynn Neillie, Karen Revill, Beth Brown, Mike Grasee, David Hochberg, Rich Takata, Bill Bass, Brett Astor, Mark DeChambeau, Scott Anderson, Sharon Bargas, Mike Guerra, Jerry McLaughlin, Donald Bielinski, Ron Paulson, Lisa Huckleberry, Soon-Chart Yu, John Prokopiak, Paula Noack, Doug Sundheim, Kathy Ferrante, Elise Dann, Dale Veno, Meg Colgate, Cindy Grimm, and Cheryl Gracie. We thank you all for your time and effort. We couldn't have done it without you.

And no list of acknowledgments would be complete without thanking Susan Zemke and Pam Dodd for their forbearance and wise advice on the progress of this project.

Ron Zemke   Tom Connellan
Minneapolis, Minnesota   *Orlando, Florida*

e-service

CHAPTER 1

REMEMBER
THE KLONDIKE

At 3 o'clock this morning the steamship Portland, *from St. Michael's for Seattle passed up the Sound with more than a ton of gold on board and 68 passengers.*

The Seattle Post-Intelligencer

July 17, 1897

WITH
↓

these words the last great gold rush of North America began. By 1902 large mineral development companies had bought up the most productive individual claims and mines and the Great Klondike gold rush had come to an end. Between end points, fortunes were made and lost, tens of thousands of fortune seekers, miners, gamblers, merchants, prostitutes, developers, opportunists, and scalawags streamed to the rugged wilds of Alaska and the Yukon Territory of Canada, and the last act in the great westward power shift was in full swing.

Seattle was transformed from a sleepy fishing and lumber port lolling in an economic depression to a robust metropolis where wealthy merchants, financiers, and import/export tycoons, proudly—and accurately—dubbed their little town "The Gateway to Alaska and the Orient." The Seattle Exposition of 1909 announced the arrival of the area as a player on the national and world scene—and a new industrial age powered by the energy and resources drawn to the glamour and promise of the place and the day.

It was a heady time that created a permanent prosperity far greater and long-lived than could have been imagined by even those dreamers and adventurers who triumphantly returned from that cold, hard tundra as high-profile gold dust millionaires.

THE GREAT CYBER GOLD RUSH: GIVE ME AN "E"

Today, e-commerce entrepreneurs worldwide are engaged in a gold rush of their own, the product of which and fallout from promises to outstrip the Klondike gold rush of 1897 in outrageous hyperbole and actual productive product.

From the beginning of this cyber stampede, press, pundits, and volunteer commentators of all types have been off to the side watching the wild and wooly action as the e-commerce frontier was explored, tamed, and exploited. These noisy bystanders have been of two minds about the great Internet gold rush. In one grandstand were the gushing, garrulous enthusiasts. These almost Pollyannaish promoters and cheerleaders burbled on about new economy versus old economy companies, paradigm shifts, and "new solution matrices." They saw boundless bounty with acres of gold nuggets in every corner of the virtual tundra.

These Klondike cheerleaders watched dot-coms explode geometrically across industry and category. Start-ups and their land-based competitors kept piling into categories that were either commodities, such as flowers and software, or that operated on the thinnest of margins, such as pet supplies and toys. Each insisted that their site was the most comprehensive flower/software/pet/toy/etc. site on the Internet, and each had an amazingly similar list of reasons why that was the case. There were a myriad of articles and press releases proclaiming yet another "change-the-world-site-that-was-going-to-be-like-no-other" frequently followed by a weird ad crying out for attention.

Predictions of revenue growth in the business-to-consumer (B2C) market soared, and predictions of growth in the business-to-business (B2B) market arched even higher—and faster. They delighted in pointing out that the number of people who logged onto the Internet daily was growing at unprecedented rates, at times logarithmically, with the Web reaching as many Americans in its first six years as the telephone did in its first four decades.

There were seemingly solid business reasons for the enthusiasm.

◆ Cisco Systems, always a good exemplar, was able to save hundreds of millions of dollars by generating an increasing percentage of its sales through the Web itself.

◆ Amazon.com redefined book selling—and set the model for managing high volumes of Web-based transactions.

◆ Ebay.com and a dozen other B2C and B2B Web auction sites proved that a most ancient form of commerce could become a hi-tech hit.

◆ AOL handily demonstrated that there's gold in cyber matchmaking.

Certainly, most venture capitalists fell into the enthusiast camp. Amazon.com and Netscape, two early players in the e-commerce space, beginning with a mere $8 million and $5 million, respectively, in venture capital, made millions for the initial investors. Indeed, these early players' successes made those investors, not to mention company founders, seem like farseeing geniuses. Others watched and learned. The rush was on! CarsDirect.com garnered an amazing $280 million in a single round of venture financing. By the time Webvan was IPO ready, it had already pulled in a whopping $429 million in venture capital funding. Life in cyberspace was good! Every new idea seemed a fundable winner and a customer magnet. Sure, most e-ventures weren't generating much profit, but traffic was terrific and investors ebullient. It was a brave new world, with brand new rules.

CYBER DUST IN THE WIND?

All the while, the dour, scowling nabobs of negativity were seated low in the opposite bleachers shaking their heads and repeatedly observing that "there's no there, there." They were appalled by the apostasies of endless sunshine and growth. They relentlessly reminded all within earshot of the frenzied speculation of the Roaring Twenties and delighted in giving lecturettes equating the cyber boom to the Dutch "tulip mania" debacle of 1637.[1]

They pointed repeatedly to the lack of profit that was being generated by many of the highly touted and respected e-commerce companies.

Then, in mid-April 2000, the world changed. The Pollyanna camp got hit with a massive dose of reality. Technology stocks in general and Internet stocks in particular plunged. IPOs were put on hold. Valuations of privately held firms were adjusted downward. "Two guys with a business plan" could no longer command an instant $1 million to $5 million in venture capital money. Talk migrated from deals that would create billions to deals that might create millions.

The curmudgeons responded almost gleefully to the NASDAQ drubbing of April 2000, raising their voices from a dour, "the sky is falling" to a higher decibeled, "we told you so." Further chanting, "the worst is yet to come," they seemed almost relieved that their dark predictions were finally being realized.

Press comparisons to the tulip mania, the Great Depression, and the October 1986 market tumble grew in number and volume. Reminders of the gold rush of auto company start-ups in 1912 and its small percentage of survivors were used with increasing frequency to suggest the worst was yet to come. Every dip in technology stocks and Internet stocks throughout April, May, and June brought questions regarding the long-term viability for this sector of the technology economy.

Flip-flop financial columnists, who had initially cheered high and loud with the best of the e-commerce devotees, started pointing out that many of these dot-com prodigies had never been through a major hit to stocks and had not proved they could weather the test of time and volatility. Stern declarations warned that the likes of General Electric and Wal-Mart were not going to let a bunch of upstarts come in and steal market share from them without a fight. "Lookout!" the omenizers warned, "You're about to learn what real competition looks like." Established firms in the auto and aerospace industries led the way by creating their own industry-wide supplier marketplaces, clearly demonstrating that they weren't about to be undone by a gaggle of clamoring twentysomethings, waving their undergraduate technology degrees and squawking about the joy of the "new economy" and the morbidity of the "old economy."

CAMP REALITY

The truth of the matter is that neither the Pollyannas nor the curmudgeons are 100 percent right nor 100 percent wrong. The truth of the Klondike is that there will be some consistent e-commerce moneymakers, some really big winners, and a lot who struggle, but never really make it big—and many, many losers.

Andy Crawford, a professor in the University of Michigan's Engineering School who teaches classes in entrepreneurship, uses the Klondike gold rush metaphor to impress upon his students the risk side of new ventures. Andy points out that 200,000 people set off for Klondike. Some 120,000 made it as far as Dawson, Canada.

Eighty thousand of those ended up actually looking for gold. The other 40,000 stayed, but decided that it was easier to make money in some other way. Of the 80,000 who actually went looking for gold, perhaps 10,000 found enough saleable ore that they became comparatively rich—for four to five years, and of all the thousands of initial adventurers, about 200 made enough money that their modern-day heirs are still comfortable.

So who is going to "make their heirs rich" in the cyber gold rush? Again, the Klondike perspective is instructive.

The most consistent money-makers of the gold rush of 1897 were the merchants who fed, outfitted, and supplied the miners. Mark Twain observed, "When everyone is looking for gold, it's a good time to be in the pick and shovel business." This is turning out to be true of the cyber gold rush as well. The most consistent money-makers are and will be those who supply the miners—the e-commerce adventurers and dot-com millionaire "wannabes," e.g., the Ciscos, Oracles, Foundry Networks, and InterNaps.

Internet commerce is obviously here to stay, and it's going to provide benefits far beyond those presently in place or yet envisioned. The Net's ruthless savings has greatly reduced friction, created enormous time savings, made customers smarter, and ushered in a whole new era of business opportunity. Just the same, our studies and those of many others suggest there is much to be done before *e-promise* becomes consistent, customer-pleasing *e-performance*.

E-commerce and technology stocks will continue to ebb and flow. Those swings are sometimes associated with value and actual productive performance, sometimes not.

But more dot-coms will fail for lack of a solid business model. The prevailing earnings before expenses (EBE) is not a solid business model. The Buy.coms of the world busy acquiring the wrong type of customer will not survive in their present iteration. Many more will fail because they haven't created value for their customers. Most of these dot-coms will have overfocused on the technology and underfocused on the customer needs. The long-term winners—those firms that are still profitably standing two years from now—will be those that have done the best job supporting customers and delivering that value in a way that seems effortless to the customer.

NEXT STEP: DIFFERENTIATION

The bloom, to borrow an old phrase, is off the Internet rose. During the dot-com gold rush daze, any HipName.com Web site that could cast a shadow drew lots of visits from lots of visitors. In addition, with any reasonable product, or service, or information offering at all, it made sales—sometimes one-time-only sales, but sales. Often, that was enough—or seemed to be. After all, the market value of the company behind HipName.com, particularly if it were a retail Web site, was increasing every day. Sooner or later, the company would become so desirable that it would be gobbled up by someone who really wanted—needed—access to the customer base HipName.com claimed as its cyberturf.

The downturn and belt tightening of second quarter 2000 has changed the rules. The future of pure dot-coms as well as the e-commerce ventures of mixed brick and click endeavors depends on economically attracting and profitably retaining customers—becoming profitable, and staying the course for the long-term.

Where and how do you differentiate yourself? Whether you're a B2B or B2C, you've got to find a point of differentiation to separate from the rest of the herd, and you've got to fight for it and maintain it. In the e-world, the competition is a click away and breathing down your neck ready to snap up your customers the moment you drop your guard. In the brick and mortar world, the "mud world" as some would call it, a primary differentiator has always been location, location, location. On the Web everyone has the same location; no place and every place at once.

Product Differentiation?

Product differentiation may work for a few product categories—temporarily. But unless you're selling rare antiques or custom hand-crafted, design-patented furniture, if you've got it to sell, then anyone else can have it to sell, too. And they will. Even if you manage to be the only online site selling your unbelievably unique merchandise, the incessant entrepreneurial spirit of the Web will surely pull that uniqueness out from under you. Sites like Fog-dog.com have "search squads" whose sole purpose in life is to track down hard-to-find items online and purchase them for their own customers for zero profit, thereby creating loyalty and discouraging consumers by dint of ease from finding new sources of products on their own.

How do you differentiate yourself on a book? You can't. It's a commodity—a book is a book is a book. How about a unique specialized kind of information? Again, maybe you can have a temporary leg up on the competition, but only for a very short period of time. Then someone else will offer virtually the same information.

It's possible to differentiate yourself *for very short periods of time* on product offering, but in today's networked and information-rich world it won't be very long before someone has a competing offer that approximates yours. The truth of the matter is that differentiating yourself on the uniqueness of product is tough.

How about Price?

While price is always a consideration for consumers, unless you intend to undersell yourself right out of business, the competition will probably meet or beat what you've got to offer. Our and other people's research makes it clear that customers will dump you if your site is clumsy, your customer service difficult to access, and your delivery methods shoddy and slow—regardless of what you charge.

You could make the lowest price in your segment your point of differentiation. But how viable is that as a long-term business model? If all you're doing is acquiring customers based on price, you're probably acquiring a customer base that won't serve you well in the long run. Price-only consumers are end users, not long-term customers; they are infamously fickle—and demanding and difficult. How about considering product your break-even point and net advertising your real money-maker? Maybe. But losing money or breaking even on each transaction with the hope of making it up by advertising is an inherently unstable business plan and doesn't seem to bode well for future profitability. There are already a substantial number of dot-coms operating on negative gross margins. A situation that can't last for long. Yes, you can gain share by competing on price alone, but the probability of being able to profitably maintain that share is minuscule.

If location, product, and price are null sum differentiators, and they won't work even in the short, much less the long run, where does that leave the fledgling e-commerce venture of a traditional company or its dot-com competitor? We suggest there is but one surefire e-commerce differentiator for dot-com and brick and click endeavors as well: Service, or perhaps more correctly, **e-service.**

SERVICE WILL SEPARATE LEADERS FROM LOSERS

Forrester Research, a leading e-commerce research organization, has boldly predicted the demise of most dot-com retailers by 2001,[2] averring that the key to survival for dot-coms rests on something most of them can't fathom—the quality of their service "Online retailers must strike back at brand confusion and product duplication by distinguishing themselves through customer service," advised Forrester's report. In another study, Forrester announced that 90 percent of all online shoppers consider good customer service to be the critical factor when choosing a Web merchant to give their commerce.[3] In our own research, customers we interviewed and surveyed told us 2:1 that poor service discourages them from making a second trip to a dot-com—regardless of product and price.

SERVICE IS THE *ONLY* DIFFERENTIATOR—AND A CLEAR OPPORTUNITY

If you can't differentiate on the product offering and can't profitably differentiate on price, the only point of differentiation is service. Service involves factors like ease of doing business, trust, responsiveness, Web site navigability, problem resolution, and all those other elements of good e-business that don't fit quite so neatly into a purely binary world, but that nonetheless, as we will demonstrate, have high value to customers.

No matter where you look, the message comes through loud and clear: Service is key to winning on the Web. Yet, few firms are doing a good job of providing that service. E-Gain reports that 50% of those who had purchased online have stopped doing business with a company due to poor customer service.[4] In December 1999 through January 2000 we sent a team of virtual shoppers out on the Net to visit sites and evaluate e-service.[5] After 755 visits to 385 sites, the results were clear: Service on the Web is woefully wanting. Allowing the most generous standard—sites named as "good" or "great" by at least one of our shoppers—we still found that only 7% of the sites met this standard. By contrast, 13.3 percent (50 of the 385) were judged "so bad I would warn others way from this site," and 28.8% were rated to be so clumsy, difficult, and uninteresting that "I would probably not shop or revisit this site."

HOW BAD IS E-SERVICE?

Few people abandon their shopping carts at the neighborhood Target or Kroger store. But set them loose in the online world, and they do so with frightening regularity. Depending on the study you look at, between 25 percent and 75 percent of all shopping carts are abandoned online. As one of our focus group participants put it, "It's easy to 'drive' to a virtual marketplace, but it's also easy to 'drive away' and leave your shopping cart sitting there. You don't even have the embarrassment of people looking at you."

E-mail? Another disaster. Again, while the exact percentage depends on the study du jour, somewhere in the neighborhood of 40 percent of all e-mail queries to companies never get answered. The answers that do come frequently take days longer than the more immediate 1- to 2-hour response time expected by today's customers.

Download times don't fare any better. One respondent in our focus groups captured the download issue fairly succinctly when she said, "Waiting for this (site's) splash page to download is a lot like watching paint dry." Again, the actual numbers vary from report to report, but the estimates of dollars lost when customers give up and leave a site due to the tedium of slow downloads reach into the hundreds of millions.

The truth of the matter is that in a world where user *experience* dictates brand, customer service *is* your brand. Doug Sundheim, senior client development manager of Internet consultancy in the New York City office of Luminant Worldwide, notes that "A brand does not, and can not, exist separately from the customer's experience. Companies now operate in a world where products are commodities, pricing wars are a zero sum game, and physical location is irrelevant. Put simply, then, your customer's experience of your service becomes your brand."

The question you need to ask yourself is, "Is the service experienced by our customers creating the brand image we want in the marketplace?" If it is, great. If your brand is as strong as you'd like, great. But if not, then you have your real work ahead of you.

WITHER ONLINE CUSTOMER SERVICE?

The bottom line is that companies have spent millions of dollars attracting customers to their Web sites and seem oblivious to the fact that acquiring customers is not the same thing as keeping customers. Not serving customers well produces hard lessons about customer loyalty and the ripple effects of poor customer care. The lesson is equally clear: Treat customers badly just once online, and not only will they never come back, but through chat rooms and broadcast e-mail they will tell potentially thousands of other consumers about your careless attitude.

The fallout from poor service online is magnified and instantaneous. E-Satisfy.com, an Arlington, Virginia-based research firm formerly known as TARP, reports that dissatisfied online customers tell twice as many people about their experience than do satisfied customers. They are also four times more likely to discuss their experience in an online chat room than satisfied customers.[6] Think about how many people that potentially reaches.

It may seem easy enough to throw up a site and watch the sales roll in, but there are an unbelievable number of ways to fail a customer at your site—all of which have been detailed in countless surveys, research reports, and high-profile press stories: Slow pages, crashed sites, lousy navigation logic, incomprehensible instructions, search engines that require a degree in Boolean algebra, unsecured and confusing order forms, Machiavellian return policies, e-mail that's never answered, and "frequently asked questions" (FAQs) that raise more questions than they answer.

These and similar malfunctions, complaints, and service disappointments undercut the best marketing plan and best advertising and send would-be customers clicking away. And yet there are few sites in existence right now that don't manage to screw up the fundamental e-service elements on a regular basis.

Customer loyalty on the Web is even more fleeting than land-based shopping. Those companies who view customer service as an afterthought—saving key infrastructure and other back-end investments until the "brand is built"—will continue to pay a steep price. As the cost of customer acquisition rises and Internet competition increases, no one can afford to lose e-shoppers after only one visit.

Meeting and managing the service expectations of online shoppers is proving to be no small challenge for e-sellers. It is a devilment often of their own making. Far too many companies' own aggressive and omnipresent advertising messages often suggest that online shopping is a breeze and that Web shoppers will benefit from fast downloads, always be a click away from what they seek, experience hassle-free product ordering, receive delivery close to instantly, and receive first-rate help from live customer service reps at a click. Most of these explicit and implicit promises go unmet. The bad news is that the first time a customer's experience doesn't stand up to the reality—that an explicit or implicit promise is breached—is almost always the last time a Web shopper visits a site.

E-shopper expectations are not just set by advertising and hype. They are also tied to the perception of the Web as an instantaneous medium. Die-hard brick and mortar shoppers accustomed to "shopping till they drop" now can shop around the clock and expect around-the-clock service and instant support on the Web—something they would never have thought to demand of a brick and mortar company.

Some of the solutions to today's stunningly poor e-service are amazingly simple. An Andersen Consulting survey of 500 people found that 95 percent said a guarantee of on-time delivery would increase the likelihood that they would buy from a Web site again.[7] A BizRate.com survey of 9,800 consumers found that 89 percent of online buyers say return policies influences their decision to shop with an e-tailer.[8] The "headline" from the Andersen and BizRate examples: Slow down the expenditure on technology and beef-up the straightforward service-oriented solutions your customers are looking for.

FALLOUT FROM POOR E-SERVICE

Those who manage B2C and B2B shopping sites have discovered there's nothing easier for frustrated e-shoppers to do than type in a competitor's URL. Or worse, they simply go back to the brick and mortar world, where they can be assured of getting their hands on a needed product right away rather than risk technology snafus, endless order form requests, late or erroneous product delivery, inconvenient return policies, and absent customer service help.

In an interview with *Fast Company* magazine, Jeffrey Rayport, a Harvard Business School professor, stressed that while poor customer service in the brick and mortar world can be damaging, in the online world it can be a death knell.[9] "People will keep going to the same supermarket (where they experienced poor service) simply because it's on the way home. On the Web, a bad customer experience can be fatal."

Without well-conceived and adequately funded strategies for handling customer problems online, e-tailers can find their call centers overrun and customer service expenses rising in lockstep when they unveil new products on Web sites or when customers start experiencing problems with existing ones.

A FEW SHINING LIGHTS

Amidst the stories of shoddy online service there are a few shining lights. These are e-businesses that understand how customer retention drives profit and who've built online models that pay as much attention to back-end concerns as they do to the investments needed to draw customers to a site in the first place. These companies understand that e-commerce is about much more than just transferring a product catalog online.

It is about e-service, first and foremost. At Lands' End, the Wisconsin-based clothing retailer, customers who have trouble finding what they want on the company's Web site simply click on a button, type in a phone number, and a salesperson calls them back in no time. The company understands that there is more to e-commerce than pretty pictures and order forms on a Web site. LandsEnd.com "gets it." A few others "get it " as well: Dell.com, Amazon.com, SmarterKids.com, Garden.com, REI.com, Gap.com, and Fogdog.com routinely get rave reviews from market researchers and their own customers for clear and easy-to-navigate sites, customer support, personalized service, return policies, service guarantees, or reliable product delivery.

The infrastructure of the Internet is largely in place. Customer loyalty, not technology, is going to be the factor that separates the winners from the losers. If you're in the competitive ballpark on offering and price, you get to play in the game. But to be a champion you need to differentiate yourself on outstanding service. Service will separate the winners from the losers—in fact it's already beginning to happen. The winners understand that, and so should you.

KNOW YOUR COMPETITION—YOUR REAL COMPETITION

CUSTOMERS

form their expectations in the darnedest ways. Advertising, word of mouth, press accounts, and simple imagination inform and shape how they envision the experience of transacting business at your Web site.

Some expectations for service at your e-commerce site are set when a customer or potential customer visits someone else's site. Those expectations are pretty straightforward. The person tapping into your site is comparing a Net transaction to a Net transaction. They have, for instance, a sense of how long it takes for ToysRus.com's home page to download and they weigh that against how long it takes your home page to open. They compare how many clicks it takes to place an order on your site with how many clicks it takes to place an order at Amazon.com or at Zinger-mans.com. Sometimes they do it consciously, sometimes not.

Rarely do they actually put a stopwatch to download time or count clicks—it's all in their *perception*. Most consumers will be certain they waited three minutes for a page to load when in fact it took less than thirty seconds. A seven-click checkout process will seem like fifteen. Does it matter that they are wrong? No. It's their perceptions that count. Customer perception in any commercial medium is reality. It's their perceptions that determine where and with whom they will shop. So whether it's thirty seconds or three minutes, seven clicks or fifteen, the point is it took too long and they are looking for something faster, better, easier. Done consciously or unconsciously, impressionistically or statistically, customers are continuously measuring load times and clicks, your response time, and service against their expectations.

There are at least three levels or types of expectation building that impact the way customers look at your organization and your ability to serve them in an acceptable fashion.

LEVEL 1: IMPRESSIONISTIC EXPECTATIONS

Sometimes customers' expectations come from direct, premeditated, site-to-site comparisons. More frequently, their expectations are less studied and direct. They come as a result, and are a by-product, of just doing business day to day on the Net. For example, someone goes to LandsEnd.com, accesses the Body Model™, picks a body type close to theirs, and "tries on" different outfits to get a sense of which will fit the best and be the most flattering. Awhile later, the next day or the next week , they come to your home-furnishing site and want to see how the curtains they're thinking of buying will look in their living room—or they're buying a corporate jet from you and wonder what different interior options look like in different color combinations. Consciously or not, they are comparing your "trying on" process to that of LandsEnd.com.

This informal comparison of company to company is e-service expectation setting at its most basic of levels. It's the process of retrospectively comparing a transaction on one Web site to a like or similar transaction on another nonrelated site. Customers compare the ease of ordering a fishing lure from Lure.com with the ease of ordering polyethylene from Chemdex.com with the ease of ordering a HEPA air cleaner from Gazoontite.com. In the end, they label one site superior to another regardless of product, price or industry. Call it a Level 1 comparison.

The same type of comparison goes on all the time in the brick and mortar world. Buyers compare a phone call to L.L. Bean with a phone call to your organization; whether it's a call to your toll-free help line for guidance with a product or a call to your corporate offices to chat with the CEO. (Think customers are going to stop calling you just because you've got a Web site? Think again, and then read chapter 9 very carefully.) Customers compare deliveries from

FedEx to UPS and USPS and if you are shipping products via one of those three worthies, your reputation for delivery reliability rests in their hands. They foul up, and your customer blames them *and* you for the inconvenience. Customers' expectations tick upward with every new positive experience and unless you continue to meet, or better yet, set their standards for basic elements like page-loading speed, call-answering haste, and delivery times, you will continue to flounder in the pool of mediocre companies that can't quite grasp the concept of differentiation.

If an informal Net site versus Net site comparison were the only expectation potential customers brought to your site, life would be relatively simple. Not necessarily easy, but simple. Unfortunately, they bring other offhanded expectations to their dealings with you as well. If they see a commercial on television with attractive, friendly service reps chatting via live text options with customers at Web sites, that becomes a standard of comparison when next they go online. When they place an order online and it arrives in two days, rather than the week to ten days they had anticipated, they revise their vision of the art of the possible. If they expect an answer to an e-mail question within the hour because that's what they experienced at OmahaSteaks.com and your reply doesn't come for four hours, you've disappointed them—regardless of how impressive you think your turnaround time is.

LEVEL 2: DELIBERATE
SITE-TO-SITE COMPARISONS

Frequently customers will make very direct, real-time comparisons. A customer—let's say someone who makes business travel arrangements for a small office—orders a plane ticket from Expedia.com, then surfs over and orders a ticket from Travelocity.com. Then, he goes to OfficeClick.com and discovers that at that site he can build a profile of each person he orders tickets for and automatically track their itineraries.

Once he gets the chance to build those personal profiles at OfficeClick.com, he expects a profile building feature at every site he visits. Before visiting OfficeClick.com he may never have considered the value of or need for a profile, but now it is the basis upon which he judges your offering. This customer is experimentally, experientially, and directly comparing ticket ordering to ticket ordering. And he concludes that without that all-important handy-dandy profile tool, all those other offerings, which may have been perfectly acceptable to him three weeks ago, just don't live up to his expectations anymore.

Every time a customer is wowed by a site's service, or gravely disappointed, he or she makes a decision about who to return to the next time—and the time after that, and the time after that.

LEVEL 3: COMPARING ONLINE TO OFFLINE

"You know," said David, a participant in one of our focus groups, "when I call my industrial supply house, the guy there almost always remembers what I mean when I say I need a gross of those thingamabobs I use for shipping. And if he doesn't remember, he can look it up pretty fast in my order history. But when I go online to try and order something, there's no one there to remember. No one to talk to. And there's no way for me to cruise through my order history and figure out what it was I ordered four months ago. You'd think these computer guys would be able to at least put something like that on a Web site. Seems easy enough to do, doesn't it?"

David was making a Level 3 comparison. He was comparing an offline transaction to an online transaction. It's a comparison that's frequently made by customers.

Those expectations are often set in ways that are much more complex, and subtle, than you may realize. The individual who clicks to your Web site may just have come from a great experience at a Marriott Hotel where he was welcomed back because Marriott's software informed the front desk that not only was he a returning guest, but also one who preferred a king-size bed and usually needs a full-size rental car. Or, he may have just returned from the Magic Kingdom, eaten in his favorite restaurant, or been wowed by someone in a Nordstrom store. It doesn't matter. Each service experience, regardless of whether it's online or offline, sets the stage of expectations for future service interactions, including those on your Web site.

If you're going to run a world-class Web site, you need to provide consumers with the same or better level of information and service than they have access to from other sources, be that a Net source, television, or a land-based shopping mall.

Gazoontite.com caters to people with asthma and allergy problems. Its brand promise is to help sufferers breathe happier and healthier. It uses multiple channels to reach its market and to reinforce the brand promise—a catalog, physical stores, infomercials, and a Web site. One of the key components of delivering on that brand promise through all these channels is education.

Quick Case
Level Three Versus Level Three In Action

Dave and Avis had been wanting a faster modem for their Compaq Armada notebook computer. On the way home from the beach, they stopped at a CompUSA store, described the computer, and gave the salesperson the model number. He listened attentively and sold them a modem.

They took the new modem home and set it aside, planning to do the installation the next day. In reality, it was close to three weeks before they got around to the installation. Step one of the installation instructions said: "Carefully remove the back of the computer." They tried. The case cracked.

Puzzled, they took the computer and the modem back to the store. It turned out they weren't supposed to remove the back of this notebook computer. They had been given the wrong modem. The nice folks at CompUSA estimated it would cost $410 to fix the computer. Dave and Avis suggested that because it was a CompUSA error that caused the problem, CompUSA should foot at least part of the repair bill. No such luck. In fact, because it had been more than thirty days since the modem was purchased, Dave and Avis were told they were "lucky to get a refund on the modem itself."

Irritated, they went home and sent an e-mail to the president of CompUSA. No reply. A call to the corporate offices generated an explanation: "Only one person is answering e-mails, so sometimes it's a couple of months before you can expect a reply." Boiled, baked, and steaming, they marched to the nearest computer and dialed in to Dell.com to buy an entirely new notebook computer. It was the exact model they were looking for—all the bells and whistles they wanted and none of the superfluous functions they didn't want. (Why wouldn't it be. They designed it themselves—online.)

As soon as they entered their order, they received an order number. They could now go to Dell's Web site and check on the progress of their order, which they did frequently over the next few days. Five days later they received their computer. It works without a flaw. They have yet to hear from CompUSA, and CompUSA will never again hear from them.

The site provides quizzes that test customers' knowledge about allergy and asthma and feeds back information and insight on dealing with chronic breathing problems. There's even a nurse on duty to answer the most complex questions from 9 AM to noon.

Why do that? It's part of fulfilling the brand promise and ties directly into expectations. People are used to getting educated from a nurse or doctor in the offline world. Gazoontite.com's customers have the same expectations of the online experience. Information is a hot commodity, especially when it comes to health, and who's a more reliable source than a medical professional? Once consumers go to Gazoontite.com and find that the quality of information and expertise is reliable, trustworthy, and immediate, it sets their expectations for every other health-related Web site they visit.

Your customers make these same Level 3 brick-to-click comparisons all the time. Consciously or unconsciously, they're comparing much more than Web site to Web site and ease of ordering with ease of ordering. They compare the overall service Gestalt of organization "A" with organization "B," regardless of their differences.

They're comparing calling you with calling FedEx or L.L. Bean.

Think about that for a minute. A customer calls FedEx to check on a shipment. Then she calls L.L. Bean to order a pair of woolen socks. Then she calls you. If your phone response system isn't as fast and reliable as those paragons of call center management, then you need to get busy.

No matter what consumers are buying, from office supplies to scented candles, there is always a common theme that links every buying experience together: The quality of service. Consumers can and will compare how they are treated in every transaction as apples to apples—no matter what the purchase, no matter where it's done, no matter how much they spend or what industry they spend it in. In the minds of consumers service is the great equalizer. They judge you as much by how you deliver it as what you deliver.

So step back from the technology you're bringing to the table. It's a necessary, but not sufficient condition for success. You may have fallen into the trap of being overobsessed with the technology and underobsessed with the customers experience.

Look at what your customers are bringing to the table. There's a person behind those fingertips and he or she has a much more complex set of expectations than you may realize.

UNEARTHING EXPECTATIONS:
THE CUSTOMER EXPERIENCE GRID

Knowing customers have expectations and figuring out how those expectations manifest are two different things. Some expectations are obvious, "I'd like the item to be delivered when you say it will be delivered." Some are far more subtle or outlandish, "I want a natural language search engine that understands and answers my question on the first try. In any language."

Can you accommodate them all? Maybe, but first you have to know how to find them. A model we use with clients to capture the sum total of a customer's experiences is called the Customer Experience Grid (Figure 2-1).

The vertical axis of the Customer Experience Grid is the outcome the customer receives. It could be a product that is shipped, software that is downloaded from your Web site, information, such as the weather in Cleveland, that is made available on your home page. The *outcome* is whatever your core offering is to the customer.

The horizontal axis is the *process* the customer has to go through to obtain that outcome. It's navigating your Web site,

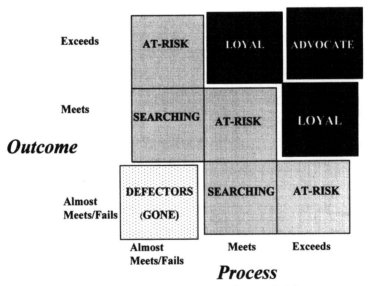

Figure 2-1. Customer Experience Grid.

printing out information, looking for pricing, ordering the product, checking with a customer service rep, opening the shipment, or any of the other myriad process contact points a customer has with you during the purchase of your wares. It is on this line that most e-commerce operations have the greatest opportunity to differentiate themselves. Most of the outcomes available on the Web are available on another Web site or from a brick and mortar operation. The process—the way they are served—is what makes it memorable, positively or negatively.

Customers who find their needs unmet on the process and the outcome axes are, in reality, ex-customers—what we call "defectors." They're history. Too many other options exist in today's business world. There are no second chances when their choices are so vast.

If a customer's needs are met on one dimension and unmet on another, they are—by and large—actively searching for ways to replace you. They are surfing for other sites, e-mailing friends, talking to colleagues or neighbors. In some way, shape, or form, they're looking for another source of what you purport to provide. Their message to you is: "You've still got my attention, but I'm actively looking around for something better." Unless you take great strides to make amends, most of these "Actively Seeking Alternatives" customers will revert to the brick and mortar world or find what they need at another Web site. Once that happens there's little hope you'll ever see them again.

The middle band of Figure 2-1, is populated with the "at-risk" customers. These are the customers whose action makes the Net such a dicey game. These are the individuals and organizations who conduct a few transactions with you and then are pulled away by a banner ad, an e-mail offer, a recommendation from a friend, an ad during the Super Bowl, or a direct mail piece. They have a sort of commercial Attention Deficit Disorder (ADD), because you've given them little or no compelling reason to behave otherwise.

Most customers who abandon their shopping carts and never return cluster in the "outcome met" and "dissatisfied with process" band. You met their outcome needs—you carry the shoes they wanted in their size—but something in the ordering process became so burdensome that they decided to forget the whole thing and move on.

You can have a great product offering, but if you combine it with abysmally poor service (Figure 2-1, upper left box), you've got an "at-risk" customer. Too many e-commerce offerings fall in that box. We call it the "we love your products but we hate doing business with you" attitude.

Focus group participants, members of our virtual shopper teams, and workshop participants have all encountered Web sites that fall into this category. The feedback can easily be paraphrased as "the site has just about everything, but it was a hassle to navigate, the pages took forever to download, and the checkout process kept locking up."

Likewise, if you have great service—and the examples are few and far between on the Web—combined with a poor core offering (Figure 2-1, lower right box) you've also got an "at-risk" customer. This customer is also around only until they find a source that better meets their needs, and in Net time that won't take long at all.

The box in the absolute middle represents the quiet, easy-to-overlook brand of "at-risk" customer. You meet their expectations on both the offering and the service. They may be tolerant, even satisfied with your service and products, but they have no loyalty to you. They know you—or someone—can do better. It's not unlike going to a restaurant where the meal was "fine" and the service was "fine." Neither was awful and neither was memorable, everything was just OK. And while there is nothing desperately wrong with having a mediocre meal in undistinguished circumstances, why would you ever go back for more?

The next band is the "Loyal Band" (Figure 2-1, top). Here, you meet customer expectations on one dimension and exceed them on the other. This is the loyal customer. They're not easily swayed or drawn away to another site or vendor. Someone recommends a source for executive gifts or incentive programs, and they say, "I'm happy with Bravogifts.com. They have good products, a great Web site, and they are very helpful." They are the customer everyone counts on for long-term, extended success in the marketplace.

Best of the best is the customer in the upper right corner of Figure 2-1—the "advocate." Each customer in this category is the economic equivalent of a banner ad that really does work at bringing people to your Web site. They gush about your service, show off your fabulous products, and tell stories at cocktail parties about shopping at your site. The best thing is that all of this kind of advertising doesn't cost you a dime.

If you want to succeed on the Web, you need to consistently manage the total customer experience in a way that draws and holds your customers in the categories in the upper three (black) boxes of Figure 2-1. These represent value-based competition. The lower three boxes: "defectors" (gone), "searching," and "at-risk," represent price-based competition. And while price is certainly a piece of the equation, it's neither necessary nor appropriate to make it your sole competitive weapon.

Leaders in e-commerce recognize the importance of the total customer experience. Walk through the halls of Dell Computer's headquarters in Round Rock, Texas and a pervasive phrase pops up everywhere: "The Customer Experience: Own It." You'll see it on bulletin boards and on the back of photo IDs. You'll also find Dell's mission: "To be the most successful computer company in the world at delivering the best customer experience in markets we serve."

That experience is the sum total of a customer's interaction with Dell—from the first click online, to dealing with a sales rep, to opening the box and taking out the computer.

The phrase comes out of Dell's Customer Experience Council, a team formed to examine every aspect of how the company interacts with customers online. Dell now formally tracks three elements of the customer experience month to month: on-time and accurate order fulfillment, postsale service and support, and postsale computer performance. Dell is the industry leader in remote resolution of customer problems, resolving 70 percent of desktop issues and 90 percent of service issues within the first fifteen minutes of contact by a customer.

How well do *you* do at managing the total customer experience? If you're like one of the 385 sites we had our teams visit, the answer is not very well. And if yours is like most Web sites, you likely fall short on the process dimension.

Fortunately, this book holds the keys to much of the wisdom you'll need to build a phenomenally successful Web presence. It is time to crawl out from under the rock of mediocrity and face the light of day. Doing business online requires a much broader and more efficient approach to dealing with customers. Don't ever be fooled into thinking you know more than they do. You don't. On the Web, consumers run the show. Now more than ever you must bend to their wishes, accommodate their needs, and learn to be humble when you fail. When you do that, you will win them.

3

HOCKEY-STICK
LOYALTY

THE

head of the FactoryOutlook task force opened the meeting: "I'm pleased to say that 89 percent of our retail store customers rate us as satisfactory or better and 93 percent of our online customers rate us as satisfactory or better. So the Web site is actually producing a little higher average level of satisfaction than the brick and mortar side of the business. Obviously we're very pleased by those results. But before we start looking at specific issues, let me ask our guests if they have any comments on our e-commerce satisfaction levels." Eleven heads turned toward us.

We had reviewed the results beforehand and knew there was considerable reason not to be "obviously pleased" by the online or offline satisfaction levels. So, we asked the obvious question: "Do you want us to be polite or truthful?"

In response to a chorus of "truthfuls" we tackled the statement: "Ninety-three percent of customers rate us as satisfactory or better." Their customer satisfaction survey asked customers a series of ten questions. Some were worded better than others, but the macroissue on the table was the "93 percent," and the possible wrong direction the task force would take the company's e-commerce effort if they didn't understand the full impact of their survey results and the apparent assumption that these results contained unremittingly good news.

The truth of the matter was that the survey results showed that they faced some severe loyalty problems. The summary items from their follow-up survey tells the tale as well as any (Figure 3-1).

That's not to say that the statement: "Ninety-three percent of our customers rate us as satisfactory or better" is inaccurate. It's not inaccurate. It's dead on. But to be pleased by those results, and more accurately the distribution of results shown in Figure 3-1, is dead wrong. And to let those results go unchallenged is to be dead out of e-commerce business at Net speed.

Studies in retail, wholesale, and Internet environments have shown that the relationship between customer *satisfaction* and customer *loyalty* is nonlinear. They don't increase uniformly together.

alty. To be sure, some of the other 15,876 could be counted on, maybe in the neighborhood of 1,500 to 2,000 in most situations. In round numbers, however, somewhere between 13,500 and 14,000 of those customers could be easily lured away to another site. They will be "at-risk" any time a competitor makes a better or just a different offer, a possibly better product turns up, or they happen upon a more interesting or more customer-friendly, easier-to-use site. They might even go to a competitor just for the amusement of trying someplace new.

Walid Mougayar, president of Cybermanagement Inc., a Toronto-based consulting firm, sounded an interesting warning in *Business* 2.0. Mougayar referred to the importance of customer satisfaction and recommended that readers "only invest in companies that score in the top 10 percent of their category. Publicly traded companies must score in the upper echelon, or they aren't worth investing in." He went on to strongly assert that when it comes to looking for a dot-com to stand the test of time, "the number of customers is the lifeblood of online businesses," and to judge one's investments accordingly.[1] We would amend Mr. Mougayar's advice only slightly:

> The number of *highly satisfied* customers is the long-term lifeblood of an online company.

Look at your own business with that perspective. Do you have enough loyal customers that you'd be comfortable putting hard cash into your own stock? Better yet, do you actually know how many loyal customers you have compared and contrasted to one-time and at-risk customers?

THE "SATISFACTION" TRAP

People in too many organizations fall into the trap of thinking that "good" and "satisfactory" ratings equate with substantial loyalty. For example, one of the largest U.S. phone companies looked closely at the loyalty behavior and attitudes of customers who rated it "good" on a one- to five-point "very bad" to "very good" scale. To management's astonishment, it learned that 10 percent of the customers who rated them as "good" on all dimensions had no intention of repurchasing products or services from the company, and 50 percent were undecided. In other words, at the "good" level, more than 60 percent of those customers were at significant risk of defecting. When the company did a similar analysis of the "satisfactory" level responses, it learned that 97 percent of customers so rating the company were "at-risk" of defecting. They flatly said they could be lured away by a promise of lower price or better service.

Auto companies find similar results. A customer who gives them a top rating (say a "five" on a one- to five-point scale) is two to three times more loyal than a customer rating them just one level of satisfaction lower. That's why the auto industry is obsessed with what it terms "top box rating." They know that customers who give a dealership a top ranking on sales, service, and product will be back for both service on their present vehicles and at least a test drive when it's time to buy a new car. General Motors, as an example, looks at customers not as the purchasers of vehicles costing $18,235 but as an asset with a life-time value of $276,000.

Coca-Cola® comes to similar conclusions about its target audience. Customers who stick with the brand over a life-time have basically written Coke a check for $6,000. No one is going to make that kind of life-time investment in a merely satisfactory experience with a product. A customer who buys one Coke a day, week after week, is affirming a positive experience. To build brand loyalty and solid revenue, you need to do the same math that GM, Coke, and the phone companies have done. Figure out the life-time value of your customers and treat them as an asset worth $3,000, $27,000, or $375,000 instead of a $14.95 single purchase and manage their experience accordingly. When you start looking at them as assets worth thousands of dollars, your viewpoint naturally shifts from one of acquisition to one of retention. You will suddenly care deeply about doing whatever it takes to keep them coming back and keep them rating you at the upper end of the satisfaction/loyalty scales.

Focus Health, an Ann Arbor, Michigan firm uses the Net to provide employees of its client firms with access to tailored health care insurance. A. David Vinson, chairman and CEO, not only understands the importance of "top box" ratings from customers, but also has a unique way of putting that understanding into practice.

Sometime in their first ninety days, every person hired by Focus Health spends a day in the life of a user to get a gut level feel for what that's like. Says David, "It gives them an intuitive sense of the user on the other side of that monitor impossible to get from reports or written descriptions. I want every person here—programmers to finance to sales—absolutely committed to creating value for our customers. This policy may seem like a small thing, but I believe it positively affects the way customers experience our brand."

The importance of customer value is an especially critical one when viewed through the hockey-stick loyalty lens. Branders.com, for example, sells a full line of promotional items for corporate and association meetings. They use a five-point scale to measure customer satisfaction, with one being low and five being high.

It's important to note that Branders' ability to service customers starts them off from a high base—even the customers who give them a one, two, three, or four have an average order size that is nearly twice the industry norm. But hockey-stick loyalty comes into play for Branders from the customers giving them a five. Their average order size is 66 percent higher than customers who rate Branders with a one, two, three, or four. The clincher is that customers giving them a five place 50 percent more orders than customers giving them a lower score.

As Dale Veno, vice president of sales and marketing puts it, "Providing outstanding service is not only the right thing to do for customers, it's also a sound business stategy that pays off on the bottom-line. There are clear lines of demarcation between a top score and everything else."

Even outsourcing firms are in the act. Danna Mezin, CEO of eAdvocate, an Avon, Connecticut-based firm that provides call center support to e-commerce firms, sees their mission as one of providing their clients' customers with "a level of service that consistently elicits the highest marks on satisfaction surveys."

IT'S ACTIVATING FINGERS, NOT JUST ACQUIRING EYEBALLS

The impact and importance of top-box loyalty ratings is hard to overemphasize. Growing top-line revenue may look nice to Wall

Street, but all too frequently the revenues don't have any loyalty or long-term profitability potential backing them up. If our friends at FactoryOutlook don't take immediate action, revenues will show the folly of management's overconfidence in six to twelve months.

The enchanting rap among and about dot-coms had been about the importance of "acquiring eyeballs." That makes some sense as a preliminary measurement of customer preacquisition, but the real measurements need to be built around "activating fingertips." E-commerce companies need to study why people come to a Web site the first time, what they do there when they arrive, and, most importantly, what makes them come back and do it again. Coming back does not happen as a result of "satisfaction"; it happens at the blade end of the hockey stick, it happens when customers are more than satisfied to be doing business with you.

The headline to keep in mind? Customer satisfaction is a poor predictor of loyalty. To keep them clicking back you need to create a sense of customer delight. You need to "wow" them with your superior standards for quality and service. You must promote a feeling of partnership through honest sharing of information and respect for their needs and always build on the foundation of a trusting relationship. If you do these things, then you will build a loyal and profitable following online.

ADD A LOYALTY METRIC TO REVENUE METRICS

The dramatic impact of moving from a four to a five doesn't mean that movement at the lower levels of satisfaction doesn't count. Any movement toward a higher level of satisfaction and repeat business intention is important because it adds revenues. But adding the same revenue dollars at the higher loyalty levels has a greater value than adding revenue dollars at lower loyalty levels. At the higher levels, the dollar amount shifts are greater, and you can be sure that loyal customers will come back again and again further adding to your revenue stream.

Consider a client of ours who put its customers under a microscope to determine just what their exact dollar values were so that it could figure out how to improve them. This direct marketer used two channels in going to market: a catalog operation and a Web site. To figure out the dollar amount associated with every customer—from the least happy to the most delighted—the company took a closer look at what the different levels of satisfaction had to do with annual revenues.

To do that, they divided customers into three categories: at-risk, satisfied, and advocate. The research showed that at-risk customers generated an average of $50 a year in net revenue, satisfied customers $150, and advocates $200. They also found that "satisfieds" were five times more likely to stop doing business with the company than "advocates," for a wide variety of reasons—most of them seeming on the surface to be petty excuses.

The company had 2 million active customers. Of these, 12.3 percent were "at-risk", 54.9 percent were "satisfied," and 32.8 percent were "advocates" (Figure 3-3).

What's the difference between an "at-risk" and a "satisfied"? Or between a "satisfied" and an "advocate"? Several functional variables predicted which category a customer would fall into. These variables formed an actionable base the firm could use to allocate resources to improve customer loyalty. So let's see what

BASE			
	Percentage	*Average Revenue*	*Yearly Revenue*
At-Risk	12.3	$50	$12,300,000
Satisfied	54.9	$150	$164,700,000
Advocate	32.8	$200	$131,200,000
Total Revenue			$308,200,000

Figure 3-3. Customer satisfaction distribution.

happens to revenue and the degree of loyalty attached to that revenue when you start manipulating variables.

As Figure 3-4 suggests, if the firm were able to shift 2 percent of the "at-risk" customers up one category from "at-risk" to "satisfied," that would produce an increase in revenue of $4 million.

Look at what happens if that 2 percent of customers was shifted into the "advocate" category (Figure 3-5) rather than just into the "Satisfied" category. On the surface, looking only at the percentage column changes, it doesn't look to be a whole lot different, but in reality it's an increase in revenues of $6 million. That's because in this example the difference in average revenue is much greater from "at-risk" to "satisfied"—an increase of $100—

	Percentage	*Average Revenue*	*Yearly Revenue*
At-Risk	10.3	$50	$10,300,000
Satisfied	56.9	$150	$170,700,000
Advocate	32.8	$200	$131,200,000
Total Revenue			$312,200,000
Net Revenue Change			$ 4,000,000

Figure 3-4. Shifting 2 percent from "at-risk" to "satisfied."

	Percentage	Average Revenue	Yearly Revenue
At-Risk	10.3	$50	$10,300,000
Satisfied	54.9	$150	$164,700,000
Advocate	34.8	$200	$139,200,000
Total Revenue			$314,200,000
Net Revenue Change			$6,000,000

Figure 3-5. Shifting 2 percent from "at-risk" to "advocate."

than the difference in average revenue gained going from "satisfied" to "advocate"—$50.

So, you say, what's the real advantage? One strategy adds $4 million in revenue. The other adds $6 million. Both nice, but nothing to do cartwheels over.

Perhaps not—at least not if you only look at the revenue dollars. But, here's the clincher. The $4 million that is added by moving customers from "at-risk" to "satisfied" is five times more likely to disappear than the $6 million represented by moving customers from "at-risk" to "advocate," because advocates are "loyal," "satisfieds" are not. The $4 million worth of satisfied customers are only there until something better comes along. Lose them—and you might—and you've got to start all over acquiring new customers to replace them, investing time and money making sure these new consumers turn into loyal advocates so they won't disappear, too.

The $6 million in revenue added by moving that same 2 percent from "at-risk" to "advocate," however, is a much more secure revenue base. Once consumers are at that level, you're able to spend less keeping them happy than you would trying to acquire new customers. In this situation, the additional revenue is only one aspect of the real benefit. Equally, perhaps more, important is the strength of the loyalty that's attached to the revenue.

Customer loyalty measured in repeat purchases and referrals is the key driver of profitability for online businesses, even more so than for offline companies, according to a series of joint studies in online retail by Bain & Company/Mainspring.[2] For example, in apparel, the average repeat customer spent 67 percent more overall in the third year of his or her shopping relationship with an online retail vendor than in the first six months.

The same research also shows that for e-tailers to recoup their marketing and operations costs, they need to convince customers to return to their site again and again. The study found that the average online apparel shopper was not profitable for the retailer until he or she had shopped at the site four times. This implies that the retailer has to retain the customer for twelve months just to break even on the acquisition costs.

The same thing likely holds true for your firm. Look at the loyalty levels attached to your revenues. If the loyalty levels are weak, the revenue is "at-risk." Where do your customers stand? When do they become truly profitable for you? If you don't know, it's time to load your spread sheet and work the numbers.

MULTICHANNEL SHOPPERS INCREASE REVENUES

It's worth noting in the case mentioned earlier, that many of the customers acquired through the direct marketing firm's Web site also became customers of the catalog channel, and they produced higher levels of revenue than those who remained online customers only. Other firms find similar results. Home-shopping network QVC finds customers that use the Internet and on-air shopping are their best, most loyal, and most profitable customers. They also know that when they find a new online customer and convert that person to television, they have twice the value.

THINK EVERYDAY LIFE

Still not sure about the importance of attending to hockey stick loyalty for your organization? Think about it in your everyday life. How many restaurants do you go back to because the meal was "satisfactory"? What do you say when your 24-year-old daughter comes home with a fiancé and pronounces him "satisfactory"? What about your stereo system? Just "satisfactory" is it? We'll bet you brag about *that* to all your friends. Enjoy sports? How many people really get a kick out of a "satisfactory" game? Or a "satisfactory" season?

Our guess is that you'll never go back to the restaurant, that you're appalled at your daughter's choice, that you'll buy some other brand of stereo next time, and that you'll switch off that snoozer of a ball team and mow the lawn.

Satisfactory doesn't cut it in everyday life, and it doesn't cut it in terms of customer retention. Not even close.

TAKE THIS TEST

Don't take our word for it. Judge for yourself the impact of "just satisfactory." Run this experiment for the next week. Every time you interact with an online or offline business give it a rating (Figure 3-6).

Next, decide what the probability is that you will return to that place to do business again: definitely, probably, maybe or maybe not, probably not, definitely not (Figure 3-7). Using the same scale, decide whether you'd recommend that business to a friend.

Notice the pattern that develops. You'll probably find that the real pay-off in genuine loyalty comes at the top of the satisfaction scale. Are you recommending sites that satisfied you or just wrapping up your business and forgetting about them? Want to add some discussion value to it? Ask your colleagues to do the same thing.

Keep this in mind: Your customers bring mental versions of this same score card with them every time they come to your Web site. Every day they're deciding, consciously or unconsciously, whether

---

How Satisfactory Was My Visit to This Store/Site?*

Name of establishment: _____

Date visited: _____

Not Satisfied	Somewhat Satisfied	Satisfied	Very Satisfied	Completely Satisfied
1	2	3	4	5

*Yes, we know this isn't a balanced scale. It is slanted toward the positive evaluation end so you can clearly see the "Hockey Stick" effect in your ratings.

Figure 3-6. Testing hockey-stick loyalty.

What Is the Probability That I Will Return to This Place of Business?				

Name of establishment: _____

Date visited: _____

Definitely Not	Probably Not	Maybe / Maybe Not	Probably	Definitely
5	4	3	2	1

Figure 3-7. Would I go back?

they'll come back and whether they'll recommend you to a colleague, friend, or relative. Do an outstanding or excellent job for them, and they'll come back again and again. Drop one notch in the ratings to good, and the loyalty level drops significantly. They slide back down the hockey-stick curve.

THE ANATOMY OF CUSTOMER-PLEASING E-SERVICE

Seven Principles, Twenty-Four Keys

NOTHING

↓

in the history of business has grown with the speed of commerce on the Internet. Nothing. By one estimate, the 1990s saw hundreds of thousands new commercial Web-based start-ups a year. Who knows. Who could know! Infinite possibility and endless optimism are part of the nature of the brave new beast. The heroic mythology and uncertain reality are part of the allure. With every rumor of new venture success, a thousand and one "What if" visions join the entrepreneurial ether and the business plans flow.

The success of Pierra Omidyar's ebay.com, started as an exchange site for Pez collectors, inspired a thousand and one hopeful hobbyists to establish a thousand and one specialty auction Web sites.

A fabric designer in rural India put her unique patterns online, was discovered there by a London necktie maker, and both prospered—mightily. Within a fortnight, a thousand and one art students and Sunday watercolorists with stars and dollar signs in their eyes had erected a thousand and one cybershowrooms.

Michael Colton and John Aboud, a pair of Harvard College chums, amused themselves by writing outrageous parodies and posting them as a Web site magazine named *Modern Humorist*. Serious venture capitalists lined up with offers to turn their hobby into a full-fledged dot-com company—the newest of the thousand and one spins on the success of the TheOnion.com, one of the Internet's earlier humor e-zines. This, too, is the nature of this brave new beast.

THE E-SERVICE CHALLENGE

Within this wild and woolly entrepreneurial context, the business of declaring a singular vision of e-service success is a daunting idea. Seeing clearly the importance of e-service to commercial Web success and knowing just how to leverage this opportunity are very different things. Just as every new business concept is almost instantly copied and/or mutated a dozen times, e-service advances rocket through the medium at blazing speed. Dell Computer spends months researching and adding a natural language search engine to its self-service options, and a few short weeks later every respectable Web-based technology purveyor has a natural language search engine on their site—or claims to.

The lightening speed of innovation is as true for e-service as it is for dot-com business plans and software innovations. Just the same, we believe that there is a short list of principles—seven to be exact—that govern the management and delivery of high-quality, customer-pleasing, company-differentiating e-service. Our research into the ways of the best e-service providers; the wants and needs of both novice and experienced e-customers; and our years of research and consulting with brick and mortar companies, brick and click companies, and pure dot-com players as well convince us that armed with this menu of seven ideas—and a little creativity—any commerce venture can meet the challenge of creating and maintaining an e-service edge.

THE SEVEN PRINCIPLES: SECRETS OF E-MASTERS

The e-service masters first and foremost have an obsession with their customers. They talk to them, study them, and learn from them. The e-masters do not, however, simply take orders from their customers. Rather, they synthesize their sense of customers' wants, needs, and expectations into unique, clever, and sometimes highly innovative solutions. And sometimes they learn the lesson of failing forward. But learn, and listen, and try again, they indeed do.

The successes of the e-service masters seem invariably to fall along seven lines. Specifically, their success at creating customer pleasing, company distinctive e-service comes from the following principles.

1. *Practice easy-to-do business with thinking.* Easy-to-do-business-with (ETDBW) thinking asks first, "how do we make it simple and effortless for customers to find and use us, and only then deals with questions of style and design. ETDBW thinking asks everyone in the organization to think first like a customer and last like a technical wizard.

2. *Design for distinction*. The look and feel of an e-commerce site sets the tone and tenor for customer expectations. A site designed with the customer and brand uniqueness in mind forms an indelible, lasting impression on the customer psyche.

3. *Personalize the e-experience.* Commerce in Internet space may be frictionless and remote, but it need not—should not be impersonal. People do business with people. Creating a sense of intimacy in the e-world is both possible and important.

4. *Deliver end-to-end service.* Also-rans believe the sale is over, the transaction completed when the customer clicks on the "submit order" button. E-service masters know that the transaction isn't complete until the product is in the customer's hands or the service has been delivered. They manage every contact point in the customer's cycle of service.

5. *Encourage human contact.* E-Commerce is by definition an efficient medium. It is a core axiom. But it need not be a bloodless, sterile medium. E-service masters know that the right balance of human touch puts a unique distinctive face on their endeavors.

6. Make recovery a point of pride. The e-savvy know that despite their best, most focused efforts, things can and sometimes do go awry. The e-service masters who know that fixing customer problems and answering customer queries, faster, better, more fully, and with style give their venture a clear advantage to customers who have seen them retrieve a lost situation from the brink and know the true strength of the organization.

7. Build a retention strategy. The most savvy of the e-service masters know that retention—repeat business—doesn't come from luck, or great product, or happenstance. Retention is a thought-out, iterated, and polished plan. It is the master goal: Bring customers back to your site—your business really—again and again. It is the goal that pulls together the other six principles.

From here to the end of the book, as we progress through the exploration of these seven principles as they are practiced by the handful of bona fide e-service masters we've encountered in our research, there are key points—specific, practical lessons we learned. There are twenty-four of them. Think of them as rules of the road for applying the seven principles to your organization's e-service efforts.

A NECESSARY WARNING!

As this book was being written, we endeavored to include as much state-of-the-art e-service technology and technique as possible. We knew, of course, that even though the publishers would do their level best to turn manuscript to finished work in record time, the odds were, that much of the technology and even some of the technique we give voice to here, would be "de rigueur" by the time the book hits the shelf and wends its way into your hands.

And there is even a chance that the state-of-the-art research we cite—some of it only days old when the manuscript was put to bed—could feel dated as this is read. Today there is both a real and false sense that things are changing so fast we can scarcely chronicle them. We concede, agree, and cheer the fact that by the time you read this, some of the highly effective, state of the art, e-service we point to could be a little passé.

However, we believe with equal vigor that the seven principles and twenty-four keys around which this book is structured can provide solid, long-term guidance for building world-class e-service. The particulars of application may change—will change—but amazing service recovery and systems designed with ETDBW in mind, to pick just two of the principles, will transcend the particulars of current practice. If we've done our work well, it will be the platform from which you, dear reader, will create the future e-service that we will all marvel at next.

PRACTICE EASY-TO-DO-BUSINESS-WITH THINKING

IN

↓

the 1990s we developed an inventory and database of characteristics and practices that distinguished between organizations that delight and retain their customers and those that marginally satisfy and frequently lose customers. In effect, it was a survey-based process that separated those that simply sold products and performed services from those that created value for their customers and strove—successfully—to create long-term business relationships with those customers.

One of the most statistically influential factors in that database is one we dub, having an "easy-to-do-business-with" (ETDBW) delivery system and attitude. Specifically, organizations deemed "easy-to-do-business-with" by their customers are distinguished externally by their ease of access, the transparency of their systems, and the reasonableness of their policies and procedures.

While it's amply clear from our data that these ETDBW characteristics are important for brick and mortar companies, when it comes to e-commerce they are the lifeblood of success. For example, a mediocre restaurant with a surly wait staff that sits in the heart of a major business district will continue to do business and profit because its proximity to a major work place gives it value. On the Web there is no proximity, or rather every business has proximity—they all reside in every office, every living room, everywhere a shopper might sit and surf. Online customers won't notice you as they wander down the street, they have to seek you out. They won't return out of convenience because they can just as easily go to a hundred other sites with the same ease as visiting yours. So, delighting them with your products and services, making yourself ETDBW, is critical to surviving online.

ETDBW e-companies make it easy for customers to obtain their products, information, or services—on their own terms—just as they make it easy for customers to reach the right individual, area, or resolution system when they have a problem or question.

Internally, organizations high on the ETDBW scale are characterized by significant employee accommodation—they work as hard at keeping their people as they do to at keeping customers. In ETDBW companies, organization policies and procedures are regularly reviewed to ensure that they make it easy and efficient for employees to deliver excellent service and quickly solve customer problems. Formal processes exist for collecting data on errors, customer complaints, and comments, and there are procedures for analyzing their significance and modifying the systems accordingly. Employees have the knowledge, skill, and permission to "do what it takes" to solve customer problems.

At Amazon.com, service representatives have broad authority for responding to customer queries and complaints. For example, they can unilaterally decide to rebate a shipping charge, offer a discount, or issue a credit. They are empowered and supported by systems, policies, procedures, and a management team that knows and believes in the importance of making Amazon.com an ETDBW company.

As we continue to meld e-commerce and "new economy" companies in this database, ETDBW persists in being a significant distinguisher between companies that customers rate as "exceptional" and those rated "run-of-the-mill." The core message of ETDBW is to focus on making it easy—to the point of effortlessness—for customers to do business with you. Every dollar and hour you spend anticipating and removing barriers to customer access, fulfillment, and support will come back tenfold.

San Francisco Chronicle staff writer Sam Zuckerman made the ETDBW point well in his assessment of the superior customer satisfaction results that J.D. Power reported for Fidelity Investments and Charles Schwab over back-of-the-pack E-Trade Group. "It is not surprising to see a gap between leaders Fidelity and Schwab, which were in the brokerage business before online investing took off, and E-Trade, which came of age in the Internet era," wrote Zuckerman. "Schwab and Fidelity have a long tradition of high quality customer service and support. E-Trade is a more technology controlled firm as opposed to a customer-controlled firm."[1]

In short, adopting an ETDBW mentality recognizes that most of your customers come to your site to have a need met, not to play with your technology. Make your technology work for them, not the other way around.

KEY 1:
MASTER THE ETDBW DESIGN BASICS

There is an emerging collection of agreed-upon basic rules of e-commerce system design that if adhered to will yield the ETDBW results you need for sustained success and if strayed from will ruin the visitor's experience and ensure they won't come back to your barrier-laden Web site. The rules are

1. Be useful. Shoppers typically don't care about the history of your founder so don't make that your opening page—or even an obvious detour. They *do* care about finding a product that fits their needs quickly and easily. Give them easy access to prices, descriptions, and checkouts. Do not inundate them with pop-up windows, banner ads, and useless information. OK, if your founder is an obvious cultural icon: Colonel Sanders, Bill Gates, Conrad Hilton, Michael Dell, Walt Disney, Steve Jobs, Jeff Bezos, Debbie Fields, Lillian Vernon, or Steve Case some voyeuristic visitors may want to read or hear their words of wisdom, even gaze on their visages. Just take care to make that a very minor piece of your Web presence. By and large, customers are at your Web site for commerce, not for entertainment.

2. *Don't waste their time.* Buyers shop online because it's advertised as being faster, cheaper, and more convenient than going to a store or calling a vendor. Keep this in mind at all times while evaluating your plans to add, subtract, change, or modify your Web site. Give them one-click access to any page from any page through a universal navigator. A ski equipment site that begins by asking for the customer's skiing proficiency level feels as if the customer's convenience and time are important considerations to your company.

3. *Make everything obvious.* The best way to do this is to make every vital link and tool accessible on every page. That includes a search field, access to the shopping cart, a direct "jump to checkout" option, shopping categories, and customer service. If the buyer has to hunt and search for anything, the experience becomes a burden.

4. Be *bandwidth-friendly.* No matter how attractive your graphics, long downloads annoy shoppers. They are not there to be wowed by your art, they are there to shop. Zona Research estimates that Web sites are losing $362 million per month, more than $4 billion annually, because of unacceptable download speeds.[2]

According to the report, the average Web buyer will wait about eight seconds for a page to download.

One way to sneak big graphics in without losing business is to have the rest of your content download first giving shoppers something to read while the graphics load. The HoneyBaked Ham Company (HoneyBaked.com) uses this tactic. Click on an item in the product list and you immediately see a delicious description of your item with phrases like "seven-pound spiral sliced ham smothered in our secret-spice glaze." About halfway through reading the description the picture pops into place, squelching any doubts you might have that spiral sliced ham is exactly what you want.

5. *Keep it simple.* Web shopping is about simplifying the purchasing process: Simple to search, to browse, to check out, to return, to get help, to find any information that might to be relevant. In fact, "simplify" is the mantra of every business-to-business buyer who wants to preselect a set of products and services from a vendor site and let employees help themselves on an as-needed basis. The Web is where corporate purchasers change their role from order taker to product purchase powerholder.

6. *Show them what they've bought.* Access to the shopping cart gives shoppers a sense of security. It let's them know what they've chosen and that nothing has been accidentally purchased or lost. At Web sites like Clinique.com, every product chosen is listed at the top of every page under "items in bag," so consumers can always keep an eye on their purchases. Barring this sort of constant view of your shopped items, a one-click link to the shopping basket on every page is the next best thing.

7. *Give them lots of search options.* Companies that understand and anticipate how customers will use their site almost always have state-of-the-art search engines. REI.com lets consumers do price searches, allowing them to narrow the list of products to only those things they can afford. Illuminations.com has a "Find a Gift" search tool that lets shoppers choose an occasion and price category and a search routine that returns a list of suggested items.

8. *Encourage customers to make contact if they want help or have a question.* Putting a business online does not mean you can reduce the customer service experience. In many cases it will increase your need to communicate with customers, and the channels used for that communication will expand. An increase in the number of options you provide for customer communication will usually decrease the cost per transaction, but not necessarily your total customer service net.

9. *Give consumers access to help on their terms.* Nothing infuriates a Web shopper more than a site that doesn't have contact information and multiple contact options.

Your 800 number should be boldly listed on every page. The "contact us" link, which must be accessible on every page, should list phone numbers, addresses, and e-mail addresses to real people who will actually respond. Sites like Influent.com have the right idea. It lists names of employees along with their job function and e-mail address so you can e-mail the person who will best fulfill your needs.

A single e-mail address to Webmaster or info@company.com doesn't cut it. "Consumers today have no expectation of getting a response from an e-mail sent to an info@ address," says Barry

Parr, an analyst with International Data Corp. (IDC), a research firm based in Framingham, Massachusetts. "They are more confident about e-mail to people with names."

10. *Answer every e-mail in less than a day.* Better yet, answer in less than an hour and do it in a personable manner. "Delight is a universal reaction to a personal e-mail response that answers a question from a real person at an e-commerce site," says Parr.

E-customers across all industries expect an acknowledgment of their e-contact within one hour, and an actual answer to their questions within one to twenty-four hours depending on the industry, according to the ICSA/e-Satisfy.com Benchmarking Study.[3] The study also shows that only 12 percent of e-customers receive an acknowledgment in one hour, and only 43 percent receive one in twenty-four hours.

Don't be the site that lets them down. A friendly, timely response to an e-mail query cements customer loyalty.

11. *Don't ever tell them you are too busy to respond.* If you send an acknowledgment that says you are too busy to answer today, but you will soon, consumers will shop somewhere else. If you can't answer a question in twenty-four hours some might ask, "Why bother?" A response to a question posed days earlier is of little value. If they had any intention of shopping they did it somewhere else.

Customers are not transactions, they are people who demand respect. If you are too busy to do business with them, surely there will be others who are not.

12. *Make it easy to navigate.* Studies conducted for this book show that regardless of the Web savvy of the user, ease of navigation is the most important element of design. In fact, the more savvy users have greater expectations of site navigation because they know what the Web is capable of.

13. "Easy to navigate" means you can get to any page regardless of where you are in the site. The Web is not a linear experience. Shoppers will not travel through several "departments" to find what they want. Sites like Clinique.com and HoneyBaked.com make excellent use of tabs and robust, yet simple navigation design to make it easy to jump around the site.

14. Put a price with every product. Consumers want to comparison shop so prices should be up front and everywhere. List them next to every initial product link and again with the product description. Don't make shoppers drill to the description to find out what it costs. This wastes their time, which is counterproductive.

15. Have simple beneficial registration processes. Registration options are the latest customer service craze at e-commerce sites. Filling out names, addresses, and shipping information is tedious. Consumers are happy to give you the information in exchange for a faster checkout. Registration is not only for companies to bulk up their contact database, it is to make the shopping experience simpler and faster for the consumer. It is one more way sites brand the experience and make consumers imagine that they could shop at this site again.

16. Tell them what the shipping costs will be long before they get to the checkout. Shipping dramatically changes the cost of a product and without that information shoppers cannot make informed decisions about what they are buying. "I want a Web site to tell me how much shipping is going to be before I go through the process of adding items to my cart, going to the checkout, and then finding out it's ridiculous," says one focus group participant. A link to shipping information on the navigation bar will give them peace of mind and increase sales.

> A study by BizRate, a company that rates online stores, found that 24 percent of customers who had abandoned an online shipping cart, did so because they found shipping and handling charges to be too high; a reason given three times as frequently as the next highest category—"technical glitches" in the site.[4]

17. Tell customers how they can return items and make it simple. If you are a brick and mortar as well as a click and mortar store system, let them return merchandise to any one of your locations. If you are a dot-com, include a return label and return shipping instructions with the package so if something is wrong with the order, the customer can simply retape the shipping box and leave it for the postal carrier.

18. In the business-to-consumer (B2C) space, make the checkout process fast and painless. Once consumers are done shopping, they want to check out quickly and easily and they only want to do it once. Three screens to check out is the expectation. You can further reduce that with quick checkout options, like the ones at Godiva.com and Amazon.com that allow consumers to save their checkout information at your site.

This is a rule that surprisingly, many existing e-commerce sites have a tough time following. When Andersen Consulting shoppers attempted to purchase 480 gifts at 100 different Web sites during the Christmas 1999 season, more than one-quarter of the sites explored could not take orders—they crashed, were blocked, were under construction, or were otherwise inaccessible.[5] Our own "Shopping the Internet Circa 1999" study found that 5.1 percent of 744 sites visited locked up or kicked the shopper offline during their visits.[6] Every time a site makes it impossible to complete an order, especially if time has been spent shopping at the site, the consumer will leave, tell others not to go there, and, of course, mark it off their own list of go-back-to sites.

19. *Deliver products on time.* If you say the product will arrive on Tuesday it had better. Need we even refer to the Christmas 1999 ToysRus.com debacle?[7] Hopefully your failures won't make the six o'clock news, but they will surely be discussed over coffee and in chat rooms for months to come.

To avoid disappointing customers, either deliver products in the amount of time promised, which begins the very moment they completed the transaction, or explain in detail at your site when an item can actually be expected to arrive.

20. *Unless your primary audience is eight year olds, get rid of anything on the site that blinks, spins, or otherwise moves erratically.* Whippy, zippy, childish features annoy adult shoppers. And while you're at it, toss out that splash page that does nothing more than make customers wait forty-five seconds to see an obscure graphic and welcome message. Nothing online says "I don't care at all about your time, but I do like to show off" like a Web site splash page that means nothing to—and does nothing for—the customer.

If you screw up apologize. It's your fault, make it better. Recovery is one of the most effective ways to cement loyalty and turn a frustrated shopper into a contented one. Dissatisfied e-customers tell twice as many people about their e-experiences—both online and offline—than satisfied e-customers, says the ICSA/e-Satisfy.com Benchmarking Study.[8] Dissatisfied e-customers are also almost four times more likely to discuss their experiences in online chat rooms. Don't take the chance of losing thousands of potential customers as a result of one mistake.

THE EXTRA RULES OF BUSINESS TO BUSINESS

Making a business-to-business (B2B) site ETDBW is not radically different from doing the same for a consumer site; but there are enough differences that you can't take the overlap for granted. Even though corporate buyers have frequently cut their Web teeth as consumer shoppers and it's where they set many of their expectations, they are much more demanding of characteristics like speed and dispatch. There are at least five features that busy, efficiency-minded B2B buyers expect from an ETBW e-commerce site.

1. *Customize the experience.* Most large companies expect online vendors to customize an online presence just for them—either on the Web or on their corporate intranet. Corporate buyers want to choose exactly what items employees can buy and have specific automated verification processes in place that ensure only certain items are bought by certain people. The expectation of custom-built sites is universal with most giant corporations, and the concept is trickling down to smaller and smaller organizations. As B2B syndicates become the structure a la mode, customization around simplicity, ease of use, and reliability will become an absolute entry level standard.

2. *Save their purchase history and give them reorder options.* If a customer plans to buy largely the same items month after month, they expect to be able to go to your site, click on their personal history and reorder the same batch of goods, with the option to modify the order. The entire process should take but minutes to complete.

3. *Give every B2B customer a sales rep whom they can contact.* Unlike personal consumers, corporate buyers want a personal sales rep who knows their account and is available to help if needed. The difference in the Web-based B2B relationship is that the buyers have greater control over the contact, calling or e-mailing only when they feel it's necessary. Oh, that account representative had better know the customer's account history deal cold, especially the problem history.

4. *Send e-mail order reminders.* Companies like Staples.com use order reminders as a big selling point of their online services. The feature should be optional and not abusive. Subtle personal e-mails that say it's time to reorder your standard shipment of goods increases sales and customer satisfaction. CAUTION: Daily special sales announcements, select customer offers, a barrage of coupons, and the like turn personal contact into junk mail assault in a heartbeat. Only send options and offers to customers who want them—and stop sending them if they appear to annoy.

5. *Make participation and self-service meaningful.* The Chubb Organization, a Warren, New Jersey-based property casualty company already allows commercial customers to review policies, track claims online, and even lets shippers write their own certificates of insurance online as they need them. To speed the forging of complex multinational policies, Chubb can, and frequently does, link agents and customers in twenty countries together with the head office to do a real-time hashing out of coverages and pricing. Next out of the e-door—providing commercial customers access to a data warehouse and analytical tools for examining and studying the business they are doing with Chubb.[9]

While these entreaties are not rocket science, surprisingly few companies, from the fledgling start-ups to the world-weary mega brands, are following any or all of these ETDBW guidelines. An IDC survey of Internet retailers showed, for instance, that while e-vendors all agreed that speed, security, and easy navigation are crucial to the success of an e-commerce site, only half felt that their sites were completely secure and only one-fourth thought they were fast and easy to navigate.[10]

Consumers, from the least to most savvy, are unwilling to struggle to do business with you online. Their expectations are simple and their choices are infinite. They expect the new technology to make something about their life or work easier. Be the one to accommodate them, and you will flourish. Ignore them, and you will join the dying breed of companies that just couldn't make online commerce click.

WHAT THE CUSTOMER DOESN'T—AND SHOULDN'T SEE—COUNTS MOST

A duck swimming upsteam is a perfect metaphor for a well-run commercial Web site. What the observer sees is smooth, against-the-current progress, while below the waterline, the outwardly calm quacker is paddling like heck. A well done e-commerce site looks and runs so smoothly it seems natural and easy. Away from the customer's view, below the line of visibility, there is an undertow of action and activity that supports, and makes possible, that customer perception and experience of buying ease.

The key is a continual customer-focused picking at, prodding, and improvement of every essential element of your e-service delivery system.

KEY 2:
START ETDBW BELOW THE LINE OF VISIBILITY

Your e-service delivery system consists of all the apparatus, physical and procedural, that your employees must have at their disposal to meet customers' needs and to keep the service promises you make to your customers. What your business plan and marketing material promise is what your system must deliver—every time.

If your promise is, "twenty-four-hour delivery on all orders—no exceptions," your e-service delivery system is everything you do and use to make twenty-four-hour delivery a reality, from your order entry system to the way you measure your performance.

In a badly designed and poorly operating delivery system, you frequently hear managers complaining about lazy, unmotivated employees; frontline employees complaining about stupid, unreasonable customers; and customers complaining about inflexible, unhelpful systems, features, people, and rules. A well-done e-commerce service delivery system is customer- and employee-friendly and has monitors and feedback mechanisms to enable the people who work in the system to correct poor results.

Your continuing quest should be to seek out ways of making it easier for your customers to do business with you tomorrow than it was for them to do business with you last year, last month, last week, and last night. Rest assured that's exactly what your competition is doing.

Rule of Thumb: Never say, "That's against company policy," unless you have a good explanation—from the customer's point of view—to back up that hard-nosed position.

KEY 3:
MAKE YOUR SYSTEMS EMPLOYEE- AND CUSTOMER-FRIENDLY

You need systems, rules, policies, and procedures to run your business. But rules, policies, and procedures are the servants, not the masters. In a world where most services and products are readily available from multiple sources, it is important to make the components of the service transaction painless and easy at a minimum, and invisible or positively memorable at best.

Your employees have nothing but your systems and their skills to delight customers. A well-designed service system must have two attributes if it is to help them do that consistently:

1. E-service delivery systems should be "easy on your employees." E-service delivery systems are not a naturally occurring phenomenon. People make them up. Therefore, people should be able to explain them, and adjust them—and fine-tune them, and change them—and even circumvent them on those occasions when a customer comes in from an angle no system designer could ever have foreseen. The people with the power to flex and change the systems should be the ones closest to the customer.

For example, at Godiva.com, point out an error in the Web site to a customer service rep (CSR) and they can adjust it instantly. "Go ahead, point something out and I'll change it," said Beth Brown, Internet marketing manager at New York City-based Godiva, as we discussed the site in a recent phone conversation. If there is a problem or they want to highlight a new product, she and others on the Internet team have the power to make changes at the site for instant updates to better serve customers.

2. E-service delivery systems should be "easy for your employees." If the rules, policies, and procedures get in the way of giving great service, your employees will stop focusing on their roles and start focusing on their restrictions. If a customer e-mails your service rep to let them know they received a damaged or incorrect product, that CSR must be empowered to make it up to the customer. Give them the control to say "Another product will be sent immediately and here are coupons for your next purchase," and everyone will be delighted. Create a wall of red tape that CSRs have to climb through to help disgruntled customers, and they will get positively surly at the mere mention of a bad service experience.

As one veteran of the e-service wars told us, "If I am on the frontline listening to customers bitch about bad pages, balky processes, and policy barriers that I cannot make better or simply bypass, I either become a bastard or a burnout."

THE HUMAN FACTOR

There's a very real people dimension to the ETDBW delivery system dilemma. It's usually expressed in the lament, "You just can't get good people anymore." Wrong. We would argue that their experience with dysfunctional and sometimes downright abusive service systems have taught your employees, and your customers, a lot of bad habits, attitudes, and behaviors. The people at the frontline have learned to duck and cover because what hits the fan hits them from every direction.

"Old economy" managers and higher-ups often preach conformity to rules and regulations, policies and procedures, accountability and control. They make a point of punishing people who try to do more than they are, on paper, allowed to do. As a result, customers faced with inflexible people and their inflexible rules long ago learned that they have to get nasty if they want to receive anything beyond a recitation of the policy manual. Today, they don't even bother to grumble loudly, they simply click away and never come back.

THE LAW OF RULES

Your core in-house management responsibility is to set up workflows, guidelines, procedures and fail-safes that your employees can readily manipulate to meet the specific needs and expectations of your customers. It's inevitable that over time rules will be written and evolve. The "Good Rules" will well serve your employees—and through them your customers . The "Bad Rules" will seek to enslave. How do you know which is which?

Good Rules are grounded in customer expectations and contribute to meeting customer needs. Making answering the phone by the third ring or e-mailing responses in one hour into a rule won't impress the customer whose call is answered in staccato fashion and who is put on hold before a word can be inserted edgewise because your people are working only to hit the statistical target. The same is true of a one-hour e-mail reply that acknowledges receipt of an e-mail and promises a detailed response within three weeks. It reinforces an already upset customer's worst fears about your organization.

Good Rules help the customer experience your organization as ETDBW. Put yourself in your customer's shoes: Do the steps you ask them to take to solve a problem or obtain information make sense or do they make extra work for you and/or your customers?

Good Rules are consistent with your service strategy. Kinko's Copy Centers work hard to be the copier of choice for college students. Consequently, the Kinko's rule of thumb is, "We accept students' checks." OmahaSteaks.com wants to be your provider for high-quality/high-value beef products. So it is not unusual for an order of steaks to contain four bonus hamburger patties. The "extra" gives the customer a sampling of a different product and adds substance to the value proposition and delight to the experience.

Good Rules have feedback woven in. They have a system-monitoring component that alerts you in prompt and actionable fashion whenever the delivery system is about to fail or break. That way you can fix it before customers experience your site crashing, their e-mails getting lost, or being dumped from your site during checkout. Delays, glitches, backups, abandonment rates, and the like should be captured and reported real-time and trends analyzed daily, if not instantly.

Good Rules allow employees who come in contact with customers to be human and humane, not robotic. They allow, even encourage, your people to respond uniquely, personally, and creatively to the full spectrum of customer needs and expectations, and especially to those that do not fit the standard pattern. Amazon.com reps are encouraged to personalize e-mail to customers instead of sending generic, prepackaged responses to questions.

LillianVernon.com's CSRs are empowered to suggest alternative sources for goods that they don't have in their own stock. Customers can't help but be impressed when CSRs go the extra mile and provide them with something they didn't expect.

Good Rules are simply guidelines to promote a value or goal, not the value or goal itself. In setting up fail-safing and continuously evaluating your service system, remember that it's the customer's need that is driving the game. As Harvard marketing professor Theodore Levitt put it, the customer would like to go from "I need a quarter-inch hole" to "I have a quarter-inch hole" without having to deal with quarter-inch drill bits and drills and hardware stores and chucks and electric cords and checkout counters. The smart e-service provider designs and maintains the delivery system accordingly. Service systems that are low on the friendliness scale, by their very design, tend to subordinate convenience and ease of access for the customer in favor of the convenience of the people within the system. Sure it would be easier if customers would follow one path through your system or be willing to fill out a ten-page checkout form to make processing easier for you, but they won't. Try to make them and they will be livid and vocal when they ditch your site and tell their colleagues about you.

SYSTEM SOLUTIONS

How good are you right now? How many times do you have to wonder, "Where did the system break down?" and "Where did the customer get lost?" and "How can we rewrite the rules, change the policies or upgrade the gear to keep this from happening again?" The more often you ask (and answer) those questions in the short-term, the less you'll face them as major, life threatening problems in the long-term.

What does an ETDBW e-service delivery system look like in action? From the customer's point of view, the "customer friendliest" delivery systems are:

1. **Accessible.** You can reach the company easily, when you want to, and in multiple ways: via e-mail, live 24-7 chat, an 800 number, snail mail, and fax.
2. **Accurate.** Whether it's about shipments, billings, status, or product usage, the information is accurate and correct.
3. **Integrated.** Customers can get all the information they need from one point of contact if that is their desire. Yes, that may mean information redundancy as well.

4. **Customer-Driven.** Customers can understand and use the information they're given without a basket of order numbers, item IDs, and billing codes in hand.

5. **Fast.** Customers never have the sense they are waiting for a very slow computer to get warmed up or that their product order is making the trip from Phoenix to Boston via rickshaw or pedicab. E-commerce sets cyberfast expectations for everything you do.

6. **Totally Transparent.** If there are hoops to be jumped through or marathons to be run, they happen outside of the customer's field of vision.

CHANGING A NOT SO ETDBW SYSTEM

◆ Do Not go out and start buying new auto responders, or new phone systems, or new routers.

◆ Do Not go out and hire a pack of expensive management consultants and page designers.

◆ Do Not blame, punish, or execute existing associates.

◆ Do start with a series of small meetings with customer contact employees and employees who directly support their work and customers' use of your site.

◆ Do Not make the meetings too small or people will be reluctant to tell you what they really think or so large that most people feel like spectators. In those meetings ask two questions:

1. What do our customers like least about doing business with us?

2 What can we do to make it easier for you to serve the customer?

Then shut up, listen, and take notes. You won't necessarily like the answers, and they may not all be immediately actionable, but they will give you a great start at making your company, department or team ETDBW.

MEASURE AND MANAGE FROM THE CUSTOMER'S POINT OF VIEW

Regardless of the business segment you are in and the size of your operation, measure you must! A commitment to service quality without a commitment to standards and measurement is a dedication to lip service, not e-service. Standards and measurement are critical to the smooth functioning—and improvement—of your e-service delivery system.

A common denominator among companies with reputations for high-quality service is their bias for setting service standards and their prodigious efforts to measure how well those standards are met. In complex e-service delivery systems like those of Amazon.com, Ebay.com or even mixed brick and click companies like Federal Express or Schwab that effort involves hundreds of standards and a multitude of measurement systems to keep e-service delivery on an even keel. In a simpler system, like that of a Troutriver.com or Coopersnuthouse.com, it takes far fewer standards and measures to keep on top of the "how are we doing?" question.

THE LOOK OF CUSTOMER-FOCUSED MEASUREMENT

Chances are pretty good that you already measure a number of things about the e-service delivery systems you manage all or part of. Just the same, it is a good idea to stop, step back from your system for a moment, and ask yourself whether your current measurement is driven by customer parameters or internal technical specs. To make sure the former, not the latter, energizes your measurement efforts, use these three general criteria for auditing, and perhaps improving, the customer focus of your e-service delivery system.

1. *Your measurements should reflect your marketplace purpose.* Nothing makes your vision or service strategy—your purpose— more real to everyone in the organization than measuring what you're doing against customer-focused norms. If one of your service promises is for "timely deliveries on all shipments," and your customers have told you that means "twenty-four hour turnaround on all orders," measure that. But don't just look inside. You're not done until the customer has taken delivery, so be sure you also measure the customer's perception of whether orders are arriving "in a timely fashion." On the Internet, customers begin measuring delivery time from the moment they complete the online transaction—not twenty-four hours later when it actually gets processed or three days later when the item comes into stock. Even if you're dead solid certain that a customer's order came and went in twenty-four hours—and twenty-four hours is twice as good as your nearest competitor—if the customer doesn't perceive that the order arrived in a timely fashion, the customer is right and you are wrong.

> Remember: For the e-customer, perception is all there is.

How can you be 100 percent "on time" but wrong about being "timely?"

◆ First, the twenty-four-hour standard is *your* technical standard, not the customer's. To the customer, "timely" is a perception, not a measurement, as it is to you.

◆ Second, "timely" or "on time" to you typically means when the order goes out your door. To customers, those same words may well mean the time the order comes in their door, is on the shelf in their warehouse, or is in hand and ready for distribution or use in their system.

Not your problem? Wrong! If your customers believe there is a problem, there is a problem—whether you think it's real or not. And you'd better have a systematic way of finding out about it. Your measurement system has to tell you about the problems customers are perceiving as soon as possible, not just comfort you with statistics about your adherence to your own technical standards.

2. *Your measurements should measure customer quality, not just technical quality. There is a difference between the two.*

◆ Technical quality is the measurement of all the hardware and mechanical and procedural things that must go right if your system is to work effectively and efficiently. Technical quality measures are internal indicators of your delivery system's specification driven performance.

Think: Speed of your site, server down time, order waiting time, order assembly time, back order volume, order turnaround time, shipments per hour, and similar measures.

◆ Customer quality is the performance of your e-service delivery system from the customer's point view. It is the assembly of elements that are important to the customer, as judged by the customer. These are the elements that are directly observable by the customer and that most directly determine their satisfaction with your e-service delivery system.

Think: Ease of contact; order correctness and completeness; upfront information about shipping costs; speed, ease and accuracy of the site and checkout process; timeliness of order arrival; look of package upon arrival; understandability of the bill; simple return procedures; and similar subjective impressions.

Technical quality measures are important to trouble spotting, problem solving, and the smooth and cost-effective functioning of the system. Customer quality measures are important to customer satisfaction and retention and to system improvement and priority setting.

3. Your measurements should measure what's important, not just what's handy.

◆ It's late at night. A man, call him Naz, is crawling about on hands and knees in the street, near a streetlight. Chaz, a neighbor, comes by, watches Naz feeling around, sifting through the dirt, and crawling about.

"What are you looking for, old friend?" he asks.
"My key," answers Naz, "I lost my door key and can't get in my house."
"Just exactly where were you when you last saw your key?"

"Oh," answers Naz as he continues his searching, "I was across the street, near my front door when I dropped it."

"Then why are you looking for your key way over here?"

"Because the light's better over here," answers Naz.

That story is more than 400 years old. But, like Naz, we're all prone from time to time to do things the easy way, not the best way. That's especially true of building service quality measures. In organizations with extensive telephone customer contact, for example, the two most common measurements of the delivery system are length of phone calls and number of rings before pickup. Yet customers we've asked about contact with such companies seldom, if ever, mention either factor. They're more concerned about getting the information they need, having their problems solved (ideally during that first contact), and not being put on hold for hours or connected to the voicemail system from hell. The same is true of e-mail to your site, live online chat with a CSR, a perusal of your "frequently asked question" (FAQ) base, or use of your information search engine—responsiveness without resolution is superfluous and only serves to frustrate the customer.

In many organizations, these measures have been automated and computerized as an employee surveillance and evaluation system. The claim is that such measurement systems improve service. They do not. They may improve productivity, which may or may not be related, but service is not the point of such measurement systems. Authority and accountability are.

Not only do they not have the desired effect on customers, they also don't do a thing to help the people charged with delivering customer service. We've yet to talk to a CSR hooked up to one of these electronic stopwatch systems who didn't (a) resent the obvious lack of trust and (b) learn to trick the system anyway in self-defense.

Are we suggesting that you not measure "number of rings before answer" or "length of chat time with a customer" or "number of e-mails replied to" or "e-mail response time?" No. We are saying that these and similar measurements, valuable as they may or may not be for managing costs and monitoring system capacity, are not necessarily helping you directly manage service quality as perceived by your customer. That means they're not helping—and may well be hindering—your employees as they try to directly improve customer satisfaction and directly build customer retention.

ADD VALUE: THE MILK AND COOKIES PRINCIPLE

Great systems, well-designed and managed, start with a simple goal: reliability—delivering on your core promise to the customer. But delivering on reliability is only enough to get in the game. Reliability wins you satisfaction ratings. To really brand yourself in the minds of your e-customers, your systems need to reliably and consistently offer something extra—an added value to distinguish your style of doing business and attract business away from your competitors.

Our favorite example of the type of no-charge extras that can be bundled in, tracked, and consistently repeated to win over and keep customers is the Doubletree Inn's Milk and Cookies program. Frequent business travelers who stay with this Phoenix, Arizona-based lodging company answer a number of personal preference questions the first time they sign in at a company property. Among

the categories. Go straight to the person sitting in front of the monitor.

1. *Customer Surveys.* Face-to-face, through e-mail or snail mail, over the telephone, or through a combination of these, ask customers to rate you on overall satisfaction, on the success of the last transaction they had with you via your Web site, and on specific aspects of your e-service delivery system. Then feed the results back into your system. Be sure to ask both importance and performance questions. Use pop-up screens to ask them about the Web site itself. Use e-mail after the transaction to check out the whole cycle from first click to receipt of product or information. Get quantitative data and qualitative data.

2. *Focus Groups*. Bringing current customers together, especially B2B customers, to discuss the good, the bad, and the ugly of what you do puts flesh on the bones of survey data. Customers can problem solve with you, rate and rank the relative importance of different aspects of your service (the "Moments of Truth" that define the shape and style of your services in customers' eyes), and explain how different elements of a Web transaction affect their perceptions of you. Employee focus groups work almost as well as customer focus groups. Bring a group of employees together and ask questions like, "What are our customers saying to you?" and, "What gets in the way of doing your job?" and, "What should we be doing differently?"

3. *Employee Visit Teams.* These teams are useful primarily for B2B. Assign teams of frontline workers, supervisors, and support people to study the customers' "points of contact" (with you as well as your competitors) from the customers' point of view. Their assignment: Bring back ideas for improving transactional quality based on customer experiences. What are the pluses and minuses of your e-service delivery system versus alternative systems when seen in this light?

4. Viewing Room Studies. Put consumers in a focus group room that is equipped with computers. Let them log onto your site while observing and videotaping them. Have a trained facilitator chat with the paid users about the choices they make at your site, their search patterns, even query them about that furrowed brow or puzzled look. Following the clickstream gives you a start. Where did that person go on the site? How long did they stay there? What kinds of information did they read? After they read "A" did they go to "B" or to "C?" This is all helpful information, but it's not enough.

It doesn't tell exactly what's going on inside their heads. You need to know what kinds of comparisons they are making in their minds about your site experience. What are they thinking about while they're cruising around your site? What's going through their mind in the four seconds it takes a page to download? How are they responding to different pieces of information? Viewing labs in which you watch consumers shop your site can give you that information.

Don't be passive about your role. Encourage them to talk. Ask questions.
- What's going on in their minds?
- How did you feel about what you just saw?
- What would you like us to know about your experience?
- What should we have asked you that we didn't?

Questions like these will help prompt the verbalizations. **This** gives you direct input about user barriers and stumbling blocks and problem procedures.

5. *Customer Advisory Panels.* Retailers and software builders often use panels of customers to help them anticipate fashion trends; electronics manufacturers look for feedback on design, standards and pricing; utility companies study environmental and consumer options. If you're working for a long-term relationship with your customers, they should grow and change with you and vice versa. This is particularly useful for B2B relations.

6. *User Groups.* In the early days of the computer revolution, owners of specific brands of hardware and software often formed groups to share information and ideas; in essence, becoming a living user's manual. Initially, manufacturers felt threatened by them. Then a few smart ones began to use these groups of dedicated users for information and design assistance. Fittingly, when Apple introduced its first Macintosh model, it did so to the members of the Boston Computer Club.

7. *Employee Surveys.* Employees are sometimes reluctant to offer opinions and advice one-on-one or in live forums. A service quality survey is similar to an employee attitude survey, but focuses on (a) employee perception of how well the organization is doing in delivering quality service, (b) how current management practices affect their efforts to serve customers, and (c) what the biggest barriers to serving their customers are.

8. *Mystery Shopping Services.* There are companies that specialize in playing the role of customer and giving feedback on customer contact performance. The best ones work with you to de-

Quick Case
Just the Cancerfacts, Ma'am

You can do something with user groups or customer panels that few e-commerce firms do. Get customers and employees together in a joint learning group. Use a facilitator to guide a free-wheeling discussion. A discussion where everyone can learn from everyone else.

Cancerfacts.com did this with very powerful results. They're an innovative dot-com with a series of powerful software tools that give patients access to crucial medical information from the most current and significant published scientific studies. With this information, patients can make informed decisions regarding various treatment options.

As part of their intense focus on creating value to their site, they pulled together a ten-member National Consumer Advisory Council (NCAC). Not because it was a nice thing to do and something that they *should* have. They did it because they believed it would help them increase the value they provided to visitors to their site.

Howard Mahran, cofounder and vice president of product development at Cancerfacts.com., reports that at the first meeting, NCAC let him have it with both barrels. "The dynamics of the meeting were incredible," he says. "We had a group of individuals who all had their own perspective, their own experience, their own insights, and their own individual intelligence that when brought together in a group made the whole exponentially again greater than the sum of the parts. It took us out of the world of science and into a very practical domain where people live, breathe, yell, scream, laugh, and cry."

As a result of that meeting, Cancerfacts.com changed the way it presented the scientific information on its site, personalizing certain aspects of the message with regard to demographics and enhancing the trust factor. They're now

> much more focused on the receiver of the information. Visitors to their site now have new graphics, a different color scheme, and more ways of interacting with the database.
>
> Cancerfacts.com, in turn, has a growing base of visitors, more people recommending the site to others, more people using the information, and, most importantly, they're providing a more valuable service to their Web site visitors.
>
> Michael Samuelson, president of Samuelson Associates in Ann Arbor, Michigan facilitated the meeting for Cancerfacts.com. He noted that in addition to the "both barrel blast," the council also commended Cancerfacts.com for the purity of its information and their extremely high ethical standards. "It's not that they were doing poorly before. It's just they had the potential to be so much more than they were. And now they are!"

velop checklists or evaluation scales based on your service strategy statement; some will even put their people through your service training so they know exactly how your people are supposed to be doing things. As a twist, you can use your own employees as shoppers as well. It is also possible to do online comparison shopping of your competition using your own criteria for good service.

9. Toll-Free Hotlines. A good service recovery system almost always has a hotline of some sort. A customer-focused new product development function or a quality team with a customer-centered agenda also has hotlines. Customers who call in to register a complaint, make a suggestion, ask a question, or have a problem solved offer extremely valuable input on your e-service delivery system.

The key to making a hotline work is data capture and analysis. It is more difficult than it sounds to get people in department A to work with people in department B on service systems improvement. This is especially true when one of the departments is seen as the "complaint-handling specialists." Incentives are usually needed—and objectives—and attention to detail.

10. *Benchmarking.* Started as a way to compare operational efficiencies with those organizations that have similar problems or challenges but aren't in your business (so data can be shared without concern for competitive consequences), benchmarking has become more broadly defined today as a way of looking for breakthrough ideas by seeing how others are seeing their customers. The original purpose of benchmarking relates directly to improving an e-service delivery system by comparing operational ideas and numbers with a world-class company in another industry. That is still the best use possible, but don't overlook the teaching examples of anyone's comparative experiences. This book is full of benchmark examples for e-service in consumer, B2B, and B2C industries. If we've mentioned a site, it is worthy of at least a visit if not close study to see how some e-commerce companies have figured out how business —and service—really works online.

One thing is pretty clear. Customers have needs, wants, and desires. Tap into those needs, wants, and desires and you have a map of how your Web site should work. Absent this map, you end up getting stabbed in a duel you don't even know you've entered. What an even clearer map? Visit customers where they actually visit your site. Chances are you'll learn even more. The resolution on their monitors is probably different than that in your office.

Maybe they're accessing your site from a production floor or at a school filled with noisy kids. Most certainly they are in an environment considerably different that that in which code is written.

Most everyone involved in e-commerce is proud of their twenty-four/seven presence. Forget the emphasis on twenty-four/seven. That's a necessary but not sufficient condition for success on the Net. Think 360. You want a 360-degree view of your customers.

C H A P T E R

6

D E S I G N   F O R
D I S T I N C T I O N

WALK

into the Godiva shop in Water
Tower Place shopping center on Chicago's Michigan Avenue and
you know you've entered a special space. With your first breath you
inhale the rich decadent smell of chocolate. The curved golden
walls, art nouveau designs, and elegant display of chocolates all
work in concert to say "come in," "browse," "take something home."
You know you aren't just buying candy, you are experiencing
Godiva.

Click to Godiva.com and you know you have entered a special Web space. While the fragrance isn't there—yet—the look, the feel, the ambiance are just what you would expect of a site dedicated to the expensive, high-quality, melt-in-your mouth, special occasion chocolates and truffles that bear the Godiva name.

As importantly, the look and feel of Godiva.com reflects the look, feel, and ambiance of a brick and mortar Godiva boutique. Just as the physical Godiva stores exudes quality, taste, and a touch of indulgence, the Godiva.com Web site sends the same subliminal "Go ahead. You deserve it" message. It is exactly what we mean by designing for distinction and branding every touch-point.

It may seem strange for us to be discussing design in a book dedicated to e-service. But in our view, distinctive design is only partly about building an eye-appealing Web site, more importantly, it's about building trust and loyalty and creating a unique service experience. There are thousands of mediocre retail Web sites that do little more than offer a list of items for sale. The successful ones imbed themselves in shoppers' memories through a smooth, effortless feeling of being well served. From the first click, shoppers are drawn in, made curious, and delighted by the display of offerings. When every link works and help is given if and when it's needed, the experience is secured in trust. Whether or not they buy on the first visit, the visit is branded in their memories, and they will return to experience it again.

Lands' End is another organization that knows the importance of making every e-space touchpoint exude the brand identity—the feel and look, the ambiance and personal care service—

that characterize the company's catalog, phone, and outlet store operations. Specialized tools, live access to customer service reps (CSRs), and multiple ways to browse and shop work in concert to convey LandsEnd.com's dedication to customer service and desire to please the customer.

Sites, like LandsEnd.com and Godiva.com, which are designed for distinction—to stand out in the user's mind—take their offerings far beyond the quaint and largely outdated storefront metaphor. They take the time to evaluate what their audiences want and present their goods and services memorably, reliably, and consistently. Shopping at these sites feels real to the consumer—whether she's a housewife in Minnesota or a purchasing manager for a Fortune 500 firm in Philadelphia. A well-branded site has a loyal, profitable following that guarantees its online success and bottom-line performance.

KEY 4:
PUT YOUR PERSONALITY INTO EVERY TOUCHPOINT

Of the "beyond-the-basics" elements that create a distinct Web site, branding is what elevates you from average and acceptable to memorable. It's the first step toward loyalty.

Having brand name recognition outside of the Web will bring shoppers to your site once. While they are there, you must win their loyalty and trust all over again through consistent memorable experiences online. Unfortunately, most well-known brick and mortar names build boring click and order sites that create no memory, or worse, sites that frustrate and annoy— even anger— visitors and *damage* existing brand loyalty. Better to stay out of cyberspace than to go there badly.

To make an e-commerce site memorable, you have to *brand every touchpoint*. A touchpoint is anywhere a customer comes in contact with your company. It's the ads, the titles, the links, the click-through approach, the search capabilities, and the order process. Think of customer touchpoints as "Moments-of-Truth," each is an opportunity for the customer to make a positive or negative judgment about your organization. Every step a customer takes through your site must be foolproof, easy, and say "you" to the consumer. At Godiva.com, it's not just a picture of chocolates that brands the site, it's the image of luxury, the consistent customer service, the helpful extras throughout the site that all project the image of a luxury brand.

Most sites have not achieved this level of brand identity consistency. Disagree? Go to any two sites that sell the same goods and look for the differences. In most cases they are minimal. For example, ToyRUs.com and eToys.com are well-designed sites, but they have little brand originality. Both sites are easy to navigate, load quickly, and have a fairly trustworthy reputation for delivering goods,[1] but the sites themselves are eerily similar. Besides slightly different color schemes there is little to set them apart.

There are likely a hundred sites that sell the same, or similar, products that you do—all within a click of your site. So what makes your site special? What will make consumers remember you—only a branded e-shopping experience.

Quick Case
Godiva.com Immerses You in the Experience

After five years and several evolutions, the Godiva.com site captures the spirit of its brick and mortar identity. It is one of the most successfully branded sites online.

"The challenge was to translate the boutique to the Web," says Beth Brown, interactive marketing manager at Godiva's New York City headquarters. "The site is not just an analogy to the shops, it's a seamless expression of the company as a whole."

Because shoppers can't touch, taste, or smell the merchandise, the designers put a lot of effort into projecting, in some ways simulating, the Godiva experience with crisp graphics and detailed descriptions. "We want people to get pulled into the site. The images and copy do that for us," she says.

But the look and feel aren't the only things that make Godiva.com special. The customer service, easy navigation, helpful content, and specialty features make it a bright spot in the Web's growing collection of otherwise unimpressive e-commerce options.

Send Godiva.com an e-mail, and chances are you'll get a response in hours if not minutes. "Our policy is to respond to every e-mail within twenty-four hours, but we usually answer them a lot sooner," says Brown.

Our Test: When we sent them an e-mail, Godiva.com's CSR responded in less than ten minutes, with a pleasant personal note that answered all the questions we asked, included the CSR's name, e-mail address, phone and fax numbers, and encouraged us to "have a sweet day." Every one of our Christmas 1999 mystery shoppers who visited the Godiva.com site reported a similar experience.

"We're very customer service focused," says Brown. "We

know consumers really appreciate personalized e-mail with a real name on it."

The site also offers a recipe index for chocolate lovers, gift reminders and suggestions, and a store locator, which at certain times of the year is the motivator for the bulk of the site's traffic. On the days leading up to holidays, traffic to the Godiva.com site spikes from people looking for their nearest outlet, says Brown. "We know some people don't want to shop online or they need to buy something right away, so we make it convenient for them to find our stores," she says. "We're sending business to ourselves."

And while chances are slim that your package will be late or damaged, Godiva will take back any item through the mail or at one of the stores. "We are a luxury brand," says Brown. "Our 100 percent guarantee and customer service sets us apart."

TRANSLATING A BRICK AND MORTAR BRAND TO THE WEB

If you are brick and mortar, the Web is not the place to reinvent yourself. Your Web presence should be an extension of your company, not just of your retail stores. It's not just about making a virtual storefront, it's about making the site a positively enhanced representation of your organization. Brick and mortar companies must learn to translate their distinctive customer experience to the Web and then learn how to use their e-commerce offering as a means to reinforce that customer experience throughout the entire business system.

If you are a pure dot-com, your Web site is your brand identity. Along with your advertising, your site is your primary point of identity and what consumers will judge you by at first click. Their experience at your site and your follow-through are all you've got to secure their loyalty. If they do not inspire confidence and demonstrate your competence and personality, you lose. There is no room for error.

Regardless of whether you are virtual, brick and mortar, or both, the experience consumers have at your site determines whether they will make a purchase. How you respond to that purchase, with the timeliness of your delivery and the quality of your products determines whether they will shop with you again.

KEY 5:
MAKE EMOTION PART OF THE MEMORY

Branding is about more than a catchy logo or a cool advertisement. Branding is the total customer experience encompassing every step, from discovery to purchase to fulfillment to postpurchase service. Tying emotion to a site is part of the branding process. A well-branded site is remembered, enjoyed, and talked about.

Companies like Illuminations.com reinforce their brand with emotion from the moment a shopper arrives. Every graphic and link is well thought-out and works to create a consistent mood. Visiting the site is an experience that will forever connect Illuminations.com with the idea of candles and bath oils in the minds of shoppers.

When a customer arrives at a site, curiosity and interest are present almost by definition. He or she is ready to be delighted by easy-to-find information that gives them what they need in as short a time period as possible. They are already predisposed to buying something, or at the very least finding out if you have anything that peaks their interest and merits bookmarking your site for a revisit. At the same time, they know they aren't stuck in your site. Irritate them and they click away. Entice them and they are yours.

A memorable experience begins before the visitor arrives, through advertising and word of mouth. According to our "Shopping the Internet Circa 1999" study,[2] these are the two most likely reasons consumers go to a dot-com site: An advertisement or a third party encouraged them to visit. The chances of them finding your site, even if they've heard of it or seen something written about it, is dependent on another branding moment: An easy-to-remember URL.

Assuming they do remember you long enough to go online and find you, the experience and the evaluative opportunities are far from over—they've just begun. Now your site must capture them emotionally. Which emotions are captured depends on your goals and products. For example, REI.com immediately excites visitors about the prospect of climbing and biking with REI gear, whereas Illuminations.com calms visitors, lulling them into a state of relaxed awareness with pictures of candlelit patios and silky bubble baths. In both cases, the sites entice their visitors, making the visit more than just another Web site. It's a unique and memorable experience.

Once they are in, a company's brand is further developed in how it treats consumers throughout the online shopping experience.

Go to LandsEnd.com and you know immediately that this company cares about its customers in a unique way. The company's dedication to customer service shines through in its specialty features, such as Lands' End Live™, which lets consumers chat online with CSRs who send them pages of products they might like or the Your Personal Model™, which uses shoppers' dimensions and coloring to create virtual models that try on clothes and suggest outfits to fit that body type.

Everything you do at LandsEnd.com is a unique Lands' End experience.

But just as it is easy to enhance the experience, the smallest mistakes can destroy it. For example, during our research, one of the sites we visited and otherwise were impressed by acknowledged an e-mail inquiry within minutes of receiving it to say they would answer the question as soon as possible. That was a plus for brand identification. However they waited three weeks to actually answer the question, which erased any points they accumulated from their impressively designed site and prompt computer-generated acknowledgment.

Turning visitors into loyal customers is a two-step process: Easy access, reliable performance, and attention to detail are the ante you pay to play in the game. Delivering on wants, needs, expectations— and dreams brings them back again.

KEY 6:
BUILD IN—AND ON—SECURITY, SPEED, AND
EASY NAVIGATION

Once the key emotional tone of the site is in place, access must be above all things, easy, fast, and consistent. No matter how beautiful your site or how well it physically represents your company, if your site crashes or is too slow, if you deliver products late or damaged, or you don't respond to customer requests, you will fail. You will be reverse branded— become known as a purveyor that doesn't deliver. When the mechanics intrude, you destroy the mood.

These three elements emerge again and again in research data on the characteristics that make a Web site successful. The Net is a new environment that changes the context by which products and services are experienced, compared, and delivered. Security, speed, and ease of use are the elements of the environment that make the experience acceptable.

Without a secure Web site an e-commerce company will fail. Even the most novice shoppers look for the padlock icon and security guarantee before offering up sensitive personal information. Seventy percent of our focus group participants said the lack of that simple signal of security gives them pause about buying from a site.

However, if security is obviously there, they will browse and consider shopping, which is where speed becomes essential. Consumers expect instant gratification from the Web and that includes instant access to pictures and fast click-through options.

The single biggest gripe about Web sites heard in our retail customer focus groups is that they don't get to the point. Consumers have very little patience for waiting time. Pages must load quickly and then have the information the shopper wants.

Web shoppers we observed in action, *claim* they will wait thirty to sixty seconds for a page to load, but as we watched, they regularly became restless much, much sooner. In reality, eight seconds seems to be pushing it.

"Every time a page must load you risk losing customers," says International Data Corporation (IDC) analyst Barry Parr. "If a page loads too slowly, gets lost, or has the wrong information, customers lose patience," he adds, "so don't waste their time with layers of flashy header pages that don't have useful content."

Once they've made their choices and put items in their cart, shoppers expect to be able to check out quickly. Access to checkout needs to be available on every page. Shoppers tell us that if they know what they want from a site, they should be able to arrive at the home page, type a search, and click directly to that product, choose it, and check out.

A great example of understanding this need for speed is Clinique.com. The company knows its customers are loyal to certain product lines. They accommodate them with an Express Shopping feature that goes to a "know exactly what you want?" page that has quick links to every product they sell for easy access to the item of choice. It's a three-click process that most consumers are coming to expect from Web sites.

Regardless of the number of pages shoppers choose to view, those pages must be well organized, easy to search, and consistently accessible. The best sites, like LillianVernon.com, offer multiple category options through which products can be accessed. Lillian Vernon recognizes that its Web site is not about the products themselves, rather it's about what the shoppers need. Consequently, the same items will appear under "gifts," "at home," and "in season." Likewise, ArchieMcPhee.com has multiple ways to arrive at the same product, picture, and description. These companies know that not all customers think alike, act alike, or look alike. Nor do they search a site the same way.

For business-to-business (B2B) sites, the needs of specific clients can be catered to more fully through the customization of vendor sites for individual customer requirements: Lands' End creates elaborate custom sites for B2B clients, such as Saturn, that include pictures of the Saturn corporate logo stitched on to every potential product. Branders.com does a similar thing. Customers can place their logo on various items, such as shirts, canvas bags, calculators, and other promotional items, and see how they'd look.

KEY 7:
COMMUNICATE TRUST THROUGH DESIGN

All of the elements of distinctive design—branding, easy consistent navigation, fulfillment of promises, distinctive uncluttered presentation, up-to-date technology, and proof of security— lead to a perception, a judgment of trustworthiness.

Online brands are built first and foremost on trust and reliability. On the Net, brand trust is only as strong as its infrastructure is reliable and consistent. If consumers believe in your company and trust your site, they will shop there and tell their friends and colleagues. The look and feel of the site are the first and most constant touchpoint for customers' assessments of your organization's trustworthiness.

Customer loyalty, measured in repeat purchases and referrals, is the key driver of profitability for most online businesses. According to a recent study of online retailing,[3] the average online apparel shopper was not profitable for the retailer until he or she had shopped at the site four times.

If trust generates loyalty, and loyalty creates repeat business, trust is a key component of e-service success.

That perception of trustworthiness begins with look. As a shopper in one of our retail e-commerce focus groups put it, "If a Web site is designed well then it is more probable that other shopping details such as delivery and correct billing have received proper attention." In essence, if you look good, I'll give you a chance to be good.

Convincing the buyer that you are trustworthy is the first and largest hurdle every e-commerce site faces to secure the first and most crucial sale. If buyers feel confident enough to give you their commerce and you respond by fulfilling your promises, there is a solid chance they will be back. This is especially true of B2B buyers who won't take the time to complete a transaction on a site that doesn't have a high potential for repeat business. B2B buyers don't have time for one-click stands.

The promise of trust must be built into every link, every form, every graphic. Every time someone clicks on your site they are looking for proof of your trustworthiness. If a link says "Men's Shoes" it had better go to men's shoes options—not to women's shoes, not to useless company fluff, or worse yet, not to an error message.

When you screw up early in the relationship, even in minor ways, customers become suspicious. How can a self-respecting business have lost links at its site, spelling errors in content, or a checkout process that inexplicably dumps the customer halfway through? Surely it means this e-commerce site is shoddily thrown together. Make customers suspicious or fearful— and kiss them good-bye.

OVERCOMING FEARS: A CRITICAL STEP IN DEVELOPING TRUST

Getting retail buyers to make the first purchase at your Web site is a monumental challenge. The implicit trust that helps drive that first purchase is even more important online than offline. Online shopping requires consumers to provide considerable personal information— names, addresses, credit card numbers, and the like. People aren't comfortable sharing this confidential information with just anyone. In fact, 60 percent of consumers have significant concerns that someone will misuse the personal information they provide online, according to a Boston Consulting Group's study.[4]

What's more, they are buying goods that they have never handled or seen, except onscreen.

As a result, shoppers, especially less Web savvy consumers, are still very wary of the Web as a place to do business. Securing their loyalty is tricky.

According to a 1999 survey by Cheskin Research and Studio Archetype/Sapient,[5] 90 percent of consumers perceived purchasing on the Web to be risky business. Similar fears were noted in the Shopping the Internet Circa 1999 focus groups. Consumers are still afraid of being scammed by shady online dealers and imagined hackers who can steal their credit information from any Web site. Even though none of our many focus group participants felt they had ever been scammed, they believe in their hearts that if they shop online often enough, they are asking to be taken.

As a result, most visitors do significantly more browsing than buying. When they do buy, they aren't spending all that much money. In fact, none of our focus group participants were willing to spend more than a few hundred dollars on any Web purchase. The money they did spend they considered expendable—a gamble that has some thrill attached to it and no real guarantee of delivery. The attitude seemed to be that money lost on a Web site transaction was a result of their bad judgment and a loss to be expected, not a woebegone transaction to be challenged. For example, a participant who had ordered and paid for stereo equipment he never received, blamed himself. "That's stuff that I really probably shouldn't have bought anyway," he said. "I just risked it and went for it because it was a really good deal and I never got it. That's all right." So even though technically he was scammed, he took the blame for making a foolish transaction. And of course, he is willing to let anyone interested know about his experience with this site, anyone *except* the site owner and operator.

B2B buyers are much less fearful of financial fraud. B2B business online is typically an amalgam of a long-term relationship and an existing contract. Buyer and seller have already tied their trust of follow-through to promises made before any procurement has taken place.

KEY 8:
BUILD TRUST FROM THE FIRST CLICK

"Consumers see the world of the Web as one of chaos," says the Cheskin Research/Studio Archetype/Sapient study,[6] adding, "While trust develops over time, communicating trustworthiness must occur as soon as interaction with a site begins." What leads to customer trust? According to the study, six fundamental forms communicate trustworthiness to e-commerce customers—and prospects:

◆ Brand Identity	Being known by the customer away from your site; having a positive reputation and broad product offering.
◆ Navigation	Having a site that is easy to access, move around on, and understand.
◆ Fulfillment	Reliably delivering the goods and services promised.

◆ Presentation	"Looking Good" and "Looking Right" count.
◆ Seal of Approval	The site bears a seal of approval from a known agency such as BBBonline, Visa, or American Express, and a technology security seal from an organization such as VeriSeal, TRUSTe1, etc.
◆ Technology	Having the attributes of employing the latest or best technology; page speed, imagery, and smooth operation.[7]

Our interpretation of the Cheskin et al. study is that e-trust, like commercial trust in the "dirt world" is a two-step process.

◆ Be 100 percent picture perfect in the attributes customers feel are core fundamentals.

◆ Show that you are working to add something special to your offering.

Who's "got it?" At least according to Cheskin et al. circa 1999, twelve organizations out of 102 evaluated lead the pack in customer trust.[8] In descending order they are:

1. Yahoo!
2. Wal-Mart
3. Netscape
4. Infoseek
5-6. Blockbuster Video and Excite
7-9. Borders, Amazon, and USA *Today*
10-12. Dell, Internet Explorer, and Lycos

Trust is about more than just creating a secure place to make credit card orders—which is a gimmie when it comes to e-commerce. Shoppers give their trust to sites that are consistent from the start. Every page is thoughtfully laid out throughout, not just the home page, and offers information in forthright attractive ways.

Brick and mortar companies that operate on the Web potentially have a giant head start in building trust and loyalty, because customers are familiar with the brands and are already comfortable doing business with them. They trust Gap.com and BN.com to follow through on their online promises because they've already developed a relationship and have a positive memory of those companies. They've seen them perform in trustworthy ways offline and assume the same will be true of their Web sites.

Pure dot-coms, on the other hand, present something of a threat. "These people open up new Web sites and they say, 'allow six to eight weeks for delivery,'" observed a focus group participant. "Think of all the money you can collect in eight weeks and then get up and go."

When asked to make a list of sites they felt comfortable doing business with, our focus group participants came up with nineteen companies, thirteen of which were either well-known e-commerce brand names or e-commerce ventures of brick and mortar establishments.[9]

"Like REI, for example. I know they're in business," said one participant. " I know they've been around for a while and they're going to treat me right. I'm not going to hook up with some Web site I've never heard of before. I don't want to get the shop out of somebody's basement that may not be there tomorrow."

Heavy advertising and word of mouth helps dot-coms get past the fears. Companies like Amazon.com and CDNow.com—dot-coms that have no brick counterparts—were listed as trustworthy sites because they were familiar names.

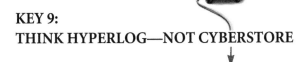

KEY 9:
THINK HYPERLOG—NOT CYBERSTORE

One of the reasons companies struggle to offer a well-designed, well-branded site is that they are fixated on the storefront metaphor. Early e-commerce sites were constantly burdening consumers with virtual product aisles and department store motifs. In reality, the shop metaphor doesn't work online. It's clumsy and the design never rings true. Consumers will never get a store experience online because it's a self-paced do-it-yourself virtual world—with different expectations, wants, and needs.

The analogy that does work online is the catalog or more accurately the hyperlog. Web designers today shy away from the word "catalog" because it sparks memories of phone book style sites, heavy and dark with lists of item after item. Those sites had no pizzazz or design finesse and were painful to scroll through.

Those sites and reactions to them by site designers miss the point. The supercatalog or hyperlog is the obvious structure for an efficient and successful e-commerce site. Give consumers access to all of your products with lovely pictures, elaborate descriptions, and an easy way to order and they will be happy. While they *may not* necessarily expect to bump into helpful CSRs while browsing your site; they *do* expect to have access to all of your products in an easy-to-navigate format and the freedom to order anything twenty-four hours a day.

With the idea of a first-rate catalog as your core structure, you can begin to add all of the flash that the Web offers in a memorable, brand-adding, customer-satisfying way. Include personalization tools, like the Looks Maker™ tool at Clinique.com that customizes a makeup regime around your favorite products. Give them several ways to get help through frequently asked questions (FAQs), e-mail, telephone, and live chat. Customers love options and abhor being forced through a linear, one-best-way process. And most importantly, constantly update the offerings so that the latest and greatest is always available.

One of the best examples of developing a hyperlog is LandsEnd.com, which should come as no surprise, because the company has been in the catalog business for decades and is famous for its personalized over-the-phone customer service. LandsEnd.com is an extension of the company's basic business model, translating that dedication to very personal, flexible customer service that is prevalent in its paper catalog business to its Web identity. The site follows all the rules of distinct design and branding with added features like LandsEnd Live and Shop with a Friend™. Lands' End sees its Web site as an opportunity to give consumers the flexibility and fun—uniqueness—that its catalogs alone can't provide.

Sites like LandsEnd.com that approach design as a hyperlog

instead of a storefront automatically have the freedom to take advantage of the two-dimensional self-paced world of the Web. And because the Web can do so much more than traditional catalogs ever could, they can easily meet and outshine the expectations of consumers.

While it's not rocket science, surprisingly few companies, from the fledgling start-ups to the world-weary mega brands, are following these simple rules well. IDC's survey of Internet retailers[10] showed that, while they all agreed that speed, security, and easy navigation are crucial to the success of an e-commerce site, only half felt that their sites were completely secure and only one-fourth thought they were fast and easy to navigate. As IDC Analyst Parr says, "An increasing percentage of people are sick of it. It shows a lack of respect for their time."

Consumers, even the least savvy among us, are annoyed with the little struggles that are too frequently part and parcel of doing business online. Their expectations are simple and their choices are infinite. Be the one to accommodate them and you will flourish. Ignore them and you will join the breed of dying companies that just couldn't make it online.

7

PERSONALIZE THE E-EXPERIENCE

FOR

↓

many people, going to a shopping mall has an attendant sense of obligation. Consider the effort involved. First there is the pressure to look presentable in public. Followed by fighting traffic to get there and struggling with the mass of other shoppers to arrive at the portal of just the right shop. Then there's the annoyance of being trailed through the store by a commission-hungry salesperson who "oohs" and "ahhs" at every piece of merchandise the shopper pauses to lay hands upon. If after all that hassle they come home with nothing, it's a precious day wasted, often the better part of a working person's Saturday shot to heck.

On the Web, there is little, if any, such sense of obligation. Shopping on the Web is a solitary and generic experience. It takes little effort or time to go to a Web site—log on, point, click. There are no sales reps to urge you to buy, and because it is a solitary and impersonal experience it feels more like window shopping after the stores have closed. Even browsing every page—every aisle—is effortless. As a result, no obligation develops, there is no sense of loss if a purchase isn't made, and no sense of patronage or loyalty develops.

When nothing happens to make the Web experience personal, it's easier for the shopper to abandon a site and forget about it than it is to make a purchase. Don't underestimate that dynamic: It is easier for a Web shopper to not buy something from you than it is to buy something from you—an important challenge, especially when compared to the self-imposed obligations of the brick and mortar store visitor. But just as sales reps engage shoppers by gushing over their selections and helping them choose more or less appropriate items, personalization of a Web experience can tie a buyer to a site and push them, pull them—even guilt them—into making that critical initial purchase.

Someday, someday very soon in fact, technology will allow a Web e-tailer to generate individual custom e-commerce sites for every shopper who happens by, based on the shopper's personal data, shopping history, income bracket, and buying needs. In the future, when you enter a site, it will harvest the necessary information to do this from your hard drive, then instantly create a welcome page designed just for you with ads, suggestions, and special deals based on your tastes and buying power. It's not that much more difficult than creating an ATM that knows your name and withdrawal limit.

That capability exists for Web sites already—in a limited sense. At Dell Computer Corp's e-service site (support.dell.com) a user can enter a service code that remembers the user's system or allows the site to search the user's system for the embedded "system service tag," which will call up all pertinent data on that unit, hardware configurations, peripherals, software etc., as well as basic information on the system owner's level of computer sophistication. Information or self-help advice the owner/visitor is seeking is edited down, screened really, based on that array of variables. Information is tailored to the customer's needs and ability to use it.

But the day of the automatically personalized initial visit hasn't quite arrived, particularly on the retail side of e-commerce. The technology isn't here yet to mass customize every online exchange, although customization and personalization of the e-shopping experience is already happening in subtler ways all over the Web.

Business-to-business (B2B) buyers, especially those with big dollars behind them, expect a customized experience from online vendors. Many larger corporate users expect vendors to build customized access sites housed on the company's corporate intranet that enable employees to explore a managed selection of acceptable, preapproved products for purchase. They also expect these sites to have built-in tracking and order status options.

(*text continues on page* 122)

Quick Case
Need Pigeon Cages ASAP?

W.W. Grainger's Industrial "Personal Shoppers" Stand Ready to Serve

Time has always been money, but it's doubly so in the E-commerce age. If you're a purchasing agent on a tight deadline with a one-time or "spot" need for hard-to-find parts or supplies, you likely dread the crapshoot of searching endless Web site databases, catalogs, or physical stores for those products.

Fixing that headache is a reason venerable W.W. Grainger Inc., a major player in the maintenance, repair, and operations (MRO) market since 1927, launched its innovative "FindMRO" service (www.findmro.com) in late 1999 as a way to leverage and apply its old-economy acumen to the Net. Tantamount to an industrial "personal shopper," the service uses a multichannel approach (Internet, phone, or fax) to quickly track down a product that's more obscure than light bulbs or industrial pumps.

To wit: One FindMRO client in the western United States called desperately looking for . . . pigeon cages. Seems a large number of the birds had taken up residence in the client's plants and seeking a humane way to remove them, the client wanted to cage the pigeons and set them free. But where, oh where, to quickly get his hands on such product? FindMRO.com to the rescue.

In another case, a large automotive manufacturer called looking for a supply of canoe paddles. Not for a company river trip or as a new disciplinary tool, but to serve as makeshift "stir sticks" for the huge vats of paint in the manufacturer's plants.

And when a New York hotel was searching high and low for 800 crystal apples to decorate its banquet room tables for a millennium celebration, guess where the hotel's frustrated purchasing agent finally found her quarry?

Find MRO accesses more than 5 million maintenance, repair, and operating products through a proprietary database of more than 12,600 suppliers and 100,000 brands. Research indicates that some 40 to 45 percent of a typical manufacturer's MRO purchases are spot buys—unplanned purchases not reflected on corporate contracts but required to keep a production line or business running.

As the previous examples show, plenty of those sourcing needs can fall outside the realm of traditional MRO requests.

"We no longer define what MRO is," says Ron Paulson, president of FindMRO.com. "It's simply whatever products or items customers need to get the job done or to keep their businesses running."

The search service has found its biggest growth "syndicating" as part of users' own Web sites. In this arrangement, a clients' purchasing agents aren't forced to travel outside the company's firewalls to find FindMRO.com, they simply log onto their own organizational Web site or intranet where FindMRO has its own personalized, built-in space.

Paulson says the service's eighty-person staff—some fifty of whom are the "hunters" or sourcing agents who track down hard-to-find product—shoots to meet twenty-four-hour turnaround on most customer requests. "In the sourcing world the company that gets back to the client fastest wins," he says, "or otherwise they can do it just as easily themselves."

FindMRO adds more than 200 newly found products to its databases each day, Paulson says, and he can "count on one hand" the number of times his staff's been stumped on a search request.

FindMRO doesn't stop when its bloodhounds sniff out and ship product; the one-stop service has a customer service department that facilitates the entire purchase transaction, from invoicing customers to paying suppliers to returns or credits.

"Our goal is to combine people, process, and technology to serve customers better than anyone else," Paulson says.

Consumers don't yet have that kind of buying power online, but they can find many personalizing features on a smaller scale. Amazon.com offers a recommended reading or music list based on past purchases. Fredricks.com makes real-time accessory suggestions to go with the apparel item a customer has selected. Coach.com allows customers to select from their luxury handbags by color, style, collection, or occasion. Avon.com will assist a customer's cosmetic selections by having visitors complete a brief survey from which they can provide the best shades to compliment skin tone, face shape, and lifestyle. At the lowest level, consumers can at least expect to see their name behind a welcome message on the home page, and if they're lucky, access to their order history.

Nearly every retail site a shopper visits these days has a registration option that gathers personal data for faster checkouts, future welcome messages, and optional shopper-controlled e-mail updates. Whether most e-tailers are able to take full advantage of the data they collect through registration for use in full-blown personalized pages, what is often called Customer Relationship Management, is still an open question. That a few organizations are beginning to recognize the consumer's desire for, and the commercial desirability of, a more personalized experience at the mass market level of the open Web, is an important beginning.

Beyond that, companies are updating their customer service through the addition of live human interaction options and expanded do-it-yourself features in an attempt to undo the growing disappointment in their e-offerings by shoppers. Fast turnaround on e-mail and live links to intelligent human customer service representatives (CSRs) are the most obvious differentiators of exceptional sites, but unfortunately the trend toward instant response to online queries is still following a very slow growth curve.

Some e-tailers are adding specialty content and tools as part of their push toward personalizing the e-shopping experience and adding value beyond the price of the products being sold. Clinique.com's Color Consultation™ and LandsEnd.com's Your Personal Model™ are custom tools that help consumers match cosmetics and clothes to their coloring and build. Some companies, like Dell Computer and 3 Com Corp., are putting free *and* for-fee, Web-based training on their sites to educate potential and existing consumers and to add value and increase visit frequency potential to their sites.

As noted in a 1999 Forrester report,[1] content is what has 75 percent of consumers returning to their favorite Web sites. Some companies are—remarkably enough—looking at the Web's past for ideas on how to make their sites more than a generic shopping trip destination. Specifically, many commercial companies are taking a step backward into Internet history and reinventing, or at least dusting off and polishing up, the original community-building aspects of the early days of the Web. Companies are creating custom spaces within and around their e-commerce offerings where people can come to chat, find help, and link to others who share their interests. Not only are they selling products at these sites, companies are educating consumers through piles of free content in the form of articles, how-to manuals, bulletin boards, and personal exchanges with other visitors.

For example, recognizing the zealous nature of its core adventurous communing-with-nature clientele, REI.com created the "Learn and Share" section of its site where visitors can find guidance on everything from riding a bike to climbing a mountain, or they can access community bulletin boards where they share their favorite rides, talk gear, or find a trip partner.

CornerHardware.com is another exceptional site that has continually updated its collection of articles and animated "how-to" guides on everything from building patios to plumbing bathrooms, as well as offering live experts available twenty-four/seven with any household project.

So while it's still essentially a one-site-fits-all e-world in retail, personalization of the Web experience is the natural next step in the e-commerce evolution. It adds value to the site and gives consumers reasons to be loyal. Giving them the tools and information they want, giving them an in-depth value package, will make them more likely to reward you with their business.

CUSTOM SITES GIVE B2B BUYERS CONTROL AND FREEDOM

Cost and efficiency are primary among the driving forces behind taking corporate business to the Web. Personalizing the B2B experience isn't primarily about the individuals who come to the company Web site. Instead, it is about accomodating the culture and needs of the coroporation, which are far more likely to lean toward control, speed, and cost advantages.

When corporations turn to the Web to buy, it's typically after a relationship with a vendor has already been established. Their

Web buying isn't frivolous and it isn't random. If they shop online it is because their vendors are making it a more convenient way to do business, and they expect to be treated as well as or better online than they are treated offline.

Those expectations translate into better prices, faster turnaround on delivery, twenty-four/seven access to ordering, more efficient capturing of data, and in some cases, personalization of products.

To deliver on this substantial list of demands, more and more vendors are designing custom corporate shopping sites that offer only specified goods and have pass code protection controlling who buys what and how much they can spend. These custom sites also give corporate buyers the ability to check order status and track purchases and prices over the history of the relationship.

Online ordering when managed efficiently saves the vendor and client time and money. It reduces the vendor's cost to complete the order by making it virtual with electronic invoicing. According to an Aberdeen Group research study, the cost to do paperless routing of corporate orders is roughly $30, compared to $107 for the paper-heavy alternative.[2]

Even if only part of the order is done electronically, the paper and mailing costs are reduced, as is time to shelf—compared with traditional ordering. "I can purchase something much more quickly via the internet," reported a senior corporate purchasing agent in one of our focus group studies, adding, "I don't have to spend time on the phone talking to a person, I just place my order and move on. It's an incredible time savings." Time spent on human contact in this buying company's case is reserved for complex problem solving, relationship adjustment, and account status review.

With a custom site, a company can limit the selection of merchandise and hold orders until bulk purchases are made so that volume discounts are applied. It gives them more control over what's purchased and logistics, while at the same time freeing employees to do resource acquisition directly without purchasing department interface and commenserate delays.

"When you make hundreds of thousands of orders in a day's time that's really a significant effort," explained another focus group participant who manages purchasing for a large airline. Deliniating what employees can and cannot buy helps her bracket and manage costs and reduces the amount of time she spends dealing with petty approvals for routine, individual purchases. "By setting up these (custom) Web sites to do purchasing, I'm taking myself out of the loop of having to place all the purchase orders," she adds. "It's a huge time savings." While her company's revenues are growing, her department is decreasing in staff size.

As vendors become more proficient at custom site design, the option will be more commonly available to small and mid-size companies. And, as more companies take their business to custom Web sites, companies like Ariba and Commerce One, makers of Internet Procurement software, will be throwing up custom e-strip malls all over the Web. Internet Procurement companies (IPCs) build B2B commerce platforms for managing all buying, selling, and marketplace commerce processes through one system. So, for example, a company might have ten vendors each with a custom site that could be accessed through a single Internet pro-

Quick Case
Land's End Showcases Custom Logoed Apparel at Saturn Site

"All companies want the ordering and functional efficiencies of doing business on the Web," says Mike Grasee director of e-commerce for corporate sales at Lands' End. The company limits customization of sites to clients who do a million dollars in business with Lands' End annually, but they are working on ways to automate the process for much smaller companies. Typically, these large customers want their employees and/or dealers to have access to Lands' End made, custom-designed logo-bearing shirts, bags, and other Lands' End merchandise in their corporate colors. But they want their employees and dealers to have access without the company itself encountering any of the order, warehouse, or transactons responsibilities—and headaches.

"Our customers are asking for this value-adding service," Grasee says. "They want the efficiency of e-commerce, and they want us to enforce brand rules so they don't have to."

Saturn Corporation, for example, has a large selection of T-shirts, sweaters, and dress shirts available at its custom LandsEnd.com site. Each product choice has specified options for the color and placement of the Saturn logo. Before the Saturn site went up, the Lands' End team met with Saturn managers to choose garment colors and logos and even stitched a variety of logos onto each potential item to be sure colors and styles matched and the stitched logos laid correctly. "Product logos look different on different materials and colors," says Grasee. "There's artistry involved."

At Lands' End, once all the rules are established it takes about two weeks to get a customer site up and running. The custom site looks and feels like Lands' End's open-to-all corporate site (LandsEnd.com), but it features only Saturn products. Every item can be viewed with the acceptable logos in the acceptable colors. Orders are made Saturn-specific using passwords through the Saturn access point.

> "We are using the Web to reshape how we work with customers," says Grasee. And it's saving customers time and money. Because Lands' End can collect small orders from multiple Saturn offices, even the small batches have volume prices. And because customers are using the Web to complete much of the order process, the number of calls per corporate account order has dropped 25 percent.

curement system. When an employee logs on to the corporate e-buying center on the company intranet, a search for polo shirts would take them to the Lands' End site, and a search for pencils would take them to the Staples site, but all final purchases are made through a single checkout system, that is the "exit door" or "checkout line" for the IPC.

WELCOME MESSAGES AND OTHER SMALL EFFORTS

On the B2C, personalization is about the whims of the individual consumer. By and large, individual consumers are less concerned about things like order tracking and speed than B2B customers and more interested in being surprised and delighted by the small but memorable value-addeds of a site. Little things like their name at the top of the page and the availability of tools to help them shop go a long way toward personalizing the site and creating a Web-based relationship.

Thanks to the almost universal use of cookies,[3] most sites will recognize you if you've visited before. Some sites are sophisticated enough to store and recall old shopping baskets, that is, a customer comes to a site, puts product in a shopping cart, then for some reason does not complete the purchase. At some sites that basket is saved and when those customers return, they are reminded that they had a basket started on the previous visit and are asked if they'd like to complete the purchase. The customer can then opt to review and resume using that basket or to delete that basket and start over.

KEY 10:
WIN THEIR TRUST FIRST—ASK FOR INFO LATER

A more complete and obvious, though slower, approach to gathering information about consumers than relying on cookie data is through registration forms, which have become standard fare at most e-commerce sites. Registration forms collect scads of personal data about shoppers that if mined and used correctly, can help companies custom target their audience for deals and couponing, as well as updating content and design at the site.

The information a seller can obtain from customers via a registration form seems to be contingent on just how boldly intrusive it cares to be perceived to be. Some sites ask for as little as a name and e-mail address and use that to send e-flyers alerting consumers to promotions. Others require consumers to answer pages of personal questions about their age, education, income bracket, and product group preferences. It is remarkable how much information some customers are willing to offer up. Most Web companies look for a middle ground between asking for almost nothing so as not to offend and demanding an aggressive amount of information that they really have no right to.

For example, along with shipping information and e-mail addresses, LillianVernon.com asks twenty questions about shoppers' interests, hobbies, and experiences with the company, but only the e-mail address and a password are mandatory. Sites like Beauty.com promise free samples if customers include information about their skin coloring and skin type but don't require it. The customers who do provide this information are, going forward, only offered products suitable for their personal look.

However, a site called E-buyersguide.com, an independent e-commerce research organization, Web research firm, *requires* that consumers provide information about their gender, age, ethnic background, education, income, occupation, and information about their e-commerce activities. In exchange, customers get access to all of the research firm's retailer information.

Whether or not consumers are willing to part with their personal data depends largely on the degree of trust and comfort they have with the vendor and whether they believe that providing it will have a significant return on their investment. The common theme is that the payoff for registering should benefit the buyer as well as the vendor. Most consumers are willing to offer up their e-mail address and a few bits of personal information if the asking is done discreetly and promises are made regarding how it will be used.

"We capture customer names and e-mail addresses from our registration option and use them to build an impressive database for our e-mail newsletter, which features special promotions and sales," says David Hochberg, vice president of public affairs at Lillian Vernon.

Additional data about shopping habits, preferences, and personal information, which should always be optional, can be used to better market your brand on the site and off.

Most commonly, retail sites will use the information they collect to speed up the checkout process. Saving mailing addresses and shipping addresses, along with credit card information can take dozens of entries and several steps out of the process. E-mail newsletters are also very popular, although typically the content is slim and they read more like press releases than a publication.

Coupons, freebies, and e-mail notification of deals are the gems of the registration offerings. For example, ZDNet's e-centives program gives consumers online coupons, free e-mail, and voice-mail, and other bonuses for registering with the site. Ivillage.com offers member deals for registrees from "premiere store partners" such as Petopia.com and iBaby. Coupon offerings and special bargains change daily. And many sites, like Godiva.com and Proflowers.com have gift reminder services that e-mail you when a gift-giving occasion approaches.

As for the rest of the personal data you collected through registration, it should only be used to assist in the checkout and delivery process and to better serve customers through improvements to a site. Any respectable site with a registration form will guarantee not to sell or give consumers' information to anyone for any reason. Based on the lack of new junk e-mail arriving during the research for this book, those promises seem to be adhered to.

With the fear and low trust of the Web still a concern in many consumers' minds, asking for too much personal information can easily scare away potential customers. Guarantees of privacy help to ease skittish consumers' minds, but don't push it. Expecting more than a mailing address and a request for a newsletter is foolish and will damage relationships with consumers. Rule of Thumb: Earn their respect and trust before asking them to divulge personal details about themselves.

KEY 11:
PERSONALIZED E-MAIL TO BUILD TRUST AND CREDIBILITY

Consumers judge online customer service by ease of contact and the speed and accuracy with which questions are answered. And while a site may have a fabulously robust "frequently asked question" (FAQ), customer opinion of the site's customer service will more likely be based on company response to e-mail. The FAQ is static—the e-mail response is a transaction between customer and company that the customer can, and does, use to judge both the company concern for the customer's unique needs and problems and the company's responsiveness skills. In short, in the customer's eyes, if you are a real player, you are geared and girded for contingencies beyond those anticipated in your FAQ file.

According to the "Driving Traffic to Your Web Site" report,[4] 37 percent of online consumers use customer service more from Web retailers than traditional retailers because of ease of use and potential for quick response times. The preferred method for resolving online consumer customer service issues is e-mail. And ninety percent of online shoppers consider good customer service to be critical when choosing a Web merchant, says Forrester.

According to the SOCAP/Yankelovich study, e-commerce customers prefer to base their preferences for e-mail service inquiries on their assumption that it will be faster and twenty-four/seven available. However, there is a limit to this preference. The SOCAP/Yankelovich study shows clearly that customers prefer a toll-free telephone number when the service they are seeking is problem-based. When in trouble, customers still prefer human contact (41 percent versus 31 percent, phone versus e-mail, respectively) .[5]

But while the potential to impress customers is as easy as a quick response to their questions via e-mail, online retailers continue to fail miserably at responding using this popular service tool. The research is overwhelming that e-commerce companies of all sizes and industries still don't grasp the importance of e-mail.

A survey sponsored by Brightware, Inc., a Novato, California, software company,[6] showed that almost two-thirds of the country's 100 largest companies, based on sales, did not respond to an e-mail asking for the name and contact information of the companies' CEOs. Only 15 percent of the companies answered the question, "What is your corporate headquarters address?" within three hours. And, amazingly, 36 percent of these companies either could not be contacted by e-mail from their Web site or made it so difficult that most visitors would be unable to do so and would abandon the effort.

Those findings are echoed by a November 1999 Jupiter Communications study that found 42 percent of top-ranked Web sites took longer than five days to answer customer inquiries, never replied, or didn't even take e-mail. And yet, Web shoppers rely on e-mail as the primary way to contact companies.[7]

It is recommended that before responding to e-mail queries, the company should personalize the message with the CSR's name, use a custom response to the customer's questions, and include a personal, thoughtful sign-off. Consumers place much greater value on personal messages than on cold computer-generated responses.

When companies do respond efficiently to e-mail queries, personalized messages hold much more value than obviously generic, computer-generated responses in the customers' eyes. The personal response says to consumers that you are, in fact, not just theoretically interested in helping them do business with you. It's the most obvious, straightforward way to personalize the experience shoppers have at your site, and it can make or break the effort and turn a shopper into a customer.

There is no question or quarrel with the fact that a well-done automated response system saves time, wear and tear, and the labor of hand-constructed answers to routine questions. At the same time, a poorly structured, rigid, overgeneric response generator can alienate. Only 1 percent of customers in the SOCAP/Yankelovich study found automated responses to problem situations acceptable.

Case in Point: One of our mystery shoppers sent e-mail queries to two companies. In both cases, he received a response within forty-eight hours. One of them was a form letter and the other was (or at least appeared to be) written by a genuine person who customized the message to answer our shopper's specific question. "I visit and purchase things all the time from the site that gave me a customized letter," he now says. He wasn't impressed by the computer-generated response. "A canned response doesn't communicate much interest in you."

One of our researchers, encountering a bulky, disappointing Web site, fired off the following complaint—once he found the well-hidden correspondence button:

> To whom it may concern:
>
> Though pretty and shiny, your web pages are slow to load and patently unhelpful. I have spent seventeen frustrating minutes trying to learn something about your E1 products, but unfortunately the only way your pages would be useful to me is if I already knew what I came to your site to learn!
>
> Next go-round, try asking customers what they might come to your site for and engineer toward that set of expectations. As it is, your site has the look of a college-marketing class project—before the professor's feedback.
>
> John Smith

OK, a little bit of a flame, but not that bad. The response, however, was a size ten shoe, size seven foot, mismatch.

> Dear Acme Customer,
>
> Thank you for contacting Acme.
>
> We do appreciate your comments and I will be sure to pass along your suggestions to the proper department for review.
>
> Thank you for sharing your thoughts with us and as always, thanks for your continued support of Acme products.
>
> Thank you for the opportunity to be of assistance.
>
> Sincerely,
>
> Acme Internet Department
>
> CCB4

Compare that antiphonal call and reply to these:

Hello,

I'm considering ordering a holiday Fab Five Cookie wreath—even though it's after Christmas. Will it last until next Christmas or will it decay? I couldn't tell if it was a real or permanent wreath.

Dear Disney Guest:

Thank you for your e-mail.

Below is the information you requested regarding item #20228, the Fab Five Cookie Wreath.

Because the wreath has sugar cookies on it, the cookies will probably not be good by next Christmas. The actual wreath is a faux wreath and is not real, so you can enjoy that for many years to come.

If we can be of any further assistance, please let us know.

Sincerely,

DisneyStore.com

Or:

Hello,

I'm considering purchasing a Seven-wood golf club—can you tell me how this will improve my game?

Dave

Dave,

A Seven-wood takes the place of your Three iron. You can even use it out of the rough, if the ball is sitting high, but normally it will take the place of the Three iron. On long tough shots where the ball will be hard to get up in the air, it will take its place. It is good off the tee and for long Iron shots, and it could win you some money, too!

Hit 'em long and straight!

Have a great day!

Andrew Reichert

Fogdog.com

The Ultimate Sports Store

Most of the sites lauded in this book responded to our test e-mails in less than an hour with personal, generally thoughtful messages. When LillianVernon.com didn't have a product we were looking for in its inventory, the company's CSR responded in less than half an hour with recommendations of several other catalog companies that might have what we needed along with the 800 numbers. She also promised to send our idea to the product managers for future Lillian Vernon catalogs. The message was signed with an actual name and she included an 800 number for Lillian Vernon in case we needed further assistance.

That's a benchmark example of a personalized response to an e-mail query and an impressive act of customer-pleasing service.

"Anyone visiting our site can e-mail a question or problem to our customer service department, and a representative will respond the same day with an e-mail resolution," says Lillian Vernon's Hochberg. "It's our standard."

It's a simple, straightforward standard, but one that seems a challenge for most companies. How do they do it? The best ones use a combination of response templates and dedicated staffers whose sole purpose in life is to read and tailor responses to ensure they are responsive to the customer's specific problem or request for information. As e-mail volume increases the combination of response templates and personal attention becomes important. Amazon.com receives up to 20,000 customer communiqués a day. To keep abreast of this volume, the 200 CSRs housed in the Baker Building in downtown Seattle have 1,400 prewritten responses to draw on – and personalize as the situation and occasion dictate.[8]

For lower volume vendors, the approach of choice is straight, dedicated personal attention. "We have a person who reads every e-mail we get and responds in less than twenty-four hours,"says Beth Brown of Godiva. We received our response from Godiva in less than ten minutes with a personal greeting, and detailed answers to our questions. The company gets anywhere from 100 to 500 queries a day.

LIVE CSRs RAISE THE STANDARD FOR SERVICE

Twenty-four-hour turnaround on e-mail queries has been touted as the industry standard, and a goal that companies pride themselves on achieving. But what if you called a catalog company to ask a question and they said they'd get back to you sometime tomorrow? Or worse, left you on hold and didn't come back for a day? It would be completely unacceptable behavior. Yet, companies on the Web have almost arbitrarily decided that a one-day turnaround standard is the best they can be expected to do, and they believe customers will continue to accept it. Customers see it differently.

Customer reality is that if someone has a question about a product he or she isn't going to buy until an answer is forthcoming. The longer the customer has to wait, the lower the likelihood they will subsequently buy from that site. And the more likely it is they will have moved on to a more responsive vendor.

While there are many queries that are noncritical, the purchase process is put in peril when a customer has to suspend purchase plans to get information. Quick turnaround on queries dramatically increases the chance you'll make a sale.

To further speedup the response process, many companies

are implementing a live CSR option, making available living, breathing humans who can talk to customers through one-on-one chat boxes while they shop the site. They are the virtual equivalent of a live sales rep wandering around a brick and mortar store waiting to lend a helping hand. These live CSRs are able to answer customers' questions immediately and offer buying advice. Not only do they tell customers about merchandise they might like, the push technology from companies like Live Person, allows them to send pages directly to the customer's browser.

Even though online shopping is largely a do-it-yourself venture, the opportunity to link to a human and get help, even if it's only for a moment, has great appeal for many shoppers and further customizes the generic Web experience.

Live chat with a CSR is a fairly easy system to implement. Typically, all that's required is a link on the navigation bar of a site. When it's clicked, a pop-up window appears within which customers can begin a text-based conversation with live CSRs, creating an avenue for instant personalized responses to critical questions.

However, the technology alone is not going to make live chat with an organization's CSRs a success. If a consumer actually links to a live chat, chances are the question he is concerned about is more complicated than "what's your return policy?" They'll expect answers to questions about product quality or complex operating issues and advice on what to buy. Live CSRs must be well educated about company products and trained to communicate freeform, or the personal exchange can leave them disappointed and skeptical of the organization's professionalism.

At one of the dot-com delivery sites we shopped, we asked a live CSR for advice on choosing a bouquet of flesh flowers that would look good on a high narrow mantel. Her advice was to browse through the company's selection of 50 bouquets. In other words, she was no help at all. With all the effort this site went through to offer live personalized service, the experience had the feel of going to a store where the clerks are all gum-chewing, bored high school students who don't know their way around the aisles.

CornerHardware.com however, spent several minutes chatting with us on techniques for fixing a sinking patio. The rep was clearly an expert on home improvements, and much of his advice was completely nonsales related. He sent a link to a free how-to guide on building and fixing patios, as well as a page with the tool necessary to pull up the individual bricks that were sinking. That's the kind of personalized service customers want from a live CSR. Their presence should be a value-adding benefit for shoppers that further customizes the Web site experience.

KEY 12:
MARKET LIVE CSRs AS ACCESS TO EXPERTS WHO CAN DO MORE THAN ANSWER QUESTIONS

CornerHardware.com encourages visitors to ask its "home improvement experts" about anything having to do with home projects. And clearly they are trained to have the answers. "We hire professionals in home improvement, people who know what they are talking about," says Rich Takata, cofounder of CornerHard-ware.com. The company also puts its CSRs through certification testing and keeps research materials on hand in case they are stumped by a complex query.

Once a consumer experiences this level of real-time customer service online, their expectations for every site they visit regarding response time and service increases dramatically. *Our prediction:* Twenty-four-hour turnaround will soon be the embarrassment of the e-service world, perhaps by the time this book is published!

PERSONALIZING TOOLS CUSTOMIZE THE NONHUMAN CONTACT EXPERIENCE

Some people—perhaps most—thrive on interacting with other humans, but others go to the Web precisely to avoid pushy salespeople and other annoying humans. For those who take no pleasure in a well-answered e-question—whether it's live or via e-mail—but still need answers and want a more personal experience, many sites are building specialty advice-giving tools. These simple software elements customize the site visit and add a little fun to the process—all without requiring any human involvement.

Clinique.com's Look Maker™ tool, Personal Color Consultation™, and library of makeup tips all exist to help customers figure out their "look" and steer them to colors and product lines designed for their features. These tools are intended to help consumers choose products that will best suit them, along with encouraging sales, but they also make the site more fun and more personal. Once a customer fills out her color profile, it's permanently stored at the Clinique.com site. Then, whenever she clicks on a product category at the site, the page automatically suggests shades and product lines that compliment her coloring and skin type and brings those products to the top of the page. Getting an online color consultation at Clinique.com is a lot like going to the Clinique counter at Bloomingdale's to get makeup tips, a cornerstone ritual of the cosmetics sales technique.

LandsEnds.com's "Build Your Own Model™" tool lets consumers type in their body dimensions and coloring, then generates a custom mannequin that tries on outfits and suggests clothes that flatter their body types. The model is saved at the site so consumers can access it on any visit and, in theory, see what the clothes will look like on them before they buy. LandsEnd.com's Shop with a Friend™ tool lets two consumers link browsers at the Web site to shop together, sending pages to each other's PCs and chatting through a text box about what they want to buy.

"It all contributes to a great customer experience," says Bill Bass, vice president of e-commerce for Lands' End. "The goal was to figure out what people do in stores that they can't do online, and then make it happen." Trying on clothes and shopping with friends all contribute to making the site more personal and realistic.

These are small additions that cause a big stir at e-commerce sites. They intrigue consumers and get them to invest more time and thought into an otherwise undistinguished e-shopping experience. By giving consumers a chance to do something out of the ordinary, like shop online with a friend or get a color consultation, these sites have made themselves stand out from the very crowded e-commerce herd. They've gotten media publicity and shoppers talking—all of which translates into more traffic and more sales.

FREE TRAINING CREATES LOYALTY, REPEAT BUYERS

Web-based training is another trend in personalizing the Web experience and building a loyal e-customer base. In fact, the Gartner Group predicts that by 2003, 40 percent of e-learning activities will be directed at customers.[9]

Dell Computer is one of the companies that has jumped on the training bandwagon. They recently teamed with CBT Systems, a Web-based training development firm, to build EducateU, a library of online courses for Dell customers and potential customers, says Brett Astor, product manager for EducateU. To accommodate the varying needs and interests of customers, the library has three categories: home PC users, business PC users, and high-end technical users, each with a selection of courses that range in cost from nothing to $200.

The categories were intentionally broken up to personalize the education experience for different types of users. "We realized that the titles for home PC users had to be different from the business or technical users to make sure the training was of value to individual customers," says Astor.

Each category offers training on similar topics but with a much different approach. For example, the modules for novice home PC users walk trainees through each process with easy-to-follow steps, whereas technical courses don't do as much hand-holding. And the scenarios in each category are relevant for each

Quick Case
CornerHardware.com Believes Customer Service
Can Be Better Online

"The Web is a more powerful customer service model than brick and mortar stores," proclaims Rich Takata, co-founder of CornerHardware.com, a Web-based home improvement store. It's a powerful statement to make in a world where "almost as good as brick and mortar," is about as bold a declaration as you'll get from any other e-commerce store.

Takata is a customer service fanatic, who launched this site with a staff of home improvement experts to bring the world a better choice for home improvement shopping. "What's missing from the brick and mortar stores is twenty-four/seven service," he says. And that's not just his opinion. The company conducted extensive consumer focus groups that overwhelmingly agreed with this belief—they want any-time access to information and customer service experts, and they can't get that from the brick and mortar stores, claims Takata.

CornerHardware was launched in the spring of 2000 with twenty-four/seven access to live CSRs, a full magazine of home improvement tips and articles, a library of animated do-it-yourself manuals, an automated tool advisor, and a community center where you can talk tools and home improvement topics with other do-it-yourselfers.

Along with all of that is a search engine that considers all the potential needs you might have when doing a search. "It does more than send consumers to product pages," says Takata. It sends you links to any information the site has on a particular topic. For example, if you search the word "drill," you'll get links to manuals on using drills and buyers' guides as well as links to merchandise. "If you do a search on drills, it doesn't necessarily mean you want to buy one," says Takata, "maybe you are just doing research."

The search engine and the rest of the site is also designed to give consumers a more personalized encounter. Tanaka notes that "Personalization is one thing that is missing from the Internet experience," and adds, "It's the personal touches and the ability to interact with someone that hooks the experience."

He believes that personalization and excellent customer service is what guarantees repeat business. "Customer service builds retention, and retention for home improvement retailers is huge," he says. "Thirty percent of customers generate seventy percent of volume. Getting people to come back to the site is all about customer service."

When asked about the sizable investment it took to launch a site with so much content, his answer was simple: "If you believe in customer service, invest in it and it will be profitable."

The company hires expert home improvement CSRs to man the live chat feature and puts them through training and certification programs to be sure they have the knowledge to answer any question that comes in. And customers are encouraged to ask the CSRs for advice on anything, not just for help making a purchase. "By giving advice, we are helping our customers. Then, if they need to buy something they'll buy it from us," says Takata. "It's a matter of trust. Credibility builds trust. If customers trust you, they'll buy from you."

group. "It's one more way for customers to get the most out of their PCs, and it drives customer loyalty," Astor says.

While the tuition for the courses will eventually make EducateU a profit center for Dell, the driving force behind offering this library of courses is to personalize the Web site, increase sales, and ensure repeat purchases. "If the training lets them do more with their computers, it increases the value of doing business with Dell," he says. "And, if people can do more with their PCs, they'll buy additional products."

CREATING CUSTOMERS THROUGH E-COMMUNITIES

Community has always been at the heart of what makes the Web thrive. Long before the term "e-commerce" was conceived, people flocked to the Web to chat, share ideas, and find companionship. They went to chat boards and community centers, never expecting to buy anything—they went to make friends and get information. The Web was a virtual neighborhood before it became a shopping mall. And many Web old-timers would agree, those were much better days.

KEY 13:
CREATE COMMUNITY TO ADD VALUE

Web site development teams who remember the good old days and have enough clout with corporate higher-ups to mold the look and feel of a site have convinced some e-commerce companies to build communities into and around their catalogs of offerings. Community simply means that a site is more than a place to buy, it's a place to learn, share, and communicate with others. It allows visitors to make the site their own by joining a conversation or learning a new fact.

People have always expected to find communities online, and they search for them. If you've got a product that excites people, then give them a chance to share their excitement.

REI.com is a model for e-commerce communities. Aware of its patrons' enthusiasms, the site has bulletin boards for every sport and activity it outfits. REI shoppers know they can go to the site to talk biking, or hiking, or climbing, anytime they want—and if they happen to need product, they'll make a purchase.

Adding community to a site doesn't mean you have to create a vast knowledge portal where a staff of experts must comment on any topic that comes to shoppers' minds. You can create community through a few bulletin boards with specialized topics where consumers can come to ask questions and share stories. For example, Villagehatshop.com, a quirky wholesaler of headwear, has the "hat community" for people who are really interested in hats. It features discussions and information on hats and anything that has anything to do with hats. There are places to buy hard-to-find hats, discussions of the virtues of hats, and a place to talk about hats in the movies. The conversation is generated by hat fanatics and requires little input from the company short of regular monitoring of the boards to be sure there are no spams and that no one is left hanging on a crucial hat question.

Adding community is actually a fairly cheap addition to any e-commerce site because visitors create the bulk of the content. The payoff is that visitors feel like the site is a place they'd want to visit again because it appeals to part of their psyche. It gives them a sense that you care about their interests and that you built your site with them in mind. A place that lets the customer link with his or her peers is far more worthy of a bookmark than a strictly e-commerce site, regardless of how attractively it's built.

However an organization personalizes its site, whether it's through customized e-mail, specialty content, or live CSRs, a little effort can go a long way toward improving a generic Web experience. Without these tools and services, a site will garner little space in the memories of its shoppers. Even if there is an initial sale, without personalization nothing guarantees that customer will come back—especially when the competition is only a click away and their sites are more fun to visit.

DELIVER END-TO-END SERVICE

IT'S

easy to believe the heavy lifting's over—that the Fat Lady's already belted out her climactic aria— when customers hit the "submit order" button on your Web site. Turning eyeballs into active fingertips seemingly signals closure to a process launched far upstream, with the dollars and sweat spent to lure customers to your site, create alluring and functional design, offer breadth of competitively priced product, and user-friendly ordering processes. The temptation to celebrate at this juncture can be large, and usually well justified.

But the reality of the e-commerce game is that some of your hardest lifting lies ahead: Mastering the nitty-gritty back-end processes increasingly means the difference between fledgling e-businesses going under or living to see another, brighter fiscal year.

It's in this "last mile" of the purchasing cycle where many business-to-business (B2B) and consumer dot-coms stumble, losing much of the momentum and goodwill gained with customers on the front end with their design, convenience, or transactional prowess. The reality is e-customers don't hand out final grades until the ordered product arrives swiftly, without error, and as promised—hold the partial orders, thank-you very much—to their delivery docks or front doors. If there is a problem midstream in a fulfillment or delivery chain, they want rapid notification—or better yet, to have online access themselves for checking inventory or shipping status. If there are questions or problems with merchandise following receipt, a sizeable segment expect to be able to get the answers or solve the problems on their own, tapping the ample self-help and troubleshooting information you make available on your Web site. Failing that, most customers expect some assurance that a capable staff stands ready to serve from behind your firewall.

And if problems prove so daunting as to warrant product returns, e-customers want return and exchange policies that are synchronized between online and offline channels, and that don't drive them up the wall—and maybe into competitors' camps—with endless conditions or convoluted machinations.

If it's distinctive e-service and repeat business you're after, it's important you give as much attention to this last half of the race as the first. Here are some ways to ensure your back-end customer support systems complete the chain of service excellence launched out of the starting gate.

1. The binding power of order confirmation (or, "If you place an order in cyberspace, does anybody really hear it?"). Placing orders computer-to-computer can do funny things to people. When we order over the phone from a catalog or parts list, whether we are consumers or purchasing agents we're accustomed to a human voice repeating back our credit card or account number, parroting the items we've just ordered, offering a total, an expected delivery date, and an order confirmation number. It's all very familiar, comforting, and expected.

But when we place orders in the faceless, voiceless world of e-commerce, that human confirmation isn't there—fueling anxiety that the order just placed, crucial to keeping a manufacturing process on tight deadline for a make-or-break project or to having just the right decorations in place for Saturday's wedding, has disappeared into a virtual black hole, been somehow misinterpreted by a software "bot," or, the mother of all fears, inadvertently deleted.

That's why most service-savvy e-businesses, recognizing electronic order confirmation as one of the easiest and most cost-effective ways to increase customer satisfaction, build such services into their order-processing chains. When an order is entered, e-mail is boomeranged back to the customer — automatically, usually within seconds or minutes — thanking them for the business, detailing the items purchased, quantity, cost, shipping fees, status (notifying immediately if on backorder, for instance), and more. If the confirmed information is wrong or products are not in inventory, quick adjustments can be made. Others take the confirmation process another step by sending e-mail to customers when an item has been shipped and include the expected arrival date. Order confirmation is one thing if you're a consumer buying a book or CD over the Internet, but the stakes get higher in B2B interactions, where if you've just ordered electronic components needed to keep a built-to-order computer assembly line on production deadline or maintenance or repair products crucial to putting maimed machinery back on the productive rolls, you want to be dead sure your order has been received and is correct down to the last zip screw or industrial pump.

And with speed a new competitive lever in the e-commerce game, the faster order confirmation gets to the customer, as long as it's dead-on accurate, the greater the impression will be.

Federal Express, Inc., gets kudos as an early exemplar of letting customers track their orders at their leisure, on demand. In 1997, FedEx made PC software available to retail customers that allows customers to tap into a system at FedEx and generate a detailed package training report on all their shipments (Figure 8-1). The net results were spectacular—call center traffic flattened as customers took to self-tracking and the number of FedEx call centers has actually decreased from 40 to 25. And of course, UPS and other competitors now have similar systems in place.

2. *Following the bouncing ball: Grant customers online access to production order process and shipping status.* Consumers and procurement specialists who shop online are, by and large, a self-reliant and impatient bunch. If they're curious or concerned about

FedEx Ship
Tracking Detail Report

Recipient:	Karen Revill			
Tracking #:	790289834019			
Reference:				
Service Type:	PL			

Activity	City	St/Prov	Date	Time
Delivered	ANN ARBOR	MI	8/26/99	9:25 AM
Package on Van	ANN ARBOR	MI	8/26/99	7:57 AM
Arrived at FedEx Destination Location	ANN ARBOR	MI	8/26/99	7:28 AM
Left FedEx Sort Facility	MEMPHIS	TN	8/26/99	3:12 AM
Left FedEx Sort Facility	MEMPHIS	TN	8/26/99	12:34 AM
Left FedEx Sort Facility	MEMPHIS	TN	8/26/99	12:29 AM
Left FedEx Ramp	MINNEAPOLIS	MN	8/25/99	9:16 PM
Left FedEx Origin Location	MINNEAPOLIS	MN	8/25/99	5:44 PM
Picked up	MINNEAPOLIS	MN	8/25/99	5:09 PM

Delivered To:	Receptionist/Front desk
Signed For By:	A.LIPP
Delivery Date:	8/26/99
Delivery Time:	9:25 AM

Figure 8-1. Federal Express order confirmation.

the shipping status of ordered product, they'd much rather you gave them real-time access to that information via your web site than be forced to ring or e-mail a service rep, where the prospect looms of being placed on hold or having to wait a few hours for a reply.

Data indicates e-customers like to be apprised of shipping status. Giving them a do-it-yourself option not only can improve satisfaction levels, it can decrease costly shipping-related phone or e-mail contact with your call center.

Ernst and Young estimates that more than 70 percent of online shoppers make more than one inquiry about their order status, via phone or on-line.

◆ At OfficeDepot.com, one of the world's largest sellers of office products, customers who establish accounts can use a powerful online order tracking tool to find the current shipping status of their orders.

◆ At SmarterKids.com, which sells educational toys and games for children, customers can track order status at multiple points in the delivery chain to find out when an order was picked, packed, and shipped. Once the product goes out the door, customers are sent a shipping confirmation number and can pinpoint exactly where a package is en route by using a UPS tracking number via the Web site. "It not only keeps customers in the loop, it cuts down on the number of phone calls or e-mails to our call center about delivery status," says Mark DeChambeau, vice president of operations at SmarterKids.com. At other dot-coms, simply clicking an "order look up" link on the home page allows you to enter an order identification number or your e-mail address to spot where a product is in the shipping queue.

◆ At Cameraworld.com, the online arm of Portland, Oregon–based photography equipment seller Camera World Co., once camera gear is packaged for shipping and loading onto a UPS vehicle, an e-mail message immediately goes out to the customer highlighting the time the package is set to be shipped. And like SmarterKids.com, customers get a confirmation number from the company so they can log onto Camera World's Web site to track the progress of their packages.

◆ At Dell Computer, where computers are made to order, customers can check the status of their machine at multiple points in the assembly process, regardless if they've placed an order by phone, with a sales rep, or directly online. Corporate as well as consumer clients can view an estimated "ship by" date on Dell.com, and once product is shipped, can see exactly where the product is in transit, including who signs for it once it reaches their location.

"We're giving our customers access to essentially the same information we give our internal service technicians," says Penne Allen, marketing manager for Dell's online support. "We want them to be able to go straight to the information they need online, without having to call our customer service support."

◆ Herman Miller.com is also big on keeping customers in the loop on manufacturing and product shipping status. Sample this explanation found on its Web site:

For each item you order, we'll tell you a 'manufacturing time,' or the time it takes us to make your furniture. In most cases—90 percent of the time with items on the hmstore.com—that's two business days. Then, it's ready for shipment. We add the time it takes to deliver your order (based on the delivery choice you make) to the manufacturing time and give you a date on or before you expect the order to arrive. If for any reason our manufacturing group delays delivery of the order, we'll immediately notify you by e-mail.

It may go without saying, but it can be deadly to delay notifying customers if product they've seemingly ordered is in reality on backorder or not inventoried.

The problem is typified by the experience of one of the mystery shoppers we hired to shop more than 350 Web sites during the 1999 Christmas shopping season.

"I placed a product order at this site and received notification forty-eight hours later that my product was out of stock and cancelled," the shopper wrote in her report. "I clicked on the `send a message to a customer service representative' button, sent the e-mail, but it was later returned as undeliverable. There was no other way to contact the company on the site."

If there's bad news regarding inventory shortages or shipping delays, customers need to hear about it sooner rather than later, so there's time to make adjustments. Responding a full two days after a customer believes the order has been processed with a "backorder and cancellation" notice is clearly unacceptable and compounded by the difficulty of finding live human help to help solve the problem.

In our B2B focus groups, the majority of participating procurement specialists, when asked how quickly they expect to be notified of backorder status when placing an order online, said "Immediately." In other words, they expect performance on par— or better—than what they'd receive if they were dealing with a sales rep over the phone. Other participants noted that they increasingly expect to have direct, online access themselves for looking up suppliers' real-time inventory.

Many of the best online retailers get proactive when it comes to out-of-stock product: The moment backordered items become available, they send interested customers an e-mail alert.

3. Build (or outsource) warehouse, fulfillment, and product delivery chains that create as much customer contentment on the back end of your service process as the front. Getting the right product to the right customers at the right time—and in one piece—is a com-

According to a study of 500 Internet shoppers from professional services firm

PricewaterhouseCoopers[2], the top complaints from those not satisfied with online

purchases made during the 1999 holiday season were as follows:

- Didn't receive product in time for the holidays. 53%
- Had to pay extra for shipping to ensure products arrived on time. 30%
- Received only part of an order. 26%
- Received a damaged or broken product. 15%

Figure 8-2. Top complaints of online shoppers.

petency that increasingly separates the fly-by-nights from here-to-stay players in the e-commerce game. While plenty of consumer and B2B sites have licked front-end design and transactional challenges, not to mention those of scalable technology, building the back-end infrastructure and mastering the logistics to move product efficiently from manufacturer to warehouse to e-customer has proved far more vexing. Those who have conquered that ground will likely tell you the time to have those systems honed and under control is *before* you launch an e-commerce site, not after.

An inability to stock or rapidly access in-demand product, missing promised delivery deadlines, or shipping incorrect or damaged goods can have a crippling effect on customer satisfaction and retention (Figure 8-2). Conversely, stellar delivery performance can add another layer of "stickiness" to your site. A 1999 Andersen Consulting survey of 500 online shoppers found that 95 percent said a guarantee of on-time delivery would increase the likelihood they would buy from a Web site again.[1]

KEY 14:
FOCUS ON FAST, EFFICIENT FULFILLMENT

The delivery challenge looms as especially large for brick and mortar organizations that have created an online arm, but without experience in the mail-order or catalog business, where distribution demands roughly mirror those required in e-business scenarios.

Quick Case
Cameraworld.com: Competing on Back-End Expertise

Cameraworld.com has understood from its cyber-beginnings how critical building the right back-end customer support infrastructure is to keeping pace or staying a step ahead of competitors. According to company representatives, Camera World now ships an estimated 90 percent of its Web orders within 24 hours of receipt (as opposed to five days for its long-standing mail-order business), carrying the breadth and depth of inventory in its 20,000-square-feet warehouse that is necessary to fuel that quick turnaround. The company's latest figures for return rates on Web-purchased product run a paltry 4 percent (return averages for all merchandise bought online usually vary from 25 to 35 percent, depending on product type and industry). No small feat, considering the ambitious delivery standards and volume of orders the site handles. In December 1999, for example, Cameraworld.com handled an average of 25,000 unique users a day, and Web sales rose by 250 percent over the previous year's figure for the month.

How do they do it? Capitalizing on long-standing relationships with quality suppliers certainly helps, as does linking real-time inventory to the Web site and customer orders that are sent from servers to an order fulfillment database compliments of a swift T1 line.

But Cameraworld.com also expanded and then redesigned its warehouse to speed up shipping, making a series of small changes that carried large impact. By relocating its most commonly ordered Web product closest to picking and shipping areas, for instance, and adding more packaging stations and personal computers to the mix, the company was able to dramatically boost delivery performance.

To wring the most from back-end investments, companies must have interconnected technology platforms that "speak" to each other. For retailers with regional or local product distribution centers around the country, that means real-time inventory and order-tracking systems linked to a Web shopping site. And for a truly seamless service system, customer service reps, sales reps, warehouse workers, and others should be able to review and check customer orders by accessing order databases from their own PCs.

E-businesses like Cameraworld.com understand how the delivery expectations of Web shoppers can vary even from those of catalog customers and that taking three to four weeks to locate—let alone deliver—in-demand product can mean a death knell for customer loyalty or any willingness of those "wronged" customers to repurchase from your site.

These established retailers have order management, warehousing, fulfillment, and delivery systems efficiently designed for the express purpose of shipping huge orders to hundreds of retail stores or outlets. Now they must reconfigure or overlay those systems to efficiently ship thousands of individual orders to single customers around the globe or build (or outsource) entirely new channels for their online customers. However, established mail catalogers who've launched Web shopping sites, such as Camera World Co., J.Crew, or L.L. Bean, to name just a handful, typically find the transition to the high-growth environment of the Internet equally challenging, but far less disruptive to existing fulfillment and delivery channels.

REI, the outdoors gear seller that boasts a catalog business of about $50 million annually, discovered from customer research that customers of its Web site, REI.com, expected even faster delivery service than its catalog buyers. According to Jennifer Lind in REI.com's public affairs group, to help accommodate those demands, the site now ships 93 percent of its orders within 24 hours and is configuring a new system that will enable it to process orders within an hour of the order being placed.

One of our "Shopping the Internet Circa 1999"[3] mystery shoppers had this telling comment about delivery performance—or lack of—on a pet supply site he evaluated, underscoring how difficult it can be in many e-business categories to compete on price alone.

> "Even though prices were cheaper than in retail stores, once you pay for shipping it's about equal—and the downside is that it takes seven to ten days to get the order—my cat would starve by then."

In your customer's eyes, your chosen shipper's ability to deliver on time reflects more on your organization than theirs. They're more likely to assign blame to your organization—regardless of who's at fault—if something arrives late, damaged, or not at all, so it's important to choose shippers wisely. While the big three, the U.S. Postal Service (USPS), Federal Express, and United Parcel Service (UPS), continue to dominate the market for shipping online purchases with their wide reach, extensive delivery fleets, and customer-friendly tools like online order tracking and Global Positioning Systems, a host of other competitors are nipping at their heels. On the consumer side, these firms understand that delivering to residential markets—individual homes—often requires an altogether different kind of supply chain and distribution network.

High-speed, high-efficiency local distribution centers and local delivery seems the future of e-commerce. This new brand of delivery service ships out of local storage facilities using personal couriers, enabling same- or next-day delivery to your front door or loading dock. Some use regional warehouses as "forward stock" locations, positioning inventory ever closer to end users, ensuring ever-faster delivery performance.

These Internet age shippers include the likes of Kozmo.com Inc., which currently delivers videos, compact discs, coffee, and even ice cream, promising its couriers will show up at your doorstep within an hour of an order; Streamline.com; and Webvan. All of these shippers not only deliver their own goods like groceries, but have plans to begin leveraging their expertise to deliver goods of many other e-businesses as well. In the B2B space, shipment consolidation and resource sharing is about to experience significant growth thanks to the Internet. Companies like justclick, which tracks load availability of automobile carrier trucks in England, are poised to bring long overdue efficiency to transportation and distribution of goods.

A LITTLE HELP FROM YOUR FRIENDS: THE FULFILLMENT OUTSOURCING OPTION

Of course, not all e-businesses possess the financial resources or expertise to build and manage new warehouses or distribution networks that can scale to match Internet growth. When e-business companies were asked by Forrester Research what their biggest fulfillment challenges would be in 2001, 30 percent respondents said "managing volumes."[4]

To stay competitive, many dot-coms need to outsource these back-end functions and train their attention on polishing core competencies. In its 1999 study of 158 online businesses, the Boston Consulting Group found 57 percent of respondents outsourced some inventory or warehousing functions, 51 percent outsourced picking/packing, and 38 percent outsourced product return handling.[5]

In many cases it makes good sense for e-commerce beginners or pure-player retailers who don't have the existing supply chain and distribution network of a Lands' End or an L.L. Bean to buy into existing infrastructures rather than start from scratch. Outsourcing can also make sense for established "name" retailers. Wal-Mart wisely understood that it didn't have expertise in the single order, pick, pack, and ship business—nor was top management in a hurry to make huge investments to upgrade or build new systems to support its online venture—so it turned to third-party logistics expert Fingerhut Business Services, Inc. to handle its online order fulfillment, with good results. Fingerhut boasts a cavernous, 1-million-square-feet warehouse and distribution facility in St. Cloud, Minnesota that not only handles packing and distribution for its own Web site, but for eToys.com and other online sellers as well as Wal-Mart.

The danger, of course, is offloading work to third-party organizations that can help you control back-end costs and reduce labor demands, but who may end up treating your customers like second-class citizens. A number of e-businesses have already reversed decisions to outsource key functions and pulled warehousing or fulfillment duties in-house.

SmarterKids.com is one of those who's reversed field, pulling order fulfillment in-house after having outsourced it to a third-party organization. The decision was made on a number of fronts, according to operations vice president Mark DeChambeau. A study that compared costs of staying with the current third-party, moving to another third-party contractor, or bringing fulfillment in-house showed the latter with a potential savings of 40 to 50 percent. The prospect of greater control over inventory and fulfillment performance also swayed SmarterKids, which has fashioned a new warehouse to speed delivery of the roughly 500 to 2,000 orders the site receives daily (orders are now processed and shipped the same day if received before 4 PM, the following day if received beyond that threshold).

DeChambeau believes many third-party houses continue to struggle while making the transition to fulfilling product for e-commerce sites versus traditional catalog retailers. In the mail-order business, catalogs are mailed with a defined life span—perhaps three months—giving third-party fulfillers the advantage of arranging inventory for those three months. In a typical system, inventory might be broken into A, B, C, and D categories, with A product being the most popular, fastest selling inventory, B the next most popular mover, and D the slowest seller. Inventory is then located to correspond in the warehouse—A product might be in carts on floor racks closest to picking stations, and D further away on upper-tier shelves.

But E-commerce smashes that model, because plenty of dot-coms change or tinker with products posted on Web pages with far greater frequency than once per quarter. "The third-party companies that have trouble are those who are trying to put the square peg of e-commerce into the round hole of the catalog shipping model," says DeChambeau. "E-businesses can change the products on their home pages every few days, so something that was a slower mover last week can be a bigger seller this week, making the third parties scramble to constantly shift inventory."

The upshot, according to DeChambeau, is that some third parties had to raise contract prices to account for those increased costs. "How to get the right product out the door at the right time has been problematic for e-commerce," he says. "But we have to earn customer loyalty, and getting product into customers' hands within three or four days is one of the best ways to do that. Our surveys and focus groups back up how important dependable fulfillment is to our customers."

In its fledgling years, Amazon.com relied heavily on book wholesalers for distribution, but has since begun building its own warehouse and distribution centers throughout the United States to support its online presence, partly to reduce distribution costs but also to curtail dependence on third parties.[6] Competitor

Barnes and Noble.com also is opening its own new distribution centers, one in Memphis, Tennessee near Federal Express, another in Nevada, to complement an existing center on the East Coast, in the hope of expediting delivery of books to customers around the country.

In 1998, Bluefly.com, an online factory outlet store, outsourced its order fulfillment and delivery to one company and call center functions to another. By Christmas 1999, however, Bluefly.com had pulled some of those critical functions back in-house, more than tripling the size of its own warehouse and distribution operations.

WAIVING SHIPPING CHARGES: CUSTOMER MAGNET OR INVITATION TO RED INK?

Until recently, free shipping has been a favored tactic, particularly over the past few holiday shopping seasons, of many e-tailers trying to attract new customers. Eliminate shipping charges, the thinking went, and a major obstacle to luring customers online goes away. While many an e-customer thrills to the prospect, the problem with offering one-time or seasonal free shipping is the difficulty in reversing course—once customers have tasted it, they have a hard time accepting reinstated shipping costs that put a product price on par or even above what they might pay in physical stores. But according to a recent *Wall Street Journal* article (June 20, 2000), a majority of e-tailers have found that, in the words of Tavalo, Inc., chief executive Kevin Appelbaum, "Free shipping and deep discounting... all they prove is that if you give stuff away, people will take it."

Other dot-coms simply build shipping prices into the cost of their products, hoping to create the illusion that customers are getting a bargain with "free" delivery.

An idea with perhaps more staying power is to offer free shipping at certain purchase levels. Placing an order of fifty dollars or more with Office Depot.com, for instance, results in free delivery within the office-supply seller's local trading areas. Office Depot.com's customers can also "self-deliver." That is, they can pick up online purchases at one of the company's brick and mortar stores in their area—items ordered before 5:00 PM on Monday through Saturday are available in four hours. Payless.com also lets customers pick up online orders free of shipping and handling charge if they'll take delivery at one of the company's 4,300 shoe stores nationwide.

KEY 15:
TAKE THE PAPER OUT OF THE SYSTEM

B2B online bill payment: The next step in "easy-to-do-business-with"? While e-commerce has streamlined the buying and selling of goods and services, the same can't be said for B2B account settlements. Most e-businesses still pay each other "old school" style, with paper-based credit applications, invoices that are faxed or mailed, and checks that are cut—all of which can hold up or undercut advances in other electronic transaction processes and impede funds availability.

But the emerging trend of online bill payment promises to make it even easier and more cost-efficient for other organizations to do business with you. Companies like Eastman Chemical Co. have already begun to authorize the credit of prospective buyers in real-time over the Web, speeding what's usually a lengthy process when handled offline and cutting paper costs. UPS also has branched into electronic bill payment through its new subsidiary, UPS Capital Corp., and more are likely to enter the fray. UPS's idea is to better manage the flow of money between online buyers and sellers. For a fee, UPS pays an e-seller the price of its goods, then collects payment from buyers within a thirty-day period. Businesses can pay for product online, but before they pay, they can track the status of their goods via a UPS shipment and potentially adjust the amount of their payment based on that data. A company that receives a damaged delivery could call UPS to withhold some of its payment until an adequate replacement arrives.

Only upon delivery is an online bill sent to a buyer's system for final sign-off, where they click the equivalent of a "I want to pay my bill" button, which credits the billing company's account.

Without such electronic payment systems, many Internet analysts feel e-marketplaces won't reach their huge potential. Although much of the core technology is in place, to date only a minority seem to be using it.

RETURN POLICIES: NEW IMPORTANCE IN THE E-COMMERCE AGE

Remember this rule of thumb, and you'll likely stand apart in the increasingly congested world of e-commerce: Make your process for returning products as easy as the process for buying them. Returns get more complicated, and potentially more irritating, when e-customers are asked to box up, drop off, and ship product back to Internet sellers often located hundreds or thousands of miles away. Limiting the pain in that process is another small way to get your site bookmarked for return visits.

B2B as well as consumer sites increasingly find that handling product returns is no peripheral issue. Research from McKinsey and Co. estimates that 25 percent of all merchandise bought online is returned, with higher averages in certain retail categories like apparel.[7]

For organizations that traffic in both offline and online worlds, one challenge is synchronizing returns between physical and digital storefronts. Nothing exasperates e-customers more—and decreases their odds of becoming repeat buyers—than return policies that don't allow return of goods purchased online at a company's brick and mortar sister store just around the corner. Having to box up unwieldy items, track down return addresses and return authorization numbers, drive to a shippers' office, and endure a lengthy wait for credit or reimbursement when they might drive a few miles and finish the whole process in 30 minutes ranks as unfathomable to today's time-crunched consumer.

When Resource Marketing, a Columbus, Ohio-based consulting group that critiques e-commerce sites, tested forty-five consumer Web sites in 1999, it found only one-third of these e-tailers would accept returns of products purchased online at their brick and mortar stores. And only ten of the forty-five had prominent guarantees offering full refunds to unsatisfied customers.[8]

Most service-savvy e-businesses guarantee customers a full thirty days to return products for refund, exchange, or store credit—and some, like Amazon.com, grant the refund minus the cost of shipping and handling. Others, like Herman Miller.com, the Web site of the office furniture manufacturer that's long competed on its service quality, pays shipping fees for customers on product returns, along with granting sixty days to return product for full exchange or refund. "We want you to be completely satisfied with your purchase," reads Herman Miller's Web site, "and that's why we offer a full product guarantee intended to take the risk out of buying furniture online."

Others seek customer input to help shape the return decisions for the specific order in question. Using automated questionnaires on Web sites, customers answer a few key questions that determine whether a return product is viable for restocking on a dot-com's shelves or needs to be transshipped to a manufacturer because it's defective—sometimes even to an online auction site where some money might be salvaged.

Supplying on-the-spot Return Authorization (RA) numbers with the order shipment also sends a message to customers that you're seeing the world from their eyes. Buyers of online goods are typically asked to attach the RA with returned merchandise, often within fifteen to thirty days from product delivery. Among its other purposes, an RA helps organizations ensure customers aren't returning merchandise purchased elsewhere.

In many cases customers have to track down and call an 800 number buried somewhere within packing materials or go back to a company's web site to get their RA number. In some—hopefully rare—cases, they actually have to write a letter to an organization to get an RA number. Once received, it's not unusual that a dot-com ask the customer to print the RA number on all six sides, and maybe a few more times for good measure, of the return shipping carton.

Bottom line: Make sure the "frustration factor" of your return authorization process doesn't undo the hard work and dollars you've sunk into drawing customers to your site by making them vow to never again darken your virtual doorway.

With returns handling a burgeoning part of the e-commerce equation, plenty of growing companies have chosen to turn the function over to third-party specialists. Delivery services are also getting into the act. The U.S. Postal Service (USPS), for example, now offers e-businesses an "E-Merchandise Return" service. The service authorizes customers to print merchandise return labels directly from a company's Web site, then drop product off at the post office. The USPS positions it as a good way to "turn customer returns into return customers."

SmarterKids.com tapped the USPS system to overhaul its product return model, says DeChambeau, with the intention of "getting customers to see that we're on their side." Rather than requesting customers use RA numbers, SmarterKids now simply slips a postage-paid, preaddressed sticker into packages that customers can use should they need to send back orders, which they can now do free of charge. "If they need to return something, all they have to do is put it back in the box, seal it, slap the label on it, and drop it off at the post office," DeChambeau says. "No cost, and no hassle."

Whether outsourced or managed in-house, returns handling

has become a large part of the e-service equation, one that plays an increased role in customer retention. Make sure, when you hold your "easy-to-to-do-business-with" meter up against your returns policies, that the needle isn't quivering near zero.

PERMISSION MARKETING: WALKING THE LINE BETWEEN PROACTIVE CUSTOMER SERVICE AND STALKING

When customers make a purchase or otherwise "imprint" at a site, many e-companies shrewdly follow up with promotional e-mail targeted to preferences customers showed in that buying experience in hopes of extending the purchase cycle and triggering add-on buys. If you buy a travel book about France, you'll likely get e-mail trying to cross-sell you books about Paris or the French Riviera, and if you purchase a "Three Tenors" CD, you'll get suggestions for a ream of other operatic or classical CDs.

Plenty of customers welcome this kind of "push" marketing of special sales, rebates, or notification of Web site updates. Minneapolis-based Northwest Airlines (NWA.com), for example, has found a wide and enthusiastic audience for its "Cyberfare," concept, e-mail that lands in customers' in-boxes each Wednesday morning detailing travel options for the upcoming weekend that must be purchased on short notice for abbreviated travel, with the trade-off being heavily discounted rates.

In other, even more customer-friendly uses, dot-coms push educational e-mail to customers following a sale, intending to teach them how to use or get more from just-purchased product or to highlight specific features they may have overlooked in their product manuals. Others send out helpful maintenance reminders and checklists via the e-waves.

But what a growing number of e-businesses have forgotten, or conveniently overlooked, is that acquiring customers' e-mail addresses isn't a license for electronic bombardment or wholesale "sharing" of that address with other vendors. Nothing can turn a potential life-time customer into a one-hit wonder faster than deluging that individual with promotional e-mail he or she doesn't want.

The key is providing customers a prominent "opt-out" each time promotional messages are sent or a chance to remove themselves from your mailing list for certain pitches or cross-sells. And by "prominent" we don't mean a paltry "if you'd prefer not to receive this e-mail in the future, check here" message buried in tiny type at the bottom of the screen, but apportioned in something approximating the size and weight of the promotional e-mail itself.

At OmahaSteaks.com, customers only receive e-mail on Web site updates, sales promotions, or new recipe ideas if such communication is first welcomed. "We never send e-mail without customers' permission, and they always have an easy-to-find option to opt out with every e-mail we send," says Sharon Bargas of Omaha Steaks.

THE DOLLARS AND SENSE OF ONLINE, POSTSALE "SELF-HELP"

Factoid: Unless faced with a mind-bending or otherwise impenetrable problem following a purchase, the majority of e-customers prefer to fix their problems or answer their questions without the prospect of waiting on hold in a call center queue, or for a callback or return e-mail from a service technician or customer service rep.

Acknowledging that preference, and eyeing the cost savings of having customers (rather than service staff) answer more of their own questions, more B2B and consumer sites have moved increasingly toward the self-service arena, making troubleshooting and other educational advice available on Web sites or extranets for around-the-clock customer access. "Frequently asked questions (FAQs), technical libraries, downloads, hot topics, bulletin boards, chat rooms, and other options allow customers to trouble shoot in real-time, without ever leaving computer screens.

Dell Computer is an innovator in providing such self-help options, breaking ground in customizing and personalizing advice to match customers' product type, configuration, or industry. Dell's research showed that if customers' perceived they could get fast, efficient, and competent technical support following a computer purchase, they'd be more willing to buy from the company. A late 1999 survey found that of customers who'd recently purchased a computer online, more than 50 percent had first visited the customer support section of Dell.com to check the quality and availability of postsale support.

Corporate customers accessing service support from Dell.com do so using a unique "system service tag." Every system shipped from Dell carries this unique identifier and when customers log onto Dell's self-help site, they access information by entering their "tag," which presents them with information customized and personalized to their specific Dell system. If the system is a desktop system, the system service tag calls up specs, files, and FAQs that apply to the configuration of that system. This presorting makes basic or advanced troubleshooting far easier for customers.

"Taking them straight to what they need cuts time and eliminates the possibility of them inadvertently going to the wrong places on the site," says Penne Allen, marketing manager for Dell's online support efforts.

Dell smartly positions its self-help support differently for corporate customers versus consumer buyers. Because of in-house IT resources, businesses are generally more technically savvy than consumers, so they're given access to more in-depth technical information.

In B2B scenarios, many e-companies find creating "extranets" is a way to show customers you're willing to take partnering arrangements to another level and go the extra mile to keep their business.

Larger than a corporate intranet but dwarfed by the Internet, extranets reach past traditional company boundaries to include customers and vendors in computer networks. While many extranets were originally built as a way to provide secure networks for monetary transactions between businesses, most companies soon realized they could also make order entry, searchable databases, and a bevy of self-serve technical or troubleshooting information available to clients. The sites have the added benefit of creating the impression that customers allowed into your extranet, beyond password and firewall protections, are a trusted part of your company's inner circle.

At Dell, for instance, corporate clients have access to "Premier Pages," extranets that provide information about those Dell products approved for purchase by a client's procurement manager. Premier Pages offer simplified purchasing, order status tracking, purchase history reporting, help desk support, and special prices to which customers might be entitled. Dell's next step is to integrate Premier Pages with corporate customers' accounting and finance systems. (For more on building quality online self-help, see the "Quick Case" featuring Great Plains Software on pages 177–180.)

USE POSTTRANSACTION AND REAL-TIME WEB SURVEYS TO GATHER CUSTOMER FEEDBACK AND CONTINUALLY IMPROVE SERVICE PERFORMANCE

Surveying e-customers as they complete interactions with your call center or service technicians or to capture impressions of Web site design, checkout process efficiency, inventory selection, or other features is a way to stay on top of ever-shifting customer perceptions and experiences with your site. It will also generate a continuous stream of customer feedback to help shape improvements in your service operations.

Done right, online surveys, including short Web-based surveys delivered in real-time, can reduce surveying costs and improve response rates compared to conventional phone or mail survey tactics, in addition to automating the collection of feedback from Web customers.

Many e-businesses use "pop-up" surveys to gather customer feedback without interfering with a shopper's buying experience. These short surveys pop-up on screen as customers exit a Web site (intercepting every Nth visitor) to gather real-time intelligence on why customers came, what they liked and disliked about specific elements of a site and to pose other relationship or transaction-oriented questions. Other such surveys are programmed to pop-up only on specific pages of a Web site or only after customers have completed specific actions, like querying a natural-language search engine ("was there a question we couldn't answer or a product you couldn't find?") or making a purchase.

At other organizations, each time a customer has an electronic "human touchpoint,"where they call upon a service rep or technician for help via live chat or e-mail, a short survey is beamed out to capture their impressions of the experience while still fresh. America Online (AOL), though not typically mentioned in the same breath with e-service exemplars, regularly queries customers in this fashion. Sample this message we received following a real-time chat with an AOL "customer care consultant" who quickly diagnosed how to decode a certain attached file sent over the Internet:

> AOL Member Services wants to provide you the outstanding customer service you deserve. We recently had the opportunity to serve you, and we would really appreciate about five minutes of your time to let us know how we did. You may take our customer satisfaction survey by clicking on the hyperlink at the end of this message. We appreciate your business, and thank-you for your time.

Quick Case
Great Plains Software: Driving Long-Term Customer Relationships with World-Class Online Support

When it comes to creating online "self-help" systems for business partners as well as end-users, not many have done it as well for as long as Great Plains Software, the Fargo, North Dakota-based seller of software that automates business functions including distribution, financials, project accounting, and more. The company's two online support services, dubbed CustomerSource and PartnerSource, serve Great Plains' end-user and independent partner network, respectively, and have captured numerous honors, including a 1998 award for CustomerSource as "best overall support site" from the Association of Support Professionals (ASP).

"PartnerSource and CustomerSource represent our desire to take internal knowledge and tech support and turn it inside out, so customers and partners have access on their own to information only our support staff used to have," says Scott Anderson, Great Plains' vice president of professional services.

Launched in 1996, CustomerSource is a password-protected portion of Great Plains' Web site where software customers can access a multitude of self-help tools including a technical support knowledge base (featuring 7,000 FAQs categorized by product and solution) a discussion database, support "Hot Topics," online training, chat sessions, downloads like updates or software "patches," a resource library, and more. For customers on maintenance contracts, the advantage is around-the-clock, at-your-convenience access to the latest-and-greatest in tech support and service help. If by some chance customers cannot find what they came for, Great Plains guarantees a one- to three-hour response time from human support via phone or e-mail, depending on contract level.

PartnerSource is expressly designed for Great Plains' extensive partner network of value-added resellers, independent software vendors, and systems integrators through which the company sells most of its software products. These partners, who are also charged with delivering a certain level of postsale customer support, can log onto PartnerSource at will to access the latest in technical and service support to pass along to their buyers. When customers install Great Plains' software, for instance, a partner usually oversees implementation and provides support at the local site, then hands support duties back to the Great Plains' call center at Fargo headquarters.

"If that customer later contacts the call center with a service issue, we resolve it, document it, and then post the information out on PartnerSource, so our partners can access it in a secured way to check on the postsale activity of their customers and find out, for example, if they've been talking to our call center about certain tech support issues," says Anderson.

In addition, should a customer send a question via e-mail to the call center, an e-mail response goes back not only to that customer, but also to a service manager in the partner organization that sold the customer the product.

"How we comanaged support with partners was a big obstacle for us to overcome, because four years ago our partner organizations were saying, `either you deliver support, or we deliver support,'" says Anderson. "But we found we could both deliver elements of support in a kind of seamless hand-off system, which PartnerSource facilitates."

Great Plains' research indicates that both online support services play a large role in retaining customers. Anderson says those who aren't connected to CustomerSource are four times more likely to leave the company for a competitor than customers who use the services.

By accelerating the company's maintenance business,

CustomerSource also morphed quickly from a cost center to a revenue generator. Maintenance contract renewals across product lines average in the mid-to-high 80 percent range, and Anderson says the support business now adds roughly 15 percent to Great Plains' bottom line.

Great Plains also is poised to launch a more proactive subscription service model, where it will "push" knowledge and tech support to specific job titles within client companies, rather than asking those clients to log onto its web sites to find certain information. For example, during payroll tax time each January, Great Plains typically sees a large spike in call center volume from customers using its human resource management software. Rather than making payroll clerks access CustomerSource or call an 800 number for answers to these commonly asked questions, Great Plains would proactively queue up and send that information to them via e-mail before the January rush.

RAMPING UP E-CONTACTS

Of course, online self-serve options can't cover all bases. Great Plains' call center still receives some 1,800 service requests a day, with 50 percent coming from partner organizations. Not long ago 98 percent of those contacts came via calls to the 800 line, with just 2 percent via e-mail. Like many firms, Great Plains sought better balance between the contact modes. An initial problem was that e-mail management and phone systems couldn't "talk" to each other, creating a double-entry quagmire. Having fixed that challenge, management launched a marketing campaign to alert and educate partners and end-users around the globe about the efficacy of e-mail inquiry. Some partners and customers were asked to beta test e-mail response, then provide testimonials to help sell others on its use. One promotion promised customers if they tried e-mail instead of phone contact, their names would go into a hat for free registration to a professional conference in Orlando.

Within nine months, the tactics helped drive e-service requests from 2 percent to about 50 percent on some product lines.

Great Plains surveys all customers after they've contacted a service rep or engineer, and in the last monthly measurement period, satisfaction with phone versus e-mail contact ran in a virtual dead heat, both coming in at a 4.1 average rating on a scale of one to five, Anderson says.

If there is a downside to mushrooming e-mail contact, it's that first-contact resolution of customer problems has been running 8 percent lower than for calls handled over the phone (but down from a 12 percent gap).

"We continue to try to cut that gap with additional training for our service staff on how to troubleshoot effectively using e-mail as opposed to the phone," Anderson says.

ENCOURAGE HUMAN CONTACT

YOU'VE

built what you think is an airtight, market-leading e-commerce site with all the trimmings: Compelling design and intuitive navigation, a bevy of customizable features, a wide array of smartly priced products with alluring descriptions, order tracking, and shipping and return policies that don't have potential customers pounding their heads against keyboards.

All goes swimmingly...that is, until Joe Consumer hits his first small stretch of white water. Seems he can't locate those hiking boots he needs in extra narrow or maybe he needs some additional insight into a camera lens he'd like to buy for his shutterbug wife—and there nothing in your site's "frequently asked questions" (FAQs) or "help" section to lend assistance, and a search engine query comes up empty.

Perhaps it's Pauline Purchasing Agent who keeps dead-ending during an order purchasing attempt, comes across a posted product with a missing price, or is steamed because a shipment of ordered supplies arrived with some missing components—parts that her operations folks needed yesterday, of course.

Suddenly the power of technology has run its course—Joe and Pauline clearly need the aid of a human. Yet, trying to find an 800 number or locate a suitable e-mail address or text chat button for firing off a quick SOS to a customer service rep (CSR) becomes like reading the pages of a *Where's Waldo?"* book. Worse yet, once they do find access to a human by conventional means, the 800 number has a forty-minute queue, the e-mail yields a nonresponse automated reply, and the chat button leads to a shutdown instead of a helping hand. And Joe and Pauline decide that it's time to move on to someone who cares enough about their business to actually work for it.

That's when you learn that sometimes there is no substitute for the wisdom and grace of the human touch. Indeed, as the SOCAP/Yankelovich study[1] found (Figure 9-1), a plurality (41 percent) of e-commerce customers prefer human contact when they need a problem solved.

What is your preferred type of contact when you have a problem with a service or product?

Base: Use Web site for customer service at least monthly (n = 4476)

Toll-free number	41%
E-mail	31%
Self-help on a Web site	18%
Talk to customer service representative in person	9%
Automated touch-tone services	1%
Postal mail	0%

SOCAP/Yankelovich Partners

Figure 9-1. Preferred method of customer contact.

KEY 16:
MAKE HUMAN CONTACT EASY, AMPLE, AND VARIED

HUMAN SUPPORT DRIVES E-CUSTOMER RETENTION

So how do you ensure retail or business-to-business (B2B) customers get just the amount of human support they want, when they want it—without sending overhead costs spinning out of control? These decisions will rest on the nature of your e-business and product or service line and the size and characteristics of your customer base. But the following will give you a head start toward ensuring you're working just as hard to keep customers coming back as you did to lure them to your site in the first place.

800 numbers are not enough. E-customers expect a wide variety of ways to access human help. Multichannel customer response systems combined with automated answer capabilities are table stakes for playing the e-service game.

Many e-companies have learned the hard way that a call center equipped to handle 800-number inquiries isn't enough. Today's e-customers also want the option of having their questions or concerns quickly addressed via e-mail, and a growing number also want "text chat" options that enable them to talk live with service reps or technical support without logging off a site. Still others want rapid phone "callbacks" from service personnel at the click of a Web site button.

While it can be tempting to put e-mail contact on the back burner amid the rush of 800-number calls that invariably accompany e-business launches, failure to implement the technology and training needed to successfully handle e-mail inquiries as well as 800-number calls, particularly if you're receiving 1,000 or more contacts a month, can mean big hits to customer satisfaction and retention.

Several studies reveal that many e-companies are still handling all e-mail manually—in other words, having reps review them one by one as they arrive—resulting in high cost per contact and little ability to react to large increases in contact volume. The

ICSA/e-Satisfy.com study found that e-mail management or rout-ing software is used by only 17 percent of 56 e-companies surveyed in the study, and only 6 percent prioritize e-contacts by type of cus-tomer. In fact, the study found that the median cost per e-mail and Web-based contact of responding companies was $5.63—slightly more than the $5.00 cost per phone contact. The authors speculate that this is due largely to the manual processes being used. Typi-cally, e-mail costs should be significantly lower (no 800-number charges, etc), so it appears many companies are missing chances to provide good service at lower costs.[2]

Taking heed, more e-companies are moving to "Web-enable" call centers, installing the on-site switching gear and scalable soft-ware for e-mail routing, queuing, and even prioritization, enabling reps to handle e-mail and real-time Web requests almost as effi-ciently as 800-number calls.

Many are moving away from a patchwork system of automatic call distributors (ACDs) to single platforms that tie together all forms of interaction—voice, e-mail, and Web. Most typically in-stall e-mail management software first and later consider more ad-vanced communication tools like text chat or customer callback features.

Charles Schwab Corp. recently discovered just how important it is to e-customers to be able to access human help at a time of need. According to a report in *The Bloomberg News*,[3] in March 2000, Schwab's co-chief executives Charles R. Schwab and David Pot-truck were forced to send a letter of apology for poor service to some of the online broker's biggest clients. The one-page letter apologized to clients who in recent months had been having trouble getting through to the site or faced long waits while trying to reach the company's automated touch-tone phone service and customer representatives. "Schwab prides itself on delivering great service and we are afraid that we may be falling short of your expectations," the two execs wrote.

IMPLICATIONS FOR B2B SERVICE

While e-mail or toll-free phone contact may not have the same high priority to B2B customers whose ordering process tends to work on a sequenced autopilot, when there is a problem or pressing question—a delayed delivery, an unacknowledged purchase order, or a technical glitch in the purchasing process—prompt and efficient human intervention is just as critical as in the retail world for cementing customer trust and loyalty.

THE VALUE OF PHONE CONTACT DOESN'T DIMINISH WITH E-COMMERCE VENTURES: DON'T MAKE'EM CALL OUT THE BLOODHOUNDS TO FIND YOUR 800 NUMBER

When e-customers absolutely, positively must call, the last thing you want is to make your customers click high and low to unearth your 800 number. Patience is likely already wearing thin and playing hide-and-seek with your contact number only exacerbates the upset. Hard as it is to believe, some retail as well as B2B sites list no 800 number at all, while others have made an art form of 800-number camouflage, placing it multiple clicks from the home page, often in a tiny point size at the bottom of a page under a "contact us" category.

Failure to list any phone contact whatsoever can be tantamount to delivering potential e-customers into the arms of competitors. And while the design concept of "planned inconvenience" might have worked wonders for mall designers seeking to route customers past stores they otherwise would never see, the same idea applied to 800-number location has far uglier consequences.

In our online shoppers focus groups the majority of participants reported they rarely used FAQs or other self-service options of the retail Web sites they shopped. If they couldn't locate a product or figure out how an ordering or shopping cart process worked, for example—and without an easy-to-spot 800 number to call— they would simply abandon the site, often never to return.

When you do send customers to an 800 number for help with a problem, remember that they carry expectations into that medium as well. For instance, it is very unlikely that a customer who has opted off your Web site for your toll-free number will be anything but upset if the first voice they hear is a recorded one. As many as 40 percent of customer service callers report a dislike for automated attendant answering when calling a company for help, with satisfaction levels dropping like a handful of stones at every option branch in the call routing system.

Forrester Research uncovered similar attitudes about e-service. The study of 17,000 online consumers shows that more than 40 percent of online buyers stopped shopping at a particular site because of unhappiness with the service received. And, of those surveyed, 51 percent of those consumers who needed customer service picked up the phone first.[4]

Omaha Steaks (www.OmahaSteaks.com), which sells steaks

and other frozen gourmet foods from its Web site, makes its 800 number omnipresent and neon-visible. In a large point size and a red color that fairly leaps off the page, the 800 number welcomes customers to call—not just from the home page, but from most of the pages customers will visit on the site. Even better, OmahaSteaks.com's service corps is staffed and trained to handle the calls they encourage. Some forty-five service reps handle phone calls, with twenty-one of the most experienced hands juggling both phone and e-mail inquiries.

Likewise, when you log onto the home page of Roxy.com, the seller of consumer electronics and personal communications equipment, among the first things that catches your eye is an image of a call center service rep, in full headset regalia, accompanied by the message, "How to Get Help Online or By Phone." Below this prominent graphic is Roxy.com's 800 number in large, white type on a blue background. Fogdog.com, the online sporting goods retailer, is another site that embraces rather than shies away from customer phone contact. "There isn't a page on our site that doesn't have our 800 number on it, because we invite you to call us," says Mike Guerra, Fogdog's customer service director. And everyone at Fogdog.com gets into the act—even the company's vice presidents have been trained to answer phones when needed.

Rather than phone contacts to call centers decreasing after new types of Web-based communication tools are introduced, often the calls hold steady or even increase following the launch of e-commerce sites. PC *Week Online* reports that toll-free calls to the call center of Uniglobe.com, a travel services e-company, stayed status quo at about 700 per day in months following introduction of its site. The company's sales cycle usually starts with a customer e-mailing for more information about travel options or asking for text chat to help navigate the site and typically finishes with the customer making a travel purchase via phone.[5]

Likewise, the ICSA/e-Satisfy.com study found that only 40 percent of e-contacts (e-mail or Web) are resolved with one online contact and that almost half of all e-contacts required a telephone call from the customer to achieve resolution.

John Goodman of e-Satisfy.com says in difficult customer situations—a request or problem beyond the ordinary—the phone can be 20 to 30 percent more efficient than e-mail response, and customers' satisfaction with the response is 5 to 7 percent higher. "How long does it take to type a paragraph rather than speak a paragraph? Much longer," Goodman says. "Plus, the customer experience with e-mail may not be as good. Unless the customer uses exclamation points, I have no idea how upset this problem has made him or her. By phone, I know."[6]

Another point worth remembering: Customers may not, usually don't, use online services as much as site designers assume they do. So if an e-mail is sent to warn a customer that, say, the case of wine she ordered last week will be delivered two days early, that message can easily go unchecked for two days—and be read too late to avert disaster. A phone call, however, is likely to be a better way to ensure gaining the customer's prompt attention.

KEY 17:
UNDERSTAND AND MANAGE CONTACT EXPECTATIONS

Customers sending e-mail queries to Web sites often assume there's a small army of service reps with fingers poised over keyboards standing ready to respond the moment messages are beamed across their screens—and that's if they think about the vendor's infrastructure at all. Others believe once they place an order, their product is loaded aboard an airplane or truck within an hour or two.

Because the Web is an immediate, twenty-four/seven medium, plenty of e-customers expect—right or wrong, achievable or unrealistic—immediate, round-the-clock service. It's incumbent on Web companies to modify and manage out-of model expectations or risk fallout from customers who continually feel you're not living up to their standards. It's easy to underestimate how the twenty-four/seven nature of e-commerce will impact business systems from customer service to order fulfillment or how the demands of new contact channels like instant e-mail will test your service staff. But in many cases it's the marketing decisions of e-companies that fan the flames of high expectations. Aggressive and omnipresent advertising messages suggest online shopping is a breeze, with easy navigation and ordering, quick access to competent human help, and prompt and reliable product delivery.

They are promises that in many cases companies aren't equipped to deliver on for lack of appropriate back-end customer support systems.

Understanding e-service expectations means understanding that because the Web is twenty-four/seven, it's increasingly harder to get away with a "9-to-6, weekday-only-customer-service-hours mentality" when operating as an e-business. As a result, REI.com now has service reps standing by to help Monday through Friday from 5 AM to 9 PM PST and Saturday and Sunday from 6 AM to 6 PM PST. Their choice: Build operating hours that are compatible with customer expectations, rather than forcing customers to follow the company's bouncing red ball—or lump it.

Not all dot-com organizations are as willing as REI to follow the customer's lead and fit operating procedures to their customers' expectations. Consider the following e-mail sent by a small, specialized antique auction site operator to its registered buyers and sellers:

It is flattering that so many users of the site are so chummy and informal and all, but this extends into orders and payments of advertising.

This is causing me and several of the largest sellers an enormous headache and waste of time. Every day I get checks for purchases of advertising, where someone simply drops the check in an envelope.

I wasted four hours today, trying to figure out who to credit advertising payments to because over forty payments did not include a copy of the invoice. I have set procedures for sending payments, and all I ask is that all payments include either the invoice for advertising or a copy of the item description on purchases. I need User Names or Item Numbers to accompany payments. E-mail is NOT ACCEPTABLE, because I process advertising one day a month, I need the information to accompany payment.

Without that information finding what to do with payments is nearly impossible. PLEASE BE CONSIDERATE AND DO NOT WASTE MY TIME.

I do not want to be rude, but a great way to get me worked into a swearing fit, is to send some money and not include the information I need. If you have a concern about your bill, don't waste your time e-mailing me. Send or fax your request. I guarantee your e-mail will be trashed while I will keep and process any faxes or snail mail messages.

Please work with me on this, because my procedures will not change.

The message: "If you want to do business with us, you'll have to understand how we do things around here—or else."

Yes, of course, there are a thousand-and-one ways to rationalize this operator's frustration. What small businessperson—dot-com or otherwise—can't sympathize with them? But the fundamental question persists: Can they, or any site operator, regardless of how big or small, specialized or broadly based, afford to be this inflexible and dogmatic with their customers?

Expectations shift with experience, and they shift more rapidly than ever before in e-space. Once a customer sends e-mail to a site like OmahaSteaks.com and receives nearly instant acknowledgment of its receipt, followed an hour later by a personalized, detailed answer that addresses a product delivery question, they'll be much less apt to put up with slow turnaround or shoddy service from your site—regardless of whether or not you're a direct competitor to OmahaSteaks.com. By analogy, in the brick and mortar world, customers who regularly experience stellar service from Federal Express have far less patience with, say, the plumbing service that shows up an hour past appointment or the corner laundry that can't ever seem to get the pleats in the customer's skirt straight.

MANAGE CUSTOMER'S SERVICE EXPECTATIONS BY KEEPING THEM INFORMED

You can adjust expectations and gain plenty of goodwill simply by keeping customers in the information loop. The cyberworld, where trust currently looms as a far larger issue than in the offline world, isn't a good place to leave customers hanging and uncertain. The basic "out of sight" nature of e-service leaves customers feeling highly vulnerable—and susceptible to panic attacks.

When it comes to e-mail contact, one of the best ways to manage expectations—and increase customer confidence—is through the use of automated e-mail acknowledgment and response systems, or what some call "digital agents." These systems begin by assuring customers their e-mail has been safely received—auto acknowledgment: "Thank you for your inquiry. We are currently researching your question and will respond within twenty-four hours. If faster attention is required, please call 800-Go-Acme." They later follow up with template-driven responses, which are often reviewed by human reps, to fully answer the questions posed. Some dot-coms supplement auto acknowledgment by clearly posting standard response times to e-mail on their Web sites. Telling a customer that e-mails are answered within twenty-four, or twelve, hours grounds their expectations and gives them the information necessary to explore another option, say your 800 number, should twelve or twenty-four hours be unacceptable. It helps the customer feel in control. And if your twelve- or twenty-four-hour turnaround is acceptable to the customer, but you respond in a shorter time frame, you get credit for exceeding expectations and promises.

At this book's writing Fogdog.com was upgrading its e-mail management systems to include new auto acknowledgment and response tools to handle basic inquiries. "Our reps tend to get a lot of the same general questions—do you carry this or that, do you have catalogs—and the automated templates will enable us to send back responses within five minutes," says Fogdog service director Mike Guerra.

These systems tend to make most sense for call centers that receive a high volume of e-mail contact or anticipate growth—in the vicinity of 1,000 e-mail contacts and up per month. For example, to maintain customer satisfaction while accommodating a growing number of e-mail queries, cameraworld.com sends out e-mail notices showing customers where their question is in queue. Other dot-coms, like auction site antiqueguns.com, keep customers up to date on their bid status by sending out automated e-mail at certain milestones in the auction process. In B2B transactions, suppliers ease minds by sending out e-mail acknowledgments on the date of promised product delivery. If products are on backorder, these sites don't wait one or two days to inform customers—they do it immediately, via auto acknowledgment systems.

When Amazon.com experiences a service-related problem, the last thing its customer-focused site managers want to do is keep customers in the dark. They adjust expectations accordingly. Sample this message received recently when attempting to log onto a portion of Amazon's site: "We apologize, these sections are currently down. Please enter your e-mail address and we'll get back to you as soon as we're back up."

Hint: Whether using manual or automatic response e-mail, it's good practice to apologize to customers if your response doesn't fully answer their question. Also, give them alternate contact information if available, and provide phone numbers of other companies that may have a product or service they're searching for. When we sent e-mail to Lillian Vernon (www.lillianvernon.com) asking about a hard-to-find product, we received the following personalized response within thirty minutes:

Dear Ms. Fister:

Thank you for your inquiry regarding the above item. After researching our products database, we are sorry to inform you this item is not found in our current inventory. We have forwarded your request for the "dress-up trunk for boys" to our purchasing department. Should you need to search further, you may try contacting these catalog companies or check their Web sites: (the message goes on to list six other companies and their 800 numbers). Customer satisfaction is of great importance here at Lillian Vernon. If we can be of further assistance, please feel free to contact our customer service representatives at 1-800-505-2250.

Auto response systems can also control costs associated with answering high volumes of e-mail. According to a Boston Consulting Group study of 158 online retailers, respondents who had installed auto e-mail response systems experienced an average per e-mail response cost of twenty-five cents, with some respondents reporting as little as five cents per e-mail. In contrast, online re-tailers without automated systems—those who answer most e-mail manually—paid almost four dollars per missive.[7]

The danger with automated response, of course, is automaton-like answers and mass depersonalization. Auto response works best to answer commonly asked, fundamental questions or to direct customers to specific FAQs on your Web site. But sending out one-size-fits all responses to what are sometimes unique or idiosyncratic questions is a sure recipe for offending customers—not to mention a way to alienate your most profitable ones, the customers most likely to expect some level of personalized service. Yet an ICSA/e-Satisfy.com recent study found only 6 percent of companies prioritize e-contacts by type or value of customer.[8]

Without state-of-the-art e-mail routing and prioritization systems and facing thousands of incoming e-mails daily, personalizing e-mail can be a challenge, to say the least. One participant in our B2B focus groups gave voice to the concern. The call center she manages receives, on a relatively "slow" day, about 10,000 e-mails. Not surprisingly, the organization has implemented template-driven auto response systems that search for key words in e-mails, and "templates" those words into responses. "There are thousands and thousands of templated responses in our database that can be sent out with no typing on the part of our reps," she said. "But there is some quality control—our reps scan the responses before they go out to make sure the answer is appropriate to the question and the type of customer," she added.

KEY 18:
HIRE PEOPLE WHO DO TEXT AND VOICE WELL

E-commerce is a new ball game, often with new burdens for service support staff. Call center employees not only must continue to handle a large number of phone inquiries with speed as well as sensitivity, many now have to write e-mail responses or review automated e-mail before it's sent to customers. Although some large call centers have begun creating specialists on staff who handle nothing but e-mail or text chat, in most cases reps are still expected to be generalists and to be comfortable with each response mode.

Believe it or not, that can be a tall order. Good phone skill doesn't always translate to good writing skill. It's dangerous to assume service staff trained to speak with cheery voices, interpret spoken clues, and master phone technologies will be equally adept at crafting clear and customer-sensitive e-mail or that they'll seamlessly pick up the new technology skill that goes with it. E-mail littered with indecipherable sentences and grammatical errors or responses perceived by customers as abrupt, impersonal, or condescending—a real danger with this mode of communication, because there's no body language or voice inflection to help interpret meaning—can do unseen harm to customer loyalty. Reps who once only had to learn phone technologies now need advanced Windows® skills and the ability to rapidly query databases.

If you have live text chat or cobrowsing technology, are your reps trained to shepherd impatient customers through an online buying process? Do they know site geography and product inventory well enough to "push" certain pages to customers? It's a package of skills not always easy to find, or hold onto, for under ten dollars per hour. At Amazon.com they don't even try. According to a story on Amazon.com service in the *Wall Street Journal*, Amazon.com hires new customer service recruits who are selected for their customer communication skills and customer service aptitude at $10.50 an hour and puts them on an up-and-out track—out to other places in the company, that is. They equip them with a library of prescripted replies, but empower them to override and modify these "blurbs" as they deem appropriate.[9]

These new skill demands not only require sound cross-training, they also require building new hiring profiles as well. Typing, grammar, and proofreading skills; the ability to give clear and gracious instruction in writing; and a high level of software applications skill (not to mention advanced plate spinning) are the service competencies of the e-commerce age.

SmarterKids.com, the online retailer of children's educational toys and games, is among those using new hiring criteria and a heavy dose of cross-training to prepare its call center staff for the challenge. The organization uses the "universal" call center agent model, meaning each service agent is cross-trained to handle phone, e-mail, live chat, and Web callback support. But reps only go "live" with more challenging chat and phone duties after they've been amply trained in e-mail response, says SmarterKids.com vice president of operations Mark DeChambeau, who oversees call center operations. "We start them with e-mail because they can get exposure to many different service situations and issues without having to perform on a real-time basis with customers," he says.

This universal or generalist model also can boost service staff morale by offering an invigorating change of pace. At Great Plains Software, the Fargo, North Dakota–based seller of business applications software, call center management initially thought it would separate phone and e-mail responsibilities on staff. That is, until it decided to survey call center reps about the idea. "The overwhelming response was that call center associates wanted more diversity in their roles by being able to handle both e-mail and phone," says Scott Anderson, the company's vice president of professional services. He added that, "Now they fight over handling e-mail response."

But not all is so rosy in dot-com land: According to an ICSA/e-Satisfy.com study,[10] half of the companies it surveyed use separate agents to respond to e-mail and Web contacts, but most have no additional hiring criteria or additional training separate from telephone-skills training. We believe this to be a dangerous oversight.

Though somewhat dependent on contact volume and industry, these increased expectations generally mean a corresponding increase in service staff. One airline industry participant in our B2B focus groups said her company had to add "significant" service staff as a result of its e-commerce venture—it now has nearly as many customer service agents in its call centers as flight attendants in its planes. This is contrary to an initial "expectation" (read fingers crossed hope) that e-mail access would decrease pressure on the service center's response load.

MATCH STAFF SKILLS TO CUSTOMER SKILLS

Some companies who view e-service as a key competitive lever go a step further—they hire subject matter experts to staff phone lines and handle e-mail, ensuring they have the interpersonal skills to match the technical acumen. At cameraworld.com, the on-line seller of camera gear, most customer contacts are answered by professional photographers (or photographers who also work day jobs), who, as trained shutterbugs, can adroitly field most of the technical questions customers have about products on Camera World's site. At REI.com, the purveyor of outdoor gear, customers who call or e-mail usually get from-the-trenches advice built by specialists who actually have used the camping stoves, rain parkas, kayaks, hiking boots, or skis customers are eyeing on-line.

All of the twenty-six customer service employees at Fogdog.com hold the title of "service consultant"—only three are sans college degrees, according to customer service director Mike Guerra, and all but four have some previous management experience. Guerra believes that stringent hiring criteria is one reason Fogdog's been able to pull off its generalist approach to handling customer inquiries—most service consultants are asked to handle e-mail as well as phone calls. "We go after high-quality people, someone experienced in the workplace, but who also lives and breathes sports or sporting goods," he says. "We pay more to get them, but we also expect more." Net net: You can staff to handle your simplest customer inquiries and problems or you can staff to handle the most complex. Make that decision based on what will enhance your brand reputation and draw customers back again, not on cost alone.

KEY 19:
PEG E-SERVICE STANDARDS TO WEB AND CUSTOMER TIME

Speed wins in the e-commerce game. Make sure standards for re-sponse time to customer e-mail are pegged to "Internet time," not to the rhythms of your own internal company systems. Both retail and B2B customers continue to raise the bar on what's considered acceptable response times to e-mail inquiries. Most studies by In-ternet market research firms in the late 1990s showed customers were happy to receive a final response within twenty-four to thirty-six hours, depending on the question's urgency, with some pre-ceding acknowledgment that the question had been received and was being processed. By mid-2000, according to the SO-CAP/Yankelovich study, 29 percent of e-commerce customers ex-pect a twelve-hour or less turnaround on inquiries and 44 percent see twelve to twenty-four hours as reasonable. Don't be surprised to see that expectation ratchet up at a rapid rate.[11]

The ICSA/e-Satisfy.com study found customers across indus-tries expect acknowledgment of their e-contact ("we've received your e-mail...) within *one hour*, and just 12 percent got their wish.

Only 42 percent of those surveyed received acknowledgment within twenty-four hours. More troubling, only 30 percent of respondents received a *final* response to e-mail within twenty-four hours, and for 18 percent, it took more than seven days to get a final answer. The biggest indictment? The study found that approximately four out of ten e-customers in potential prepurchase situations (requests for literature and questions about a product or service) never receive a response to their e-contact.[12]

The team of mystery shoppers we asked to evaluate the service performance of retail e-commerce sites during Christmas season 1999[13] were similarly unimpressed with response times. After shopping 385 sites and testing e-mail response times, the shoppers judged "speed of response to inquiry" as acceptable in only 55 percent of the cases.

While the task of responding swiftly and accurately to e-mail might seem daunting when you're flooded with thousands of contacts every day, the reality is that many e-companies, usually employing the latest in e-mail management and auto response software, are getting it done. OmahaSteaks.com sets a goal of answering e-mail—answering, not just acknowledging receipt—within twenty to thirty minutes, depending on the question's complexity and level of research needed, according to public relations manager Sharon Bargas. Lest you think that lofty goal is a function of only having to handle a small number of basic questions each day, in December 1999 the site's service staff handled approximately 16,000 e-mail inquires.

Somewhat skeptical, we tested their standard with a question about the company's shipping practices for meat and other gourmet food products. It was answered in detail within fifteen minutes—almost tantamount to having a real-time text chat with a service rep.

Making it easy for customers to locate the appropriate e-mail addresses on your site is another important associated issue. All too often when customers click on a "contact us" button, it simply launches an anonymous, preaddressed e-mail screen, with no information on who the message is going to or when the sender might expect a response. Customer-sensitive companies sidestep this bland, customer-annoying practice by placing e-mail contacts into specific categories, with some even using personal e-mail addresses of specific employees. At REI.com, customers can click on e-mail response categories for gear-related questions, product ordering questions, member services questions, and more.

EVALUATE THE ROI OF IMPLEMENTING LIVE TEXT CHAT, COBROWSING, AND CUSTOMER "CALLBACK" SYSTEMS

Although not yet in widespread use, live text chat technology, where customers can "talk" with CSRs via boxes on a screen without having to exit the Web site or call in on a second phone line, is being added to a growing number of retail and even B2B Web sites.

These systems acknowledge that many retail e-shoppers have only one phone line in their homes, making it impossible to call an 800 line and get help from service or technical staff while still logged onto a Web site, which is often the most effective way to problem solve.

Cobrowsing technology, similar to text chat, enables the customer and service rep to look at Web pages together live, allowing the rep to direct or "push" customers to specific pages to answer their sizing, product availability, billing, or other questions.

Although text chat and cobrowsing are often viewed as limited in application, they offer a less-expensive alternative to 800-number phone service for e-businesses.

Among retail dot-coms using the technology are LandsEnd.com, EddieBauer.com, SmarterKids.com, and clothier-Rampage.com. Intuit, the company known for its Quicken personal finance software, uses live chat to assist customers with software installation. Some e-commerce companies position text chat as a high-end service, restricting access to their biggest or most profitable customers, giving it a unique panache.

Use of text chat and cobrowsing can have direct revenue benefits. Some companies have found introduction of real-time chat has reduced their rate of shopping cart abandonment from 5 to 10 percent because reps are able to intervene before frustrated or meandering customers log off, never to return.

A November 1999 study from market analysis firm Datamonitor[14] estimated that of the 184 million abandoned transactions in 1998, some 8 percent of all visits—or an estimated $1.6 billion in sales, at an average $85 per transaction—might have been saved by e-commerce sites implementing some form of online customer service with a human element, be it e-mail, Web chat, collaborative browsing, Web callback support, or voice-over Internet options.

A growing number of retailers and B2B sites are beginning to see value in using "callback" technology, where customers can schedule a quick callback from a sales or service rep if they have questions or problems while on a site. Customers simply click a "call me" icon on the site, enter their name and phone number, describe their request, and add a time they'd like to be called back.

USE THE PHYSICAL TO SUPPORT THE DIGITAL: IN-STORE "TEST DRIVES" AND FACE-TO-FACE CONSULTS BUILD CUSTOMER CONFIDENCE FOR DOING BUSINESS ON THE WEB

The absence of a tactile buying experience—the inability of e-customers to feel, see, inspect, and use products before buying—remains one of the biggest bugaboos of Web commerce, particularly when it comes to customer confidence in purchasing bigger-ticket items.

Some click and mortar operations have begun using physical assets to get around this, offering customers the all-important "hands-on" as a prerequisite to online purchasing, easing fears and building confidence to transact business online in the process. For example, when Gateway Computers researched customer preferences, it found a majority of its first-time buyers wanted to touch, use, and inspect its computers before agreeing to turn over large sums of hard-earned cash—one-third of those surveyed were not comfortable using the phone or Web to make a computer purchase. So in 1999 the company created 200 "Gateway Country" stores dedicated to the sole purpose of letting customers test drive Gateway desktop or portable computers before buying. The stores carry no inventory, but allow prospects to experiment with computers and ask sales advisors questions about features or use. The storefronts also allow salespeople to pitch add-ons—a complete line of peripherals, including printers, scanners, and digital cameras are on display.

Having so tested the product, many customers then return home to buy via Web or phone. When they do order, Gateway custom-builds most of the machines within forty-eight hours at a central assembly plant and then ships direct to customers. Gateway management believes that the Web provides a more effective means for order taking, ongoing technical support, and other tactics that can build ongoing customer loyalty. That said, they see the brick and mortar product demo centers as vital to expanding their market by easing less-technical customers into the Gateway fold.

The click and mortar operation is reaping another dividend. It appears that there is an emerging segment of customers who prefer their commerce to be multichannel. That is to say, these customers want to be able to browse on the Web and then buy in the store, or browse in the store and buy on the Web. The more such options you give them, the more likely you are to capture their repeat business, most likely for your Web operation.

In cases where customers have understandably high anxiety about sharing sensitive information or transacting certain kinds of business over the Internet—online banking or investing, for example, offering face-to-face contact and a bit of the personal touch as a preface to going directly online can help win over skittish customers. Charles Schwab and Co., the San Francisco-based financial services company, allows customers pondering online investing the opportunity to first stop into a Schwab branch near their homes for a consultation. Many customers feel more comfortable disclosing sensitive financial data and transferring funds in-person before launching into an investing arrangement in the virtual world.

Schwab also offers ninety-minute educational "Webshops" to teach participants how to build and manage portfolios online. The company got the idea from a survey by Harris Interactive that found a good percentage of potential investors weren't investing online because they were afraid of making technical mistakes that would cost them money, were worried about security, or simply believed online investing was too difficult to learn. Some 34 percent of respondents to the Harris survey said a class or tutorial on how to use online investing tools would persuade them to become online investors.

WHEN SELF-SERVICE IS THE ANSWER: REPLICATE YOUR BEST CSR

Of course, live human help isn't always the answer. In many cases the last thing a retail or B2B e-customer wants is human intervention mucking up the waters, forcing them to wait for return e-mail messages or placed in 800-number queues to get answers that can make or break a purchase decision. The do-it-yourself, be in control oriented customers want to get into and out of a site in a hurry, thanks very much, and find whatever information they need using self-service tools available on a Web site. Eliminating the human factor is, after all, one reason they shop in the digital world in the first place.

Self-service can be a cost-savings boon for e-companies. Not only do self-help features cut service-related costs (800 line charges, labor expenses) they offload work from typically overburdened call center staff, freeing up reps to dedicate more time to unique, challenging service issues than to the tedium of answering rudimentary questions.

The trick is making sure self-service features replicate your best, not your worst, or most mundane CSR, and that they create more satisfaction than frustration. And be forewarned: Your self-service options had better be very, very sharp. Dell's Penne Allen cautions that "Customers' expectations are far greater when they opt for self-help on your Web site." Following is some straightforward advice on making self-service work well.

◆ **Use FAQs, *glossaries, and educational articles.*** A list of FAQs, gleaned from the collective insight and in-the-trenches experience of service reps manning 800 line and e-mail posts, service managers, frontline sales reps, and others with intimate knowledge of customers' most common concerns, offers round-the-clock access to sometimes vital information.

You'll diminish the impact of FAQs, maybe even create more rather than less work for call centers staff, if this self-service tool is not:

1. Extremely easy to locate from a home page.
2. Written in simple, clear language, devoid of company jargon.
3. Substantial enough to cover all the basics, but not so ambitiously comprehensive that it means having to cram a myriad of answers into one page in microscopic point size. Differentiating point sizes or font types between questions and answers also makes navigating easier for customers.

Also, avoid writing answers that take up two or three screens of text. Give customers simple explanations to questions, then if additional information is needed, offer it one click away for those needing more depth.

You might also want to consider building two types of FAQs—one category for prospective or new customers with basic questions, another for continuing or repeat-user customers already familiar with your products or services. In that regard, designing for the equivalent of registered or authorized customers, you might answer questions about such things as when particular software programs might be upgraded or a software glitch fixed. Restricting entrance to this more advanced level of FAQ can also add a little brand panache.

FAQ visits, like complaint data, can serve as an early-warning system of sorts. Heavy use of certain list questions might indicate problems with your advertising, packaging, or product-user manuals, warranting a follow-up check. It can also be used to reorganize your site or your checkout process. For example, if 20 percent of the FAQ hits are a search for shipping and handling costs, you know to move that information to the front of your site. That "watch the customer and react accordingly" principal is practically an operating bylaw at Dell Computer. Says Dell's Penne Allen, "If we find that customers are going to one area of our site more than others to troubleshoot a question, we can elevate and differently position and rank that information so it's closer to what they need and where they need it."

Some e-commerce sites also include a "glossary of terms" designed to help less-experienced users of products or services understand technical terms or product descriptions they come across on a site (and avoid calling 800 line or sending an e-mail for an explanation). Cameraworld.com explains the purpose of the glossary on its site this way:

"The photo, video, and digital electronics business is saturated with jargon and technical terms. To assist our customers, we've created a glossary with brief, easy-to-understand definitions. Each word or phrase is listed alphabetically, i.e., Aperture is under A', Depth of Field under D.' Click the letters below to find a word or phrase you'd like defined."

Other sites post informative "soft sell" articles or interviews with experts intended to help users with buying decisions or simply add value to a site. In its well-conceived "Learn and Share" category, REI.com posts feature articles on topics as varied as how to choose a kayak or hiking gear, and content is often written by REI staff members who've used the equipment, not by professional copywriters. Fogdog.com has an "Ask the Expert" feature and also posts buyers guides ("how to buy a putter"), comparison charts of sports equipment, and a bevy of other value-added information.

◆ **_Explore natural language search engines._** Ask Jeeves (www.ask.com) and Northern Light (www.northernlight.com) are popular search engines known for letting users conduct searches using ordinary questions, such as, "How do I install a new faucet?" instead of having to outguess the cumbersome search engine's keyword structure. Using these free-form text queries, a search engine retrieves the most appropriate answers from a knowledge base and presents them to a user, with the most likely solution first. In addition, the number of matches is greatly reduced, and this responds to a common complaint of many search engine users—response information overload.

More retail and B2B Web sites have begun incorporating the feature, now available from a handful of vendors, to reduce fruitless or frustrating keyword-driven search processes. With sometimes thousands of products available on the largest B2B or retail sites, these search engines also remove some of the pressure on service reps to answer questions about inventory the reps may not have detailed availability to and that customer-driven database queries can answer faster and in far greater detail.

Dell Computer, for instance, has long had its "Ask Dudley" natural language search option. DrugEmporium.com and B2B site OfficeDepot.com were among early adopters of the search tools on their sites, according to *Inter@ctive Week* magazine.[15] Drug Emporium leased and built the Jeeves Answer and Jeeves Advisor products from Ask Jeeves Inc. into its site.

One added benefit of these natural language search engines: They often keep customers on a site longer, allowing e-businesses to do more cross-selling.

◆ *Online bulletin boards and forums let customers help customers.* More e-companies are creating online bulletin boards and forums as a way to encourage experienced users to help novice customers with problems or basic questions. Turning customers into defacto technical or service support—building a community of avid troubleshooters—is one of the most cost-effective self-service tools available to you. Some of these boards are moderated, while others use software systems that automatically manage the receipt, review, and message-posting processes.

These "virtual water-coolers" also are a good way to get an unfiltered look at how customers perceive your products or services. Unlike your design teams, who create products in controlled environments, your customers are using your products in the real world and facing real-world situations with them. When they share their stories and their problem-solving techniques at your Web site, they are giving you valuable free data about your products and how they are used. For example, Hewlett Packard (HP) has a forum on its site where customers share code they've written to be used with an HP chemical analysis machine. Not only are customers finding solutions from peers instead of calling HP, they are sharing data about how they use machine code with the company.

THE LIMITS OF WEB SELF-SERVICE

Giving customers access to carbon-based life forms—competent human help—at the time of need is increasingly what separates wheat from chaff among business-to-consumer (B2C) and B2B e-businesses. Creating such capability—attaching a welcoming voice, or face, to an often faceless business process—can turn undecided, fickle, or annoyed e-customers into loyal patrons who return to your e-resource time and again.

This idea, of course, runs counter to a powerful belief set about what draws people to e-commerce in the first place—the prospect of a "people-less" buying experience. For consumers shopping retail Web sites, much of the Web's attraction is the thought of not having to fight traffic on the way to the mall, no wheel-to-wheel combat for parking spots, no long waits in checkout lines, and no hovering or ill-advised salespeople. For B2B Web customers, the promise is greater accuracy and faster service. They no longer have to play phone tag with sales reps waiting to get product, price, or delivery information, there are fewer in-person sales pitches, and less chance that fax- or phone-placed orders will be misinterpreted or lost. They also they have access to more detailed, accurate, and up-to-the-minute product and process information than even the most well-informed sales reps can provide. It's a bit antiseptic perhaps, definitely business lunch- free, but it's fast, efficient, reliable, and oh so hassle-free.

In other words it's a people-less process, that is, until an offbeat problem or question arises that only a human can deal with and that renders a search engine or the most extensive FAQ list impotent. Or, in the case of skeptical or fearful customers who are transacting business online for the first time, it's the comfort of a human voice or personalized piece of e-mail confirming that an order has indeed gone through and has not disappeared into the electronic ethers and that your product will arrive Monday morning guaranteed, thank-you very much.

Self-service tools we've been discussing, like FAQs, real language, Ask Jeeves-like search engines, and online bulletin boards have deservedly captured the imagination of retail and B2B e-commerce site managers. They slash service-related costs, answer basic customer inquires, and free-up overburdened call centers or help desks to focus on more challenging service problems. However, the reality is there's no substitute for well-trained, knowledgeable, sympathetic human help when e-customers hit a brick wall. Emerging technologies save dollars and are scalable, but they can't offer the idiosyncratic, personal touch, critical to setting yourself apart in highly competitive e-commerce markets.

Customers who don't receive the human support they need when they need it, says e-Satisfy.com's John Goodman, are not only less loyal, they're more apt to spread the word about your determined inaccessibility. In a study done in conjunction with the International Customer Service Association (ICSA) in late 1999, e-Satisfy.com found that only 36 percent of 9,500 responding customers were satisfied with their e-contacts (e-mail and Web). It also found that poor handling of e-contacts created from 30 to 48 percent lower customer loyalty among the two-thirds of customers rating themselves unsatisfied with their service experiences.[16]

Even more ominous, according to e-Satisfy.com data, is that dissatisfied e-customers tell twice as many people about their poor service experiences than satisfied customers and are almost four times more likely to discuss their experiences in an online chat room—with potentially thousands of readers—than satisfied e-customers.

Quick Case
Fogdog's "Search Squad": An Antidote to "Sorry, We Don't Carry That"

Can't find those running shoes you've been scouring the planet for or that North Face jacket everyone and their brother seems to be sold out of? Perhaps you're a memorabilia buff and have been striking out trying to find a jersey from the 1975 Boston Red Sox.

Not to fear, Fogdog.com's Search Squad is here.

The Search Squad is two part-time Fogdog service consultants dedicated full-time to tracking down items customers can't find on Fogdog's sporting goods site or anywhere else in the known galaxy. Frustrated customers simply click on an easy-to-find "Search Squad" link on Fogdog's home page, describe in detail what they're looking for, add a price range, and the Search Squad's bloodhounds are unleashed.

Search requesters aren't billed unless Fogdog finds the product, there are no charges for search labor, nor are prices marked up or any commission charged once a product is found. Customers are billed the actual product price including shipping and applicable sales tax. "It's a personalized shopping service for consumers who haven't been able to find what they're looking for, whether on our site or elsewhere," explains Mike Guerra, Fogdog's customer service director. "If we locate the item, we'll pay retail if need be to get it for the customer."

How often does the Search Squad find its quarry? In about 20 percent of searches, says Guerra. That modest success rate is due in part to people frequently asking for items that have been discontinued, are out of stock, or aren't yet in stock because the product is a new release. In other cases, people are simply enticed by the challenge of trying to stump the Search Squad. "A lot of times people ask for something just because they know it can't be found," Guerra says. "We try to let customers know up front if they're asking for something we know is going to be next to impossible to find."

If the Squad does come up short on a search, it issues the requester a fifteen dollar coupon to use against a purchase on Fogdog's site.

The Search Squad recently began taking credit card numbers from people making requests. "We had so many people requesting things, and the Squad would find a ton of it, but the requester would already have found it somewhere else or decided not to take it after all," Guerra says. "Now we simply take a credit card number and tell them if we find the item within two days, we'll just go ahead and ship it out to them. That tends to separate the serious from not-so-serious requests." An act of self-preservation and protection that at one and the same time is potentially an act of convenience from the customer's perspective.

10

MAKE RECOVERY A
POINT OF PRIDE

AT

the core of every commercial contract and social compact is a promise. Keep that promise as a company and everyone profits and comes away from the transaction a little bit better for the effort.

But fall short of that promise, and all manner of bad things can happen to everyone concerned. There are direct and indirect economic consequences for buyer and seller, giver and receiver. Most customers who feel cheated or greatly misled by a merchant—online or offline—demand their money back and swear never to do business with that merchant again.[1] And perhaps even more importantly, they warn others to steer clear of that merchant.

However, if the merchant fixes the problem—commits an act of effective service recovery—and its done faster, better, and with less imposition on the customer than he or she had dreaded, they will sing the merchant's praises. And come back. And trust the company anew. They will have seen the company at its best, and they will know it and appreciate it all the more.

Service recovery is the art of fixing what went wrong for the customer and mending the damage that the error, mistake, or misstep did to your relationship with that customer. Yes, service recovery is first and foremost about fixing those missteps, but as, or more, important, it is about restoring trust when your customer is most vulnerable to doubt and has second thoughts about ever clicking your way again.

THE BENCHMARK FOR EFFECTIVE RECOVERY

Doug Sundheim, senior client development manager for Internet consultancy, Luminant Worldwide, ordered a boxed set of five CDs from Amazon.com's site on a Saturday afternoon. When the discs arrived the following Wednesday, one of them wouldn't play. Sundheim e-mailed a note describing the problem to customerservice@Amazon.com. Being a tech savvy sort—Sundheim sells Internet consulting services after all—he expected a reply he says, "sometime in the middle of the next week." To his amazement, an hour later he received an answer that not only acknowledged his note and his problem, but proposed a solution.

"Got your message. Sending a new set along with a postage paid package for return of the entire first set. Don't want to take a chance that something is wrong with the others."

Impressive. Once again the clock in Sundheim's head went to work, and he mentally set the middle of the next week as his "See what's going on" follow-up date. Friday—two days later—he arrived home to find a package with the replacement set of CDs and the postage-paid return envelope on his doorstep. "They just wowed me – and won me over for keeps," he recalls.

A happy accident? Hardly. What Sundheim experienced was the end result of a carefully planned, worked out process, the goal of which is to fix not only broken promises, but bent, stapled, and mutilated customer relations as well.

Amazon.com, Inc. founder Jeff Bezos has long been known as a vocal advocate of the position that e-commerce will, in the long run, rise or fall on the quality of service it provides to customers. Living up to Bezos' theorem is the job of 200 customer service representatives (CSRs) resident on the fourth floor of the Decatur Building in downtown Seattle, Washington. Those live, flesh and blood human beings are charged with dealing with the 20,000 e-mails, faxes, and phone calls— customer service moments of truth—the company is inundated with every day of the week. It was one of those 200 customer service reps working with Amazon.com's preplanned, finely balanced recovery system, who made a believer out of Sundheim.

KEY 20:
MASTER SERVICE RECOVERY BASICS

FROM BRICKS TO CLICKS—RECOVERY COUNTS

Providing prompt, high-quality recovery for Amazon.com customers, or for that matter, Ritz-Carlton or Federal Express or Billy Bob's Bait Shop and Basement Barbecue Bar and Grill customers, is a rush for the provider and a treat for the customer. But is "doing whatever it takes" to create value for a disappointed or disgruntled customer worth doing from either a business plan or a P&L statement point of view? It is important to know the art of the possible to benchmark your progress and evaluate your investment.

The research and results numbers for traditional companies are more than convincing, and the most current studies of dotcom and e-commerce companies are highly suggestive that they also can profit from focusing on distinctive service recovery.

According to John Goodman, president of e-Satisfy.com,[2] studies his firm has conducted during the past fifteen years all find that when customers' problems were satisfactorily handled and resolved, their loyalty and repurchase intentions were within a few percentage points of self-reported loyalty and repurchase intentions for those customers who had not experienced a product or service failure.

Even more intriguing are four proprietary e-Satisfy.com studies that surveyed, respectively, industrial customers of a Canadian chemical company, high-value customers of an American bank, customers of two global computer companies, and professional photographers who were customers of a European photographic supply company. These studies found that customers whose complaints were quickly satisfied were more likely to purchase additional products than even those customers who experienced no problems with the organization or its products. (Figure 10-1).

In the United States, instant camera manufacturer Polaroid found that customers who telephoned to ask about the product or report problems with camera gear can be sold additional photographic equipment once the subject of the call has been handled to the customer's satisfaction. This and similar findings casts substantial doubt on the once commonly held notion that a high-visibility service recovery effort is always a loss leader. It can, in fact, be a direct profit generator.

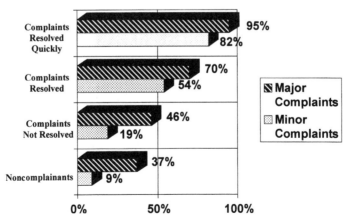

Figure 10-1. How many of your unhappy customers will buy from you again? (With permission from e-Satisfy.com.)

In other words, e-Satisfy.com's research strongly suggests that swift and effective service recovery enhances customers' perception of the quality of the products and services they have already purchased, as well as their perception of the competence of the organization and its personnel. This also enhances the perceived quality and value of other products and services the organization offers.

The same SOCAP/Yankelovich study mentioned earlier in this chapter found a high correlation between online customer care and customer loyalty[3] for e-commerce customers. A majority (70 percent) of online customers surveyed, rated themselves as "very likely" to repurchase products and services from e-commerce companies that positively responded to and resolved their problems.

On the "flip side" there are clear indicators that ignoring recovery opportunities can damage future business opportunities for e-commerce organizations.

The ICSA/e-Satisfy.com study[3] found that:

◆ Poor handling of e-contacts create 30 to 48 percent lower customer loyalty among dissatisfied customers than would be the case in a comparable brick and mortar situation.
◆ Dissatisfied e-customers tell twice as many people about their experience than satisfied customers.
◆ Dissatisfied e-customers are almost four times more likely to discuss their disappointing experience in an online chat room that satisfied e-customers.

The latter, dubbed "word of mouse" by Melinda K. M. Goddard, director, service quality and customer service at Roche

Laboratories, can be most devastating. The damage done via traditional word of mouth is modest compared to what happens today on the Internet. With today's technology, bad service experiences now travel at warp speed and to far corners of the globe. Traditionally, a disgruntled customer might tell five to ten people about his or her unhappy experience on a one-to-one basis. Now, however, thanks to Web chat groups, bulletin boards, online user groups, and broadcast e-mail, the medium of choice for venting upset with a company has become one-to-many. Frustrated or angry customers can deliver a screenful of damage in information about your company to hundreds or even thousands in an instant. There are even Web sites operated by specific consumer advocacy groups that solicit reports of poor customer service and disappointing experiences with company and agency products and service. One of the strongest, most visited sites chronicles the complaints and woes of commercial air travelers (www.passengerrights.com), but there is a whole subindustry growing in cyberspace that encourages upset customers to take their grievances public via third-party complaint resolution sites of which there are already dozens.[4] Sound crazy? According to e-Satisfy.com, 50 percent of upset retail and 25 percent of disgruntled business-to-business (B2B) customers never bother to tell you directly that they are miffed. If you aren't encouraging your customers to tell you when things aren't right, there are apparently an ample number of entrepreneurs out there ready and willing to take up the slack—for a price. And don't think the competition does not use those publicly posted rantings and ravings to study your weaknesses and look for vulnerabilities.

Surprisingly, those public complaint boards or "company hate sites" as they are sometimes referred to, have substantial credibility and usage. The SOCAP/Yankelovich study found that 20 percent of online users surveyed had visited a "company hate" site, and 46 percent of those visitors found the information posted there to be "extremely" or "very credible."[5]

Not long ago, Sony Corporation got a taste of Internet information whiplash when a computer scientist for the National Institute of Standards and Technology took offense to a Sony ad that ran on MTV. In the scientist's view, the ad was extremely sexist and deserving of comment. She took her protest, via an electronic bulletin board, to members of Syster, a group composed of some 1,500 women in the field of computer operating systems research. After describing the commercial, the scientist declared over the e-waves that she would not purchase any Sony products until the commercial was withdrawn from the air. In an interview with the *Wall Street Journal*, she sounded a sterner warning, "An electronic bulletin board can mobilize a grassroots movement within hours, and the collective outrage can be focused at individual companies." The commercial was soon pulled from the air.

Although such consumer protests can create a stir, the real damage is done in B2B or tightly niched, narrowly focused operations. Sample, for instance, the harping that goes on in bulletin boards and chat rooms where people discuss computer hardware, software, or service support issues. People writing these scathing commentaries are not corporate lightweights. Many are charged with making repurchase decisions for their companies.

Frederick Reichheld of Bain & Company and W. Earl Sasser of

Harvard University have looked at research such as the ICSA/e-Satisfy.com and SOCAP/Yankelovich findings and taken them a step further.[6] They calculated the value of customer retention over a five-year period for nine industries. They considered not only base profits but profits from increased purchases, profits from word-of-mouth referrals, and profits from price premium purchases. Reichheld and Sasser found that profits from a single customer are not static but increase over time. In other words, a customer who has been with you for five years (depending on your industry) can be up to 377 percent more profitable than a customer you have only recently wooed to your products or services. Their bottom-line calculation is that by focusing on customer retention tactics, such as service recovery and reducing annual customer defections by a mere 5 percent, an organization can boost pretax profits 25 to 125 percent.

The bottom-line is that there is as significant a benefit to attending to service recovery in e-commerce as there is to attending to it in conventional commerce, and significant risk inherent in ignoring customer pleas for your aide.

STATE OF THE ART

Just as it is clear that recovery counts, it is equally clear that e-commerce companies either aren't very good at service recovery or aren't very interested in it.

In 1999, for example, the National Consumer's League received up to 1,000 complaints a month about online service providers, compared to just 600 a month in 1998. The Federal

Trade Commission received an average of 4,800 online complaints a month in 1999 up from only 2,000 in 1998, not encouraging results.

And there are other, more case-specific studies emerging, indicating that e-shoppers' service-related problems are neither abating nor are the companies involved becoming much more recovery savvy. Resource Marketing, a Columbus, Ohio-based consulting group that critiques e-commerce sites,[7] tested forty-five consumer Web sites in the summer of 1999 and found that only 60 percent bothered to respond to customer e-mail inquiries at all. Less than ten of those sites had prominent guarantees offering full refunds to unsatisfied customers. And only one-third of these e-tailers would accept returns of products purchased online at their brick and mortar stores. In another study, market research firm Jupiter Communications[8] sent e-mails requesting help to 125 highly respected, high-volume Web sites. Almost half (46 percent) took five days or more to respond to the request, never responded, or did not post an e-mail address on the site for customers to lodge a complaint or even ask for information. That number was up from 38 percent in 1998.

The ICSA/e-Satisfy.com study[9] reinforces these dismal results:

◆ Though e-customers across all industries expect an acknowledgment of their contacts, whether for information or error redress, within one hour, only 12 percent of customers received an acknowledgment within that hour and only 42 percent report receiving even an automated acknowledgment within twenty-four hours.

◆ Only 30 percent of e-customers received a final response to their contact within twenty-four hours, and 19 percent of organizations took more than seven days to respond. Nearly four out of ten respondents reported that they never received a final response to their most recent complaint.

◆ Only 40 percent of e-contacts are fully resolved with one online contact— even though this is a widely held customer expectation. Almost half of complaints customers logged required a phone call from the customer to the organization to achieve a final resolution.

Despite all the evidence that (a) e-commerce customers are unhappy with current service recovery efforts and (b) that heeding the warnings pay off for e-commerce companies, a Boston Consulting Group study[10] found that e-commerce companies spent on average of one-fifth (20 percent) of what traditional retailers and catalog companies spend on after-sale service and customer retention activities like planned service recovery.

> The ICSA/e-Satisfy.com study summed up the current state of e-commerce service recovery in bold letters:
> ◆ E-customer service currently is not effective nor efficient.
> ◆ Poor e-customer service has and will continue to have a major impact on corporate profits.
> ◆ E-customer service operations are missing the real opportunities.[11]

KEY 21:
DEFINE RECOVERY FROM THE CUSTOMER'S POINT OF VIEW

THE FIVE AXIOMS OF HIGH-QUALITY SERVICE RECOVERY

Axioms are the self-evident truths that underlie a course of action, a process, or a philosophy. All these are true of the axioms of service recovery. These five axioms are the research-based, customer-centered ideas and ideals that form the philosophy and principles upon which effective recovery is based.

Axiom 1: *Customers have recovery expectations.* Expectations are the building blocks of all customer transactions; the embodiment of all the customer's wants and needs. A customer's expectations can be as unique as the body shape and inner functioning of a doctor's patient. However, as in medicine, there are fundamental similarities that can guide our efforts. The basic alikeness of two different human kidneys enables physicians to perform kidney surgery using a reliable set of norms, protocols, and prognoses. There is an apt parallel in e-service—and service recovery—expectations. We all want personalized treatment, but our individual visions of what that entails can share a lot of similarities.

These expectations fall into five categories that, according to the Berry, Zeithaml, and Parasuraman research,[12] cover 80 percent of the differences between high and low customer satisfaction scores. Following is an explanation of these five factors.

Reliability. *Reliability* encompasses all the actions that telegraph organizational competence. First and foremost it means keeping promises or doing what you say you will do. You exude reliability when things work as they were supposed to, or the way you said they would. Reliability is the backbone of dependability and trust. Reliability is the most critical of the five attributes of customer service and the key to understanding upset and ire when things go amiss. Why?

Customers relish a high degree of predictability. They are comforted knowing that the sun will come up every morning...and not on a random basis. When things do not happen as we predict or as we tell customers they will happen, it leaves them with high anxiety and a desire to put things back in balance. Breaking mutual agreements shatters any semblance of trust.

When ebags.com promises fast replacements for any damaged travel products, and the replacement arrives before the rollie bag with the bad wheel is even in the return shipping box— they get top box reliability scores.

Assurance. *Assurance* is about confidence; it signals that things are going as they should. The doctor acts just like a doctor is supposed to act. The clerk acts knowledgeable, the pilot

> **NOTE:** Internet customers can't see you working on their behalf. You have to tell them you are trying to solve their problems or answer their query if you are to get physiological credit from the customer for your efforts.

sounds self-assured, and the wine steward has a French accent (we made that last one up, but you get the point). Assurance is an array of cues that tell the customer to "be assured, all is well, and everything in its place." When service breakdown occurs, assurance has a deeper, more poignant meaning.

Assurance is an unspoken guarantee or pledge. Customers often enter a service transaction with specific notions about what it ought to be like. We—and they—know our place, our lines, and our role. If, for reasons beyond your control, the service provider refuses to participate in the fashion expected, consumers feel out of control and in need of reassurance. A heavy dose of authenticity coupled with a generous helping of confidence-building actions are required in the recipe to quickly right the scene and honor the pledge. In service recovery, assurance is really reassurance that everything is OK or will soon be made so. When Amazon.com or OmahaSteaks.com send their disappointed and inquiring customers progress reports on their efforts to redress the complaints, they are responding to the customer need for reassurance.

Empathy. *Empathy* includes all the actions you take to declare to customers that you genuinely care about their business. Active listening when your reps are 800-live with customers, for instance, makes customers feel valued. Communicating regularly while you are working on a complex recovery problem tells customers that you're attentive. You show empathy when you respond to customers' specific needs; when you keep them informed of important changes; and when you act in ways the customers deem fair, compassionate, honest, and thoughtful.

Empathy means understanding. And to understand at an emotional level requires a sincere *connection*. When trust has been challenged or threatened, the bridge to recovery starts with the most fundamental component of being human...a pure, genuine, and considerate link. It means someone in your organization must obviously and without reserve reach out to the customer when things go wrong. The task is to be aware and sensitive to your customers expectations and level of upset. When your CSRs respond with empathy, they stay calm and in control. Only then are they at their absolute best: Ready, willing, and able to help the customer.

Showing empathy for customers actually allows CSRs to be professional and caring at the same time. It also makes customers feel like important individuals. Empathy cannot be handed out by a machine; it's something one person does for another. There is no substitute for the human touch. Even across the Net customers can tell when you are sincerely concerned about an error. When a member of our research team complained to

> Dear Jill,
>
> Well, I am glad to know you made it to *your* destination in one piece! I am very sorry for all your trouble. What can I do to make it up to you? We can send you something, or a partial refund, etc.? Hope your holidays are great.
>
> TroutRiver.com

TroutRiver.com that a Christmas order arrived broken and had to be hand repaired by her to ensure it would be under the tree on time, the response was admirably empathetic.

Responsiveness. *Responsiveness*—doing things in an appropriately timely fashion. It means the service provider's actions happen fast enough for the customer not to feel neglected, but not in a panicky way. It's more than the pace of service, it's also the perception of that pace. The auto repair shop that takes two hours to get a needed part gets lower marks than the one that takes the same two hours but keeps the customer posted on where the part is and when it is expected. We Homo sapiens hate to be kept in the dark. Questions and answers are a fundamental building block of interpersonal communication. Without communication we feel isolated, alone—and powerless in the face of a service breakdown.

Order a computer online at Dell or Compaq, and you can see where your order is from the moment you check out to the day it arrives on your doorstep, all with the click of a button. If parts are on backorder, they alert you with an e-mail, or you can use your order number to track where the order process is at the site—in preproduction, production, or delivery preparation. When it's shipped, you can automatically link to Federal Express' order-tracking system to watch its progress.

Providing this sort of transparent access to the purchase process eases the minds of consumers who are willing to wait for a product, as long as they know what's going on.

The dark side of responsiveness is not nonresponsiveness—it's indifference. Customers interpret the truancy of reply (i.e., the faltering of action) as a calculated and calloused affront to their need for an answer. They are left angered by its absence—and doubly angered by their dependence upon it. Their deep-seated reaction suggests that they expect communication to be rapid and regular following service breakdowns and that responses prove sufficiently abundant to rebuild their reserve. Both the ICSA and the SOCAP studies make that point. The SOCAP study found 73 percent of respondents expect their problems to be resolved within twenty-four hours, while the ICSA/e-Satisfy.com study found final resolution expectations varied by industry with auto/electronic/computer customers expecting resolution in one hour, financial services customers expecting resolution in four hours, and consumer goods customers willing to wait twenty-four hours. Both studies found that customers expect their problem notification to be acknowledged within one hour—whether by e-mail or phone—just be sure to put some "e" in this effort.

Tangibles. *Tangibles* are the physical "stuff" that goes with the service experience. By "goes with" we mean where its presence is appropriate and its absence an alarm. When the plumber shows up with dirt under his nails, we assume he's been busy and we're ready to open our basement doors. But if the dentist shows up in the same unkempt fashion, we assume he's lost his allegiance to hygiene and we're reluctant to open our mouths. Tangibles work in support of the other four attributes; flowers make empathy more poignant, and spit-and-polish makes assurance more credible. Clean, accurate paperwork tells us we are working with precise professionals.

While tangibles may not be lead culprits in turning customer content to contempt, they amplify our upset or unease and underscore our perception that the server's ambition is to disappoint us. When the hotel leaves cigarette butts in the ashtrays or when the auto repair shop leaves grease on our windshield, we are insulted by their disrespect for our association—and insulted by their disregard for our assets. When your Web site makes it hard for the customer to figure out how to complain to or communicate with you, you net negative on the "tangibles" scale with your customers.

When CDW.com sends the customer a return label, postage, and instructions to "just leave it out for UPS to pick up," while at the same time including a replacement modem, they are exhibiting confidence in themselves, the customer, and their process.

Axiom 2: *Successful recovery is psychological as well as physical*: Fix the person, then the problem. Customers who have a problem with your product or service expect you to solve the problem. Just as important, but less easy for customers to articulate, is the need to be "fixed" psychologically. Often a customer who has a bad experience with your company or product loses faith in your reliability—your ability to deliver what you've promised. The repairperson who goes straight to the copier or laser printer, completes the repair task, and quietly leaves for the next call may be practicing good technical work-unit-per-hour management, but not good recovery. The customer contact person who needed to use the broken machine and was under pressure to get it fixed needs to be "repaired" as well. If nothing more, the service person needs to give the contact person an opportunity to vent his or her pent-up frustration. It's part of the job.

The core of the psychological aspect of recovery is restoring trust; the customer's belief that you can and will keep both the explicit and implicit promises you make. Trust is particularly at-risk when customers feel vulnerable; that is, perceive all the power to set things right in your hands and little or nothing under their control. That sense of vulnerability, and the customer's reaction to the breakdown, is the loudest when the customer feels he/she lacks one of four things:

Information: The customer doesn't know what is going on, or how long it will take to set things right.

Expertise: The customer can't fix the car or computer or fouled–up reservation or replace the product on their own. All the "smarts" are on the vendor's side of the table.

Freedom: There is no option for fixing the problem aside from dealing with your company. The customer perceives you as their only hope. It is a disabling, anxiety-rousing situation.

Recourse: The customer perceives that when it comes to this computer, or car, or malady it's you or nobody. They may be free, contractually, to ask anyone else they can find to do the problem "fix" but there is no one else, or at least they see it that way.

Restoring trust is accomplished by involving the customer in solving the problem, "Tell me again exactly what was happening when it stopped," or "Can you give me a rundown on the history of this problem," reassures the client that the problem is not only fixable, but that it will be fixed.

When a self-employed home office worker buys software that won't install, he expects a CSR to calmly walk him through a list of scenarios that are guaranteed to get the program loaded and working. And, even if it is entirely the fault of the consumer who doesn't know enough to double click, responding seriously, without snickering, and taking responsibility for the confusing nature of the software installation instructions is the only appropriate approach.

Processwise, it is critical to fix—deal with and reassure—the customer before plunging into fixing the problem. The most important "customer-fixing" skill your people can develop is listening. Letting the customer tell their tale (live or via e-mail), blow off steam, and give their point of view—plus giving the customer a sincere apology—goes a long way toward the needed psychological fix.

Axiom 3: *Work in a spirit of partnership.* Our research suggests strongly that customers who participate in the problem-solving effort are more satisfied with the problem resolution. There are, however, limits and provisos to this dictum. When the company clearly causes the problem, asking the customer what he or she would like to see happen next gives the customer a sense of regaining control. That regained sense of control can be vital to calming customers who feel that the organization treated them unjustly, in some way abused them, or are bordering on a perception that they have been victimized or treated unfairly.

When the customer clearly caused the problem, asking him or her to do something to help facilitate solving the problem is highly appropriate and increases the probability that the customer will feel satisfied with the solution. The solution, in both situations, becomes the *our* solution, not *your* solution.

Critical to creating a sense of partnership is the way you invite the customer into the problem-solving process. The query, "So, what do you want me to do about it?" may be seen as shifting the responsibility for managing the service recovery process back onto the customer.

Remember those old movies when the doctors send the father off to "boil water" in preparation for a home birth? By and large, the water-boiling assignment was a way of keeping the father out of the way, occupied, and feeling a part of the process. Even if all the customer can really do, metaphorically, is boil water, the effort has palliative effects.

The bank customer who failed to endorse a paycheck when it was deposited and thereby caused a string of bounced checks, feels better about the recovery effort when given a part in the redress. An assignment like "Give me a list of all the people you've written checks to" or "call the people you've written checks to and ask them to resubmit them for payment" gives the customer back some sense of psychological control.

The TroutRiver.com CSR who asked our associate to name the recompense she would like for the inconvenience of having repaired the broken item herself was putting a measure of atonement control in the customer's hands.

Axiom 4: Customers react more strongly to "fairness" failures than to "honest mistakes." Researcher Kathleen Seiders,

Babson College, Wellesley, Massachusetts,[13] has found that "When customers believe they have been treated unfairly, their reactions tend to be immediate, emotional, and enduring." In other words, if the customer feels he or she has been shortchanged, given the short shrift, or been disrespected on purpose, the reaction is heated and long lasting.

When ToysRus.com reneged on its "delivery by Christmas" pledge, you can bet customers felt that their trust was being betrayed. And few felt the atonement offered, the $100 store certificate, was a fair exchange for the hassle they incurred as a result of the breach.

There is but one course of action when the customer feels he or she has been treated unfairly— extreme apology and atonement. Sure, the customer's prescription may indeed be the result of a misunderstanding of something said or done and not intended. That is irrelevant. Once a customer feels unfairly treated, you are dealing with an at-risk customer who, according to Seiders, is a prime candidate for overt, hostile, retaliation, and a sure bet to complain about you on a hate board. According to Seiders, communication (explaining what went wrong) and compensation (atonement) can repair a perception of unfairness. It is important, she adds, to cast the explanation in terms that do not attempt to put the full responsibility for the faux pas on the shoulders of a third party or a "misunderstanding." The direct, simple, "I'm sorry this has occurred and I'll make sure it is cleared up right away" is as close to a magic bullet as there is in service recovery.

Axiom 5: *Effective recovery is a planned process.* Airlines and hotels overbook. Trains and planes have weather delays and cancellations. If uncontrollable conditions can cause problems for your customers, creating a planned process makes imminent sense. However, you must institute and apply the planned process in a highly responsive, customer-sensitive fashion. Customers remember uncaring, robotic recovery long after they forget the incident that necessitated the solution.

It is important that frontline service employees know what you expect planned recovery to look like and where the limits to recovery lie. It is also critically important that they regularly practice implementing the plan. Customers remember two things from well-designed and well-implemented planned recovery: The quality of the solutions offered and the skill of the people offering it. Of the two, the latter is the most memorable.

"Planned Process" means all the things you do to make it easy for your customers to complain to and communicate with you and for your people to solve problems and dialogue with your information-hungry customers. It is the quality of your recovery system.

At Amazon.com, 20,000 customers a day call or send e-mails with questions, suggestions, or complaints. They are all dealt with in a decidedly planned, yet amazingly flexible fashion. To respond to the press of all that hot correspondence, Bill Price, Amazon.com's head of customer service works to ensure three things: First that he hires only people who share his passion for customers; second he makes sure that they have state-of-the-art equipment, processes, and solutions to work with[14]; and third they are empowered to use their best judgment when responding to customers. One part of the latter is a database of 1,400 plus prescripted remarks, written by the CSRs themselves, that are selectively queued up as customers' queries come in. CSRs are free to modify, amend, or even discard the prewritten "blurbs," as they are referred to in-house, if they feel the nuances of the customer's incoming correspondence requires a more individualized or tailored response.

At the same time, Price is aware of the pressure that is part and parcel of a first-rate customer service, service recovery operation. His operation pays well—from $10.50 an hour for beginners to $16 an hour for senior reps who take on some minimal supervisory tasks. Internal promotions to other units within Amazon.com are not uncommon, and CSRs are regularly recognized and rewarded for above-and-beyond performance. Those who succeed in unsnarling particular messy situations or calming especially upset customers are awarded "CPR" certificates—short for "Customer Permanently Retained."

BUILD A RETENTION STRATEGY (OR, OUT WITH THE TEFLON, IN WITH THE VELCRO)

E-COMMERCE

↓

has grown up. From its childhood in the mid-1990s to adolescence in 1998 through 1999, Internet businesses have been fixated on customer acquisition, or finding new ways to identify potential customers and lure them to their sites. The prevailing language and metrics mirrored the priority: Capturing eyeballs, hits, click-through rates, and more. In these teen years, revenue and market share, fueled by Wall Street's cheerleaders, sat high above profitability on the e-totem pole.

However, as more e-businesses move into adulthood, they've begun to see the folly of strategies that are all-consuming in their pursuit of new customers—that strive to continually refill the cupboards—at the expense of efforts to keep more of the same customers around for the long haul. Many have learned an "old economy" lesson the hard way—it's a lot cheaper to keep customers than to continually troll for new ones.

KEY 22:
PRACTICE RETENTION PLANNING

A study conducted by Harvard University's W. Earl Sasser and Bain & Company's Frederick Reichheld found that the longer you are able to retain a customer, the more profitable the relationship becomes[1] as shown in Figure 11-1.

The longer you keep a customer coming back, the more profitable that customer is to your business. Why? Longevity leads to increased purchases, less price sensitivity, reduced operating costs, and high quality referrals.

The costs of acquiring customers on the Web can be forbidding compared to the cost of retaining customers, a factoid increasingly true for "pure-play" retailers, or those who've launched their businesses on the Internet and don't have the existing brand-

Company Profit Index

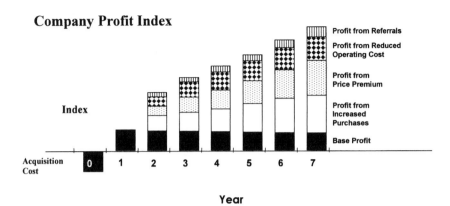

Figure 11-1. The economics of focusing on customer care.

ing or a brick and mortar lineage with which to build significant market awareness out of the gate.

The Boston Consulting Group[2] found that multichannel retailers, or those with a physical or mail-order presence as well as a digital storefront, had an average customer acquisition cost of twenty-two dollars per customer, while pure-play retailers had an average cost of forty-two dollars per customer. It won't be long before both numbers seem conservative.

To recoup those high costs—let alone consider moving into a profit phase—e-businesses have to keep customers coming back not just for one or two additional purchases, but often and far down the road.

In a study of 2,116 online shoppers, conducted jointly by Bain & Company/Mainspring Communications Inc.,[3] Bain examined factors leading to customer retention in the apparel, electronics, and groceries businesses.

In the apparel industry, the study found the average Web

shopper wasn't profitable for the retailer until he or she had shopped at the site four times, "implying that the retailer had to retain the customer for twelve months just to break even," study authors wrote.[3] Online grocers faced an even stiffer challenge—they had to retain a customer for eighteen months to break even. Except for a very few high-ticket items, online retailers were not able to break even on a single, initial visit customer purchase.

Bain and Mainspring also found that the longer the relationship between customer and online retailer, the more money the customer will spend in a given period. This is due in part to more frequent visits and to higher-value transactions. In the grocery industry, for example, online customers spent 23 percent more in months thirty-one to thirty-six of a relationship than in the first six months of using the grocer's services.

Their consciousness raised by such data, more e-businesses, with one eye still trained on acquisition performance, are embracing a new metric: "conversion" rates. Conversion rates measure the number of customers who come to your site in a given period divided into the number who take some action there—those who register or make a purchase. In most industries, a conversion of 8 to 10 percent is considered exemplary. Once "converted," the challenge becomes bringing those customers back for repeat performances.

The good news is that, using Bain's research and the experience of the brick and mortar world as a guide, even small percentage increases in retention levels can have a big impact on profit levels over time. The bad news is that many e-businesses have yet to deploy formal customer retention strategies.

SERVICE FACTORS INFLUENCING RETENTION

An e-customer's decision to continue to do business with you—and better yet, to evangelize about the merits of your site to friends, family, chat room buddies, or anyone within crowing distance—rests on many factors, only one of which is your price/value quotient. Factors carrying the greatest weight are transactional, or the customer's A-to-Z experience in using your site, from ease of navigation to order checkout to product delivery to postsale support. In this sense, at least, the formula for retaining customers is deceptively simple: Make your site easy to use, create a compelling cache of inventory, keep your delivery promises, have resources available to promptly and accurately answer customer questions, and if you do happen to screw up, create a fair fix for the customer that includes an apology.

Despite the nervous talk of customers' heightened service expectations in the online world, in reality, most of these expectations are more modest than outrageous. Above all, e-customers are looking for you to remove the complexity from their lives. Doing so quickly sets you apart from the crowd and often reserves a spot for you in the coveted bookmarked list of "favorite places."

Master the service basics, this thinking goes, and retention tends to fall in line. Sharon Bargas of OmahaSteaks.com puts it this way: "If customers try us once, can get around the site easily and find what they want, have product delivered as promised, and love the way we work with them if they need help, that's the key to bringing them back again."

KEY 23:
MAKE THE FIRST THREE VISITS MEMORABLE

Make no mistake—getting service right the first time is important. The Boston Consulting Group's research clearly shows,[4] and common sense confirms, that once customers have had a few positive experiences at a site, it takes a rash of subsequent bad experiences for them to consider abandoning ship for another suitor. The consulting firm found that it takes approximately three visits for retail e-customers to "imprint" on a site. The first visit is a "trial" purchase, where consumers cautiously dip their toes in the water of the online buying experience. The second is a "confirmatory" purchase, with customers returning to see if the first experience was an aberration or to see if the Web site repeats its round-one performance. A third visit "cements" the relationship, marking the beginning of customer loyalty that presumably could last for years.

How you manage the customer's experience during those three formative visits is critical. It is during these visits that you must roll out the proverbial red carpet and draw them in with open arms. Are you doing that? Do you welcome new customers and ask them to evaluate their experience? Do you offer to enroll them in your select customer program? Do you track their transactional and contact satisfaction? Do you compare their revisit cycle time to what you know about your best, most loyal customers?

Retention isn't just a result of a user-friendly Web site. It is a function of getting service right the first time on the back end of the purchasing cycle or order fulfillment. The Bain and Mainspring study found improvements in order fulfillment dependability can have a significant impact on customer retention. In both the apparel and grocery industries, improving customer satisfaction scores on order fulfillment by just one-half of a point (on a scale of one to five) increases "implied" customer retention rates—customers' stated likelihood of returning to that site—by more than 2 percent (significant, given that the survey's average implied retention rate for all Web sites is 86 percent, with a "definitely will return" statement implying 100 percent retention, and a "probably will return" 70 percent).

Reliable order delivery isn't a given in e-business, and developing expertise in that area provides another chance for you to stand apart from the competition. Authors of the Bain study said a surprising number of surveyed customers reported that "they didn't receive exactly what they thought they'd ordered, were not made aware of the total price when they placed their orders, product delivery was late, and return policy and service commitments were not met."[3] It was a surprisingly often heard comment from the focus groups in our own study "Shopping the Internet Circa 1999: The Good, the Bad, and the Ugly".[5]

PRICE IS NOT THE PRIMARY MOTIVATOR FOR RETURNING TO A SITE

What role does price play in e-customers' repurchase decisions? While offering competitive prices is critical, Internet market research shows that in most industries, it's only important that customers receive a "fair" price and that online prices meet or beat prices they could get offline, but not that your site offer the lowest price compared to online competitors. In other words, your biggest competitors—in the mind of today's customer—are not other dot-coms or Internet vendors, but brick and mortar companies. Even then price is only one part of a customers' "value scorecard" that also assigns weight to inventory selection, ease of doing business, reliable delivery, and other transactional and relationship factors. There's no denying that most dot-coms could improve "conversion" rates in the short term simply by cutting prices. But there's a good reason Internet market analysts refer to that strategy as "renting" customers.

E-businesses also no longer have location as a retention lever. While plenty of run-of-the-mill brick and mortar operations can retain a certain amount of business simply by virtue of their location, location, location strategy—the supermarket, video store, or gas station where the working person stops a few nights a week after work, simply because it's on his or her route home—dot-coms have no such advantage. Customers generally aren't going to "drive by" your site without strong motivation.

THE POWER OF LOYALTY MARKETING PROGRAMS

Apart from transaction-based retention strategies, e-tailers are using another class of tactics to keep customers returning to their sites: loyalty marketing programs.

KEY 24:
USE INCENTIVES TO INCREASE SPENDING

Taking a page from the success of frequent buyer programs used in the offline world, these "frequent clicker" plans typically feature point systems, loyalty cards, and other incentives that encourage online customers to keep their business in one place and to increase purchase frequency.

A 1999 study by the Carlson Marketing Group, a relationship marketing company in Minneapolis, Minnesota, suggests that some consumers spend as much as 46 percent more with companies that offer compelling loyalty programs.

SmarterKids.com, the online seller of children's educational toys and games, uses "ClickRewards" as a way to add additional stickiness to its site. Customers earn two frequent flyer miles for every dollar spent on the SmarterKids site, and 100 bonus miles with a first order of fifteen dollars or more. The miles that customers earn in the program (called ClickMiles) are redeemable on eight major airlines, as well as for hotel stays, rental car discounts, and other merchandise.

SmarterKids.com also encourages customers to spread the word about the site to friends, family, others with children, or anyone who might be in the market for the site's products. By sending in the e-mail address of friends, both the customer and the friend receive a five-dollar coupon (in addition to a SmarterKids.com e-newsletter) to apply to a future order of twenty-five dollars or more.

Cameraworld.com uses a frequent buyer concept called "Bonus Bucks." Under the program, when customers buy qualifying products online they receive 1 percent of their purchase as a credit toward future purchases. Customers can view credits accumulated in their accounts each time they visit the Camera World Web site, and credits don't expire until January 1 of the second year following a first qualifying Bonus Bucks order. So a credit from July 1, 2001 wouldn't expire until January 1, 2003. And if customers can convince a friend to place an order, 2 percent of the friend's purchase total is added to the customer's Bonus Bucks' account.

To qualify for Bonus Bucks, customers must fill out a personal profile, which also allows them to participate in other site "exclusives" like express checkout services—and provides cameraworld.com with more information about its buyers.

Other e-commerce sites dangle membership status as a way to glue customers to a site. At REI.com, shoppers can become "life-time members" for a one-time fee of fifteen dollars. Membership entitles them to an annual patronage refund, a dividend based on the total amount of the customer's regular-priced REI purchases from the Web site, mail order, or REI stores and pegged to REI's profits, with a goal of returning 10 percent of a customer's annual purchases; special member-only merchandise deals; a 20 percent discount on REI's in-house repair services of any damaged gear; and other discounts.

Likewise, Fingerhut.com offers customers its complimentary "Gold Key" membership, which promises e-customers who join a smoother and faster shopping experience—express ordering and checkout, 24-hour online access to order status, special members-only updates, and more.

Hotel chains also are getting into the act, using their Web sites to build repeat business and coddle frequent visitors. Hilton Hotels has "frequent guest pages" on its Web site, where guests can create their own pages to search for available rooms matching their preferences, such as bed size or floor level. Members of Hilton's frequent guest club also can get 1,000 or more "bonus points" for booking stays online in certain calendar periods. They also can check account balances and redeem points online, services also offered at Marriott, Hyatt, and Sheraton hotel chains.

Other hotels send promotions directly to customers' e-mail addresses, not relying on them to log onto Web sites to check the latest in deals. Holiday Inn sends out e-mail each Tuesday with lists of hotel bargains available throughout the country for the upcoming weekend. USA *Today* reports (September 1999) that 50,000 people signed up for inclusion on the list in the first six weeks it was offered.

Dot-coms with experience in the mail-order industry also understand the power of the little "extras" to keep customers coming back for more. For each order a customer places at OmahaSteaks.com, the company throws in a choice of freebies like two top sirloins, eight gourmet burgers or franks, or free cutlery. If customers choose, they can have those free gifts sent automatically from the site to a friend or family member.

(*text continues on page* 254)

Quick Case
Branders.com: Build Customer Focus into the Fabric of Your Company

Walk into Branders.com and you get a sense of intense customer focus. Branders.com is a player in the business-to-business (B2B) space offering promotional items, including canvas bags for association meetings, awards for sales meetings, pens for gifts, and other items for the corporate market. They aim to be the number one portal in the $13 billion promotional products market. Jerry McLaughlin, CEO and president, did something fairly rare for a start-up. He and his team spent three months mapping all the business processes associated with their segment.

As you walk around, you can see flow charts for every single business activity in the company. Each chart is accompanied by the metrics measuring the output of that activity and the name of the individual who is responsible for that process.

If a new hire asks, "What's my job going to be?" the answer would be, "Let's look at this screen together." Click. "Here's a high level map of the company." Click. "Here's your department." Click "Here's what you do. These are the inputs and outputs. And right there are the names and pictures of the people you'll touch."

Branders.com bases all of its decisions on how well what they're looking at matches up with what the *customers* value. McLaughlin lists five areas that comprise the core of customer value at Branders: (1) finding the perfect product, (2) a well-priced product, (3) delivery as promised, (4) a process that is as easy as possible, (5) the confidence that all those things will happen.

Every action or decision is held up to examination in the light of those five values. How and when do you reply to customers? When a customer communicates with Branders, the reply is in the same format unless an alternative format is requested. E-mail them and within five minutes you'll get an e-mail that says, "Hi, thanks for your message. My name is Dana Williams and I'll be back in touch with you in about sixty minutes if that works for you." Fax them and they'll fax you. Call and they'll call you. They're not only answering quickly—remember the disasters from chapter one—but by matching your preferred style, they're also building trust and confidence.

Easy as possible? In the ninety days before we completed our interview with Jerry, they had taken 120 clicks off their site. Their goal is three clicks to do anything on the site. Three clicks to find the product that's right for you. Three clicks to decorate with your corporate or association logo. Three clicks to buy it. In short, never more than three clicks away from a completed piece of transaction.

Branders.com naturally knows your purchasing patterns. But they also know the purchasing patterns are for various industries and job titles. If you're not ordering as frequently as their algorithms tell them you should be, you'll get a call to make sure you're not upset with them for some reason. If you've made a certain number of purchases from them and not gotten a referral, they'll check up on that, too.

Every customer gets a quick call, "Did it show up right?" "Did you like this experience?" It takes less than a minute, but they find out if something wasn't exactly the way the customer wanted it.

The icing on the cake is that Branders.com also goes back up the value stream. They are 100 percent dependant on their suppliers. They have helped lean out their supplier's processes so that Branders.com *can do a better job of meeting their customers' needs*. In partnership with key suppliers, they have brought in lean manufacturing experts to remove time and waste from the total value stream.

B2BS BENEFIT FROM INTERCONNECTED DATA SHARING

Retention might seem a lesser challenge in B2B transactions than in the business-to-consumer (B2C) variety. After all, in retail, there's not much keeping consumers from pulling up stakes and moving on to another URL that has promised a better product selection or fewer service hassles. Plenty of businesses, however, go through an involved process of integrating computer networks and sinking technology roots into partner organizations as they launch a B2B relationship. Whether it is legacy electronic data interchange (EDI) systems or more evolved extranets, today's B2B procurement usually requires that suppliers synch computer systems with customers so they can check suppliers' inventories or internal databases online, use customized, personal Web pages to make purchases and for other seamless, direct electronic communication.

Companies such as Wal-Mart and Procter & Gamble (P&G) find great advantage in their systems interconnections. Inventory specialists can look at P&G production schedules and supply line availability to plan purchase lead times. In turn, P&G planners can track Wal-Mart shelf turnover data to do long-range production planning. The two have a win-win data interchange service partnership. Once such interconnected systems are up and running—their compatibility itself a major accomplishment—popular thinking is that it usually takes more than a handful of service snafus for a customer to consider "unplugging" and looking elsewhere. But the reality is, as in the B2C world, businesses are just as likely to pull the plug if suppliers experience chronic inventory shortages or delays in delivery, give late notification on backordered product, or if they don't have trained staff standing by to help if there are problems. In times of need, access to human help is just as important in B2B settings as in the consumer arena.

B2B sellers also have more stakeholders than just end-user consumers to look after. Many create alliances with other businesses to gain access to larger audiences or better distribution channels. Those partner relationships need to be carefully nurtured and managed; the potential for cross-channel conflict with resellers, distributors, dealers, and retailers looms large in the e-commerce age. Fear of alienating resellers runs especially rampant with manufacturers who are selling direct to consumers through Web sites for the first time.

GRACIE GOLF SENDS "RETRIEVAL SQUAD" AFTER AT-RISK CUSTOMERS

E-businesses might also take a page or two from the increasingly scientific approaches used by their brick and mortar and mail-order brethren to begin identifying customers at risk of defection and take preemptive steps to ensure they don't drift away to the competition.

Gracie Golf is a pseudonym for a U.S. catalog and Web site company that markets clothing and gifts to the over-50, male and female golf enthusiast set. Gracie management places its customers into one of three classifications based on their buying behavior[6] and how they describe their satisfaction with the company.

◆ "Apostles" are customers of three years or more who order about $200 in goods annually, give the company high marks for service, and promote Gracie to friends and acquaintances.

◆ "Satisfied users" also have been on board for three years, order $80 to $120 a year, and are generally satisfied with Gracie, but don't evangelize about the company to others.

◆ "Marginals" purchase only sporadically—primarily from clearance flyers, order less than $80 per year, and give Gracie less than sterling reviews.

A detailed analysis of the customers' purchase and repurchase behavior showed that many "satisfied" and most "marginal" customers also could be classified as "at-risk" customers—buyers who competitors might lure away for a small price or selection differential. As a result, Gracie began packing short, bounce-back customer surveys with each product order it sent to these two groups. Survey results showed that a number of areas, including the look of Gracie's catalogs, the breadth of product selection, price/value, and the customers' experience with basic service (specifically, ease of credit issuance, timely product delivery, and product return policies) had high "sensitivity" factors or were dimensions where substandard performance could lead to low repurchase intentions by Gracie customers.

Rather than bemoaning low scores, Gracie saw the results as an opportunity to intervene on the customers' behalf. Specific response patterns on these surveys—those related to the sensitivity factors—now trigger follow-up phone calls to high at-risk customers (primarily the marginals) from a member of a specially trained crew called the "retrieval squad." A squad member thanks the customer for his or her order and feedback, then probes for more detail. If a specific service problem is at the root of a low rating, the service rep offers a replacement or a refund. If the problem is with, say, a discounted golf club, the rep will offer to take it back, upgrade it with a better club at a minimum cost, or give the customer a special credit against a future purchase. If two or more problems are mentioned, the rep offers the customer a gift certificate and complimentary shipping charges for the next order.

In the first year of implementation, at-risk customers who were pulse-called—customers who rated themselves as likely to stop doing business with Gracie—averaged $100 more in total annual purchases than at-risk customers who were not contacted by the retrieval squad. *Due to that effort, the company realized a $2 million net improvement on a two-million client base, traceable directly to pulse-called, at-risk customers* Equally important, a significant percentage of at-risk customers, or those initially in the "marginal" range, could be reclassified as "satisfied" customers after the next quarterly long-form customer satisfaction survey.

HARRAH'S ISN'T GAMBLING WITH CORE CUSTOMERS

Harrah's Entertainment also has developed new marketing strategies designed to make more frequent gamblers of the core customer group that constitutes the bulk of its casino business and to intervene when that business shows signs of trailing off. At the heart of this strategy: Increased knowledge of customer preferences.

According to a report in the *Wall Street Journal*,[8] the new strategy "scores" gamblers on how profitable they can be to Harrah's based on data from their previous behavior in casinos. Using data from "frequent gambler" cards customers present before they play, budgets and calendars are set for gamblers, as is a "predicted lifetime value." The information tells the casino that Customer Smith, for instance, might respond best to a cash offer—say, vouchers for $200 to use at the slot machines, while Customer Jones is more motivated to make return trips to the casino with an offer of a free hotel room.

When a gambler bets below the expected norm—maybe they've missed a weekly or bimonthly visit—Harrah's steps in with a letter or phone call offering a free meal, a cash voucher, or a free show ticket.

GETTING A CUSTOMER RETENTION STRATEGY STARTED

Planning for retention means understanding all the variables and dynamics that keep customers coming back and those that send them packing. It means ensuring that you take advantage of the former and guard against the latter—and have recovery systems and processes in place, just in case. Above all else, planning for retention means tracking customers closely and using what you learn about and from them to even better tailor your offerings to their changing wants and needs.

What can you do tomorrow to begin building greater Web site loyalty? Strategies vary by industry and in a B2C or B2B setting, but there are a few tactics most e-businesses can use to help turn uncommitted customers into motivated, frequent buyers.

◆ *Survey your repeat customers.* To find out what brings customers back, you first need to identify repeat users. When you do, survey them to determine the service dimensions that keep them coming back—be it quick access to human help, a "wizard" that helps them through the ordering process, or reliable product delivery. Use the surveys to uncover those transactional or relationship elements where if you don't meet expectations, it will significantly decrease customers' repurchase intentions. Then start to regularly measure customer satisfaction in those areas.

Taking it a step further, identify some customers who've left you for a competitor. Send them an e-mail asking why they defected and use that feedback to help protect against future losses or even to lure the lost sheep back into the fold.

◆ **Communicate during down times.** Communicating regularly with customers can be a cost-effective and potent retention tool. The majority of insurance customers, for example, only hear from their agents at renewal time—and even then, usually in the form of a letter and accompanying bill, not face-to-face. Although most of these customers articulate a decision to renew near a termination deadline date, in reality that decision is often made long before. If customers' concerns about their policies get addressed months before, when they teetered in the "defection zone," an agent might have time to devise a strategy to save them.

If you only communicate with a customer when one of you needs something, the account is continually at-risk. You're far more likely to forestall unforeseen cancellation of policies or accounts if you're in semiregular contact, monitoring clients' satisfaction with the relationship.

Consider the possibility of creating a "community" among

your frequent customers on your site. As mentioned in chapter 7, these features can personalize the experience, but they also serve the dual purpose of brining your customers back again and again. REI.com, Ivillage.com, and garden.com, all create bulletin boards, chat rooms, "learn and share" areas, and access to expert advice to extend the perceived utility and value of their sites beyond simply a buyer/seller exchange. Better yet, when customers have multiple reasons to bookmark and visit your site, the "out of sight, out of mind" effect has little chance of taking root.

◆ *Follow up after the sale.* Revisiting an e-customer after a sale is made or an account is activated lets the customer know the relationship hasn't ended with the sale. Circling back to answer customer questions about the product, pushing educational content about the product or service to customers via e-mail, reinforcing the buying decision, and again thanking the customer for his or her business not only staves off buyer's remorse, it lays the groundwork for long-term relationships. Follow-up is a proven way to add points to the customer's all-important overall satisfaction rating.

◆ *Concentrate retention efforts on your most profitable customers.* Although all customers deserve a certain level of service and to be treated with respect and dignity, it's also true that not all customers have the same long-term value to an organization. As e-businesses mature, they add more customers to their rolls who, due to the size of accounts or frequency of spending, rank a cut above other clients. Most of these e-businesses also have "loss leader" customers whose value is marginal at best.

Segment your customers by value to the organization, then design retention strategies appropriately. Airlines, for instance, expect cabin crew to treat million-mile frequent business travelers differently than the sporadic vacation flyer.

◆ **Consider automatic replenishment programs.** Products or services you sell online might lend themselves to regular e-mail updates reminding customers it's time to "replenish the

---

Making the Case for Customer Retention

The current buzz about the power of customer retention in e-business is more than just idle talk or speculation. Plenty of solid research supports how the hard work of retaining customers can translate to a more robust bottom line.

Bain & Company, a Boston-based global consulting firm, has been at the forefront of research into the effects of customer retention on profit levels for more than ten years. In a now-famous study, Bain's Frederick Reichheld and W. Earl Sasser of Harvard University calculated the value of customer retention over a five-year period for nine separate industries. The two considered not only base profit from retaining customers, but also the profit from increased purchases, from reduced operating costs—attainable through increased knowledge of a customer's requirements over time, from word-of-mouth referrals, and from premium price purchases. Their findings? A customer that a company has kept for five years (depending on the industry) can be up to 377 percent more profitable than one who's using your product or service for the first time.

Reichheld and Sasser's bottom-line calculation is that by focusing on customer retention tactics that reduce annual customer defections by a mere 5 percent, an organization can boost its pretax profits 25 to 125 percent.[7]

Reichheld cites that and continuing research for his belief that customers who stay around tend to buy more, are cheaper to serve, create more word-of-mouth advertising, and are more accepting of premium prices. The net learning from the research is that customer retention strategies pay, and pay well, whether it be in an online or offline business setting.

shelves"—and spur repeat sales. Companies like Webvan.com and HomeGrocer.com, for example, maintain shopping lists for customers, so if every three weeks customers run out of laundry detergent, they can schedule automatic deliveries.

A SEVEN-LESSON CRASH COURSE IN E-SERVICE IMPROVEMENT

WHEN

↓

we do focus groups with e-commerce end-users, one of the little devices we use is called the Academy Award question. As a focus group discussion comes to a close, we fold up our notes, close our notebooks, and go through all the other nonverbal cues that we're just about to wrap up.

Then we set the stage for the Academy Award questions:

"Well, we're just about done here but we've got another ten minutes, so let me just ask one more thing. If someone were going to be given an Academy Award three years from now for the best e-commerce Web site, what would they have to do between now and then to get that award? What would that Web site look like? What would it do? How would you be interacting with it? How would it be different from what you are experiencing today? How about if fourteen purchasing agents were the people who decided the Academy Award. What would a site have to offer to get the award from them?

This line of questioning tries to tap the participants' unspoken needs. Throughout the earlier parts of the focus group discussions, participants tried to come up with the best sites or the right answers without necessarily stepping back and questioning whether those things actually exist or not. The Academy Award question points that out to them and gets them thinking not about what is available and what they are willing to settle for today, but what the art of the possible might look like.

The answers we get to the Academy Award question tell us what their real, or at least future, expectations are. These are, we humbly suggest, the expectations you should set for your own e-commerce venture.

The preceding chapters of this book focused on capturing and achieving consumers' current and evolving Academy Award expectations. In our view, today's consumers are looking for and will continue to shop at beautifully designed and branded sites that are easy to do business with, have personalized and human touch elements to them, fulfill promises from start to finish, and rapidly make amends when something goes awry. This is the sort of e-commerce site that they seek right now—consciously and subconsciously, though they rarely come across all of these elements in one e-package. Rarer still, in encountering a site that astounds or delights them.

How well do you measure up? This chapter outlines seven "lesson plans" for finding out.

These "lessons" aren't, however, armchair, thought exercises. They require that you go out on the Web yourself and do a little comparison shopping. See what's out there, what's good, and what could be better, then compare what you've learned to your own venture. Basic competitive analysis.

E-SERVICE 101: HOW TO RESEARCH THE COMPETITION

When you surf the Web to gather your own data, don't just click in and look around. You need to visit specific sites with specific goals in mind. Think of these sites as cars you are test driving. Any car, from a Neon to a Porsche, will come to a slow stop or take a turn at twenty-five miles an hour. If you really want to see what a car can do, you challenge it. You get it up to sixty and then take a corner or slam on the breaks. That's when you uncover the flaws in handling or the exceptional shocks.

Do the same thing at the Web sites you test drive. If you're checking out their customer service, send a question that will stump the CSRs. Try to find obscure information on the site or send something back when it arrives and see how easy it is to get a refund. Send an e-mail and time how long it takes to get a response and rate them on how accurately and personably they answer your questions.

You don't have to visit a thousand sites to learn what's good and bad and different from what you are doing now online. If you use your research time effectively, look for specifics, and note what you find, you'll tap into a rich vein of knowledge that, if mined and used, will help you build, or rebuild, a commercial Web site that carries your company into a successful Academy Award e-commerce future.

The seven lesson plans are organized around—what else— our seven principles and twenty-four keys.

LESSON ONE: DETERMINING YOUR EASY-TO-DO-BUSINESS-WITH (ETDBW) QUOTIENT

Making your company ETDBW is about empowering employees as well as customers. An empowered employee can accommodate the needs of clients faster and more effectively. Consider these two scenarios:

◆ An irate customer connects with a CSR through live chat at a Web site to tell him she received the wrong color blouse, or a broken socket wrench, and she wants a new one sent immediately.

(a) The empowered CSR promptly apologizes, gets details on the expected item and sends out a new one that day, asking the customer to send the wrong item back at her convenience. The customer is suitably impressed, thanks the CSR, and moves on with her day.

(b) The unempowered CSR also apologizes, then tells the customer he's not allowed to send out new items until the old ones are returned. That CSR then spends the next ten minutes reading nasty messages in his chat window and trying to explain the company's procedure regarding return policies to the customer—even though he understands that it's the company's error. All the while he's leafing through the want ads and drawing unflattering caricatures of his boss in the margins.

Which of these scenarios is most likely to be a snapshot of an organization with positive, energized employees? The answer is obvious. How empowered are your CSRs and employees? How ETDBW is your site and the people behind it?

THE ASSIGNMENT: PHONE HOME
PART ONE: TEST THE EDTBW SITE DESIGN

1. Go to your site and attempt to buy something, anything—do it in seven clicks or less starting from the home page. Ideally, if you know exactly what you want, it should take no more than four clicks—but we think seven is acceptable if not totally respectable. Think it can't be done? Then go to OmahaSteaks.com and experience impressive site design in action.

2. Click on a product at your site and actually time—to the second—how long it takes for the graphic to load. Do this for three separate items. Remember, regardless of what people tell you, eight seconds is all they'll wait before getting edgy or moving on.

3. Choose a specific product section of your site. Now, from

the home page get to that product page in one click. Do the same thing from the frequently asked questions (FAQ) page, from anywhere in the checkout process and from another product page.

> Can't do it? Then your site fails this basic ETDBW design criteria. Get your designers on the phone and explain the concept of universal navigation—visitors must be able to get to any section from any section without being overwhelmed by link options. If you still don't understand the concept, go to Illuminations.com and try this assignment out there.

There are countless other "test-your-own-site" activities that can be built around the twenty-five ETDBW design basics in chapter 5. Go back, reread them, then rate your site. The basic question you are trying to answer is simply this: Is your site designed to impress your friends in the business and the e-commerce press or is it built to make it fast, easy, safe, and even, perhaps, fun, for people to do business with you?

PART TWO: TEST YOUR CSR EMPOWERMENT LEVEL

An easy-to-use site is only half the battle of achieving ETDBW status. How ETDBW are your employees and the processes and tools they have at their disposal? If you and/or your management team are control freaks, you'll not do well on this assignment. Empowerment—letting your people take some risks and make it up—is the key. Say it to yourself: "I will empower my employees to make their own decisions to better serve my customers." If you didn't shudder inwardly, you're ready to go.

◆ Disguise your online persona as a regular customer, then e-mail or access live chat with one of your CSRs and demand something out of the ordinary from them, something that is difficult, but, in theory, doable. Perhaps you want a new piece of merchandise sent immediately because the one you received was broken. (Make sure you have an actual product you purchased on hand so you don't come off as a crackpot, or online con artist.) Be a tiny bit rude and obstinate and see how they deal with you. (OK. If you are afraid to do this for fear of annoying the troops and being accused of doing something nefarious, then ask a friend or a mystery shopping group like Shop 'n Check to do it for you.)

◆ Or tell them a sob story about how you need the item that day. And even though you know they don't do same-day deliveries, it's important and could they please help you?

How do they deal with your requests? How long does it take them to respond? Do they resolve your problem immediately, or do they send you to someone else to get an answer. Are they empowered to help you or at least to try? They should be.

If you want to see empowered employees in action, make the same request at Fogdog.com, BravoGifts.com, or Godiva.com. It can and is being done, and the results are dedicated customers who brag about their e-encounters.

HOW'D YA DO?

Up for a little score keeping? OK. Rate your ETDBW by circling the number in the box that best represents your assessment of your site's current ETDBW rating.

A. How well have you designed ETDBW into the basic features of
   your Web site?

1	2	3	4	5
Yikes! Most of our features are clunky and hard to use.	Some of our features are clunky and hard to use.	We aren't the best—or the worst. There's room for improvement.	Not Bad. A lot of our features are pretty slick and easy to use.	Wow! Are we good. Our features are fantastic.

B. How empowered—trained and encouraged to think on their
   feet and respond to unique difficult customer requests—are
   your CSRs?

1	2	3	4	5
Duh! Do we really treat customers this poorly? Are we always this difficult?	Oh boy, are we not friendly or helpful! It's like pulling teeth. I'm embarrassed.	Hmm. They seem, well bored, and not nearly as knowledgeable as I'd hoped.	Good. Very good. I'm proud of these people!	Wow! These people are fantastic!

LESSON TWO: DESIGN FOR DISTINCTION— WHAT MAKES YOU SO SPECIAL?

Making a site distinctive goes far beyond the basic rules of Web design. There are thousands of perfectly good sites that are not distinct in the least. Is yours one of them? Ask yourself these questions:

◆ Does the look and feel of our site reflect our stores and/or our
   intended corporate identity?

◆ From the first click to the last does it communicate our brand to visitors?

◆ Does visiting our site evoke any emotional connection to our products?

No matter how you answered these questions, chances are you can do better. The best branded sites put enormous amounts of thought into the look and feel of their Web worlds. They spend hours in the stores with designers (when they have brick and mortar stores), they pour over corporate strategies and market positioning papers, they ask customers and employees what they want through focus groups and surveys, and they go through several test/retest iterations before they get it right.

THE ASSIGNMENT: TASTE THE EXPERIENCE OF YOUR SITE

To judge your site's distinctiveness, compare the experience of visiting it to the experience of visiting a known well-branded site, such as Godiva.com, Illuminations.com, or any other site you've found to be impressive.

To complete this assignment, think of a specific item you wish to purchase from your site and one from the well-branded site you've chosen. Go to both of them and do the following:

1. Write down the first things you notice when you arrive. What is your immediate reaction to this site? Do you like what you see on the home page? Why or why not? What are you drawn to when you arrived? Does anything annoy you? Is anything missing?

2. Roam around the site thinking about the brand that is being promoted and communicated and the overall experience you are having at the site. Does it evoke emotions? Do you feel like buying something you didn't necessarily come for? Do you feel like you are in a unique place with an experience attached to it, or does it feel generic; interchangeable with a dozen others? When you think about this question, imagine other stores or sites that sell similar products. What, if anything, makes this site distinct from its competition? Is there anything distinctive and memorable about this site?

3. As you roam around the site, write down all of the things you like about it—as a visitor not an owner. For example, are there great product descriptions? Can you do multiple types of searches? Do you like the graphics? Can you discern the products, even in the thumbnails? Was it easy to find the item you came for? Do you always know where you are relative to the home page?

4. Now write down all the things you don't like. Is it hard to find your way around? Did the search engine turn up piles of useless info? Did anything fail to load or confuse you? Was it easy to find contact info on every page?

Use these notes to rethink the next update of your site. Every touchpoint is part of the experience of your site. Creating that experience carves out a place for your site in the minds of users. It's very easy to be ordinary, and ordinary sites create little or no memory. No matter how fast your site is or how reasonable your prices, if no one remembers it they won't come back.

HOW'D YA DO?

C. Again, rate yourself by circling the number that best represents your view of your own site.

1	2	3	4	5
Argh! This site wasn't designed. It came in a spare parts box. It's even a little silly—not professional at all.	Embarrassingly generic. The design hangs together, but it isn't exciting or even memorable. There is no feel, nothing unique.	Well, it's not embarrassing, but it's hardly unique or memorable.	Some very nice elements. And it hangs together pretty well. It has a feel to it. It's subtle, but it's there.	Smooth look. It really tells our story without hitting the customer in the face. Very classy and memorable.

LESSON THREE: PERSONALIZING THE EXPERIENCE— WHAT'S IN IT FOR ME?

The Web is nothing if not redundant, especially when it comes to retail shopping. Unless you are looking for a rare coin or an antique piece of furniture, almost anything you shop for can be found at 100 different sites, all for around the same price. And, since going from store to store online can be done in an instant, shopping around has become a national past time for Web surfers. What—if anything—is going to make them stop and buy at your site?

Personalizing the experience of your site ties shoppers to you and encourages them to stay longer. Personalization comes in many forms, from one-to-one customized B2B sites and do-it-yourself tools that help customers find the item that best fits their needs to personalized e-mail responses to questions, help from live CSRs, and access to peers.

How many of these features does your e-commerce effort have? What makes your site a personal experience for absolutely everyone who shops there?

THE ASSIGNMENT:
PART ONE: LEARN SOMETHING NEW ONLINE

Visit the following sites and experience their personalized features. Are they better or worse than yours? Think about what you like about the experience and how it would work on your own site. Commit to incorporating at least one of the personalizing tools you experience at these sites into your site in the next six months.

1. Come up with a home improvement project you don't know how to do. Now, go to CornerHardware.com and using the sites content, figure out how to do it. You can ask a live CSR for help, use a how-to manual, or access the community bulletin boards—all are excellent examples of personalizing a Web experience.

2. Schedule time to visit LandsEnd.com with a friend and shop for a specific item through their "Shop with a Friend" tool.

3. Go to REI.com and plan a bike trip in your area. Use its Learn and Share center to get recommendations from other biking enthusiasts for good trails, find a list of the gear you'll need, learn how to change a flat, and read the bicycling touring basics.

PART TWO: RATE YOUR E-MAIL SYSTEM

Go to any three sites in your industry and send them an e-mail asking a specific question, such as the price of product X, where they are located, what their 800 number is, and so on. Time how long it takes them to respond with an answer. Note your reaction to the response. Did it seem personal? Did it use your name? Did it include the CSRs name? Did they actually answer your question? Did it seem personal or overly generic?

Now go to your own site and ask the same question. How does your e-mail response time compare to theirs? How is the tailoring of the response you received? Use this as a benchmark and even if yours was the best of the bunch, set a goal to improve turnaround on e-mail and add personalizing touches to responses.

HOW'D YA DO?

Evaluate the personalization of your site by circling the number of the box that best represents your site.

D. How customized or personalized to you as an individual are the tools of your site?

1	2	3	4	5
Yuck! Faceless, nameless, one-size-fits-all. Our site is rigid and unyielding. The DMV is more personal.	Eh. Our site doesn't take much advantage of what we know about our customers. Very little tailoring or responding to my unique needs/wants.	OK, I guess. E-mails are responded to in a reasonable amount of time, and I'm called by name once in awhile. My questions are mostly answered.	Not bad. My name gets used and I get the product/service information I ask for. And it's a pretty fast, responsive site.	Marvelous! This site feels as if it was designed with only me in mind. I'm called by name and only the things I'm interested in are shown to me.

E. How effective is your site at tailoring responses to customer inquiries and problems?

1	2	3	4	5
Boring! A Ouija board could have constructed a better response. It was almost gibberish. It certainly wasn't English.	Automated, manual-like language. About like looking something up in an owner's manual. Certainly not personalized.	Well, it was a response. It mostly answered my question and dealt with my problem. It didn't feel like I was talking with an expert.	Good! I don't know whether the responses were auto response or personally constructed, but they were what I needed.	Great! I got a unique response to a unique problem/ situation. It felt like I was talking to/ corresponding with an expert one-to-one.

LESSON FOUR: ADDING A HUMAN ELEMENT—COME OUT, COME OUT, WHEREVER YOU ARE!

No matter how robust your FAQ, how lickety-split your e-mail turnaround time, or how user-friendly your Web site is, sometimes consumers just need to talk to a human being. You will never completely eliminate the need for a call center and hiding your 800 number or tying up phone lines is not the answer.

Even with e-commerce, you've got to be prepared to actually talk to some of your customers. And, to avoid making contact with them only when they have reached the point of seething with anger and frustration, the best scenario is to give them easy access to your CSRs and to encourage them to make contact for any reason necessary.

It continually amazes e-consumers around the world how difficult it is to find a simple phone number at a Web site. You'd think companies were giving away the password to their bank accounts based on how cleverly they've hidden this important piece of information at the bottom of pages housed deep in the bowels of their sites.

Could your company be accused of such deceptive behavior? How easy is it to make contact with a human being from your Web site? Find out.

THE ASSIGNMENT: MAKE CONTACT

Go to your Web site and browse to a product page. Now find an 800 number for a CSR. How many clicks did it take? Now go to the checkout section, the FAQ section, and the Home page and do the same thing. Note how many clicks it takes to find your phone number from each page.

By the way: It shouldn't take *any* clicks from any page to find a phone number. Your 800 number should be listed boldly on every page of your site.

HOW'D YA DO?

F. Again, rate yourself by circling the number that best represents your view of your own site.

1	3	5
Rats! Finding a way to contact a human through our Web site is a "needle in a haystack" deal all the way.	Well—you *can* find a way to contact us, and the phone *does* ring—and ring and ring—and somebody *does* answer, and the waiting queue, isn't all *that* painful.	Shazaam! Perfect score! It's easy to find a way to contact a live human, and it actually worked. And there is a person available at the other end—without a long wait in the queue.

LESSON FIVE: END-TO-END SERVICE—CAN YOU ANSWER MY QUESTIONS?

The savvy surfers among us know that if you order a product from a respectable online outfit it will be delivered to you—maybe not on time and maybe not unbroken—but it will come. The rest of the world, however, is still semicertain that every so-called "dot-com" online is out to steal their credit card information and run. With each potential purchase, they envision e-commerce con men laughing with their thieving mates about the naivete of the suckers who are foolish enough to turn over their personal information to an anonymous Web site. Worse than getting suckered, nobody likes to be made a fool of, and you can be sure many consumers are still thinking about that every time they make a transaction.

Even if you are Reliablemegabrand.com, consumers won't really trust you until the product they order is in their sticky little hands. If it happened two or three times, they'll probably start to relax and trust you.

To ease their fears and to prevent them from making countless calls to your phone center to verify their online order was received and is being processed, you have to reassure them with constant updates and acknowledgments.

How do you update customers? Or, are you among the masses of e-commerce companies who foolishly assume that consumers will blindly trust you to deliver on your promises? Do you even know how many calls to your call centers are verifications of orders made at your Web site? Can you calculate what every one of those calls costs you?

THE ASSIGNMENT: PART ONE: MONITOR A PURCHASE END-TO-END FROM ORDER TO DELIVERY

1. Purchase a product online from your Web site. (Again, have a mystery shopper do this if you dread being `found out' by your colleagues.) Time how long it takes for an order confirmation e-mail to be sent to you. (Note: We think ten seconds is great, ten minutes is acceptable, an hour sluggish, any longer than that and we get concerned.)

If you don't have an order confirmation system, you fail this assignment flat-out. You are also causing unnecessary logjams on your chat, e-mail, and phone lines from wary customers "just checking in" to make sure you got their orders. Auto acknowledgment costs pennies to activate and frees your CSRs to handle more poignant customer requests.

2. Wait a day after purchasing this product, then go to your Web site and check on its shipping status. Can't do it? Again, you fail, and your CSRs are probably tearing their hair out from the stream of "when's it gonna get here?" messages. Do everyone a favor and empower your customers to keep an eye on their own packages from start to finish.

Think this is a ridiculous request to make on behalf of impatient consumers? Complete the same assignment using products purchased from cameraworld.com, Dell.com, or etoys.com and see for yourself how much control these customer-centric dot-coms are willing to give to consumers to make them happy and get them to stop calling.

PART TWO: FIND THE ANSWERS TO
COMMON QUESTIONS

Keeping customers guessing is a throwback to the pre-Internet dark ages. Customers expect access to every relevant piece of information you've got—from prices listed up front with product descriptions, to known bugs in your software, and logjams with your order delivery system. Many of those consumers who have no interest in interacting with your CSRs want to find answers about your products, services, and processes by themselves. And they expect to be able to do that faster and more efficiently at your Web site than they can at your call center.

Don't scoff. Their desires, if handled correctly, will save you a fortune. Just as customers who have the ability to track their purchases online will leave your CSRs alone, the customer who can find answers to questions on his or her own at your site doesn't waste time and money tying up lines at your call center. That is, of course, if the answers are available, easy to find, and reasonably comprehensible and comprehensive.

Are they? Is your FAQ comprehensive without being overwhelming? Do you have easy-to-follow instructions for checking out? Are the ten most common problems with your product, service, or site explained under a link showcased on your home page?

◆ Check your call center logs and find out what the three most common problems are that callers present to your CSRs.

Next, go to your Web site and try to solve those problems without calling the call center. Note how long it takes to find the answers, how many clicks it requires from the home page, and your level of frustration when and if the answers are finally found.

If you didn't find the answers, shame on you. This is basic stuff. As homework, you must now find out how your CSRs answer these questions, compile their answers in a FAQ or Knowledge Base, and post them prominently at your Web site. Also, instruct every CSR to mention this new and fabulously helpful FAQ to all callers, as well as adding information about it to your recorded hold message.

If you did find the answers, good for you. Now think about why none of your customers seem to be able to find them. Are they hidden? Confusing? Cryptically written? Unsearchable without a Masters in corporate jargon?

Once you have these answers adjust your site accordingly. It's a revolutionary thought, but you might consider putting answers to your most frequently asked questions prominently at the front of your site. Perhaps you might even list one or two of these questions in a box on the home page with a link to the answer. In other words, answer the questions before they get asked.

This little exercise, if followed through on, will almost instantly save you money by freeing call center agents to handle more serious queries.

HOW'D YA DO?

G. How good are you at keeping customers informed of the status of orders, problem investigations, or answers to complex questions.

1	2	3	4	5
Nuts! We don't acknowledge anything. And forget about updates and status info. And requests for updates and status seem to go into a black hole.	Hmmm! Boy, are we slow. Sure, we do send some tracking information, but not very often. It is not really sufficient.	We're slow, and we surely aren't proactive. But there's enough information coming out to keep most people content.	Pretty OK. Not speed demons, but we're pretty responsive, and we do send regular updates. It's certainly enough to stave off an anxiety attack.	We're not only good, we're fast. Acknowledgments come within minutes, and status updates are timely. I can even go into the system and read order status info.

LESSON SIX: MAKING RECOVERY A POINT OF PRIDE— I'M SORRY, HOW CAN I MAKE IT BETTER?

The opportunity to screw up greatly increases when you go online. In a brick and mortar store, the customer is unlikely to walk out with damaged merchandise or clothes that are the wrong size, material, or color. If they buy it in a brick and mortar store they will leave with it at the moment of purchase, so delivery time, damage due to shipping, and backorders are also not going to be at issue.

But put your business online and suddenly you can make mistakes at points in the sales process that you didn't even know were at-risk. There are so many opportunities to fail, in fact, that how you recover when they occur can go as far or further in establishing trust and loyalty with consumers than doing it right the first time. A contrite CSR who responds with apologies and solutions can be such a shocking experience for most consumers that it renders them happier than if they had no problems with your product or service at all.

But, respond rudely, take too long, or ignore them altogether and they will broadcast your failures to the ends of the earth—literally.

How well do you recover? The hard part of answering this question is that very few consumers who are disappointed with their purchases will bother to tell you, only about one in four. So, even though you may have effectively and efficiently helped the one guy who called to complain, how many of your customers are abandoning you for failures you don't even know about? Have you ever bothered to ask? What sort of follow-through plan do you have in place for one-time shoppers and regular clients who suddenly disappear off the face of your virtual planet?

THE ASSIGNMENT:
PART ONE: CHECK UP ON LOST BUSINESS

Go through your records and find the names and contact information of every customer in the last year who purchased only one product from you or stopped purchasing products after a time. Call or e-mail them with a survey asking why they stopped. Ask specific questions about their satisfaction with your products and services, and then offer them benefits or coupons for returning to your site. You will compile valuable data about undiscovered flaws in your system, while at the same time luring strays back to the fold.

PART TWO: SPY ON THE EXPERTS

Are you suitably dazzled by your own company's recovery system? Probably not, but even if you are, be prepared to be even more wowed by some of the best in the e-business.

Your next assignment is to buy something from a site your colleagues think well of and then try to return it. Call their 800 numbers and be insistent that you are disappointed with the product. Demand restitution. Pay attention to how they respond.

If your CSRs aren't as friendly and accommodating as these CSRs, it's time to rethink your recovery process and the importance you place on it. If they are, congratulations.

HOW'D YA DO?

H. How easy was it to return the product and extract a promise of restitution?

1	2	3	4	5
Oh man! You really have to persevere to get us to take anything back. And we are hostile to boot!	Really hard to get any cooperation, but at least the people weren't nasty.	Well, they took it back and promised to cover shipping. But first I had to get a special return shipping label—took about two weeks.	Nice—very nice! Our people are helpful and don't make an issue out of a return.	We're good! We're good! It's easy to get an apology and help to return the product.

LESSON SEVEN: RETENTION—ARE YOU PAYING ATTENTION TO YOUR MOST PROFITABLE CUSTOMERS?

You invested all that money in Super Bowl ads, highway billboards, and flashy Web design. As hoped, customers came, they were wowed, and they bought something. Congratulations, you successfully crossed the greatest hurdle of e-commerce—getting customers to make the first purchase.

Your investment in getting them to make those initial purchases was surely substantial. The cost of acquiring customers on the Web can be forbidding, especially if you are an unknown dotcom that doesn't get a lot of word-of-mouth traffic. All of the marketing tools carry a price, and if you happen not to be one of the golden children on the Internet coasting on a cart full of venture capital, you may not have the unlimited wealth it takes to run a one-purchase per consumer outfit.

If your budget is limited and your ultimate goal is to turn a profit, invest your energy in making sure those first-time buyers come back. Remember, every time customers return to your site they become more valuable to your business. Why? They buy more, they are less concerned about prices, and they tell people about you. In other words, if they come back they are impressed by your entire package—from the television ad that got them there the first time to the shipping system that delivered their products intact and on time.

How much are you investing to make those newbies repeat performers? How's it paying off?

THE ASSIGNMENT: EXAMINE WHY *YOU* BUY
AGAIN AND AGAIN

If you have successfully made it through this course—actually doing some or all of the assignments—you should have a feel for the value of your site compared to others in your field and to e-commerce sites in general. You know where you stand, and you should know by now where you need to improve.

Retention is about getting the whole experience right. It comes when the site is fast and easy, there are no surprises or hidden information, your service people are smart and friendly, and you deliver on all of your promises. All of the assignments in this chapter test those qualities.

Now you need to sit down and think about yourself as a consumer. Where do you regularly shop, online and offline? Ignoring location as a motivator, what is it about the grocery store you shop at that makes you return week after week? Do you buy all of your batteries and toiletries from Target even though you could get them just as easily at ten other locations near you? Why? Why do you do all your gift buying online when you work five minutes from a mall?

1. Write down five stores you've shopped at more than three times, at least two of which are online, and list the reasons why. What do they do that brings you back? Is it just price? Are they nice to you? Do they provide you with services that make your life more pleasant? Do they deliver products and services that place them beyond the offerings of their competitors?

2. Now think about your e-commerce site. Does it have the same qualities that are on your five lists? Do you make life more pleasant for your customers? Do you go beyond the minimum requirements of customer service?

Whether you are selling candles or Cadillacs, the qualities that bring people back to your site are the same—great dependable service from a company that obviously and demonstratively values consumers' business. If you aren't demonstrating to your customers how much you appreciate their business, you will not win them over as loyal—profitable—repeat shoppers.

HOW'D YA DO?

Rate yourself—and your retention strategy—using these last two questions.

I. How good a job are you doing at enfolding customers into the company—long term?

1	3	5
Oops! We are totally passive. We don't do much at all to make 'em feel like family—or even noticed.	We send product announcements and do some couponing. We try to touch our customers at least once a month.	We really enfold them. We've got chat areas, member services, clubs, special deals, newsletters, and more. We've built a virtual community for our customers.

J. How are you doing at tailoring offerings and services to your customer's personal specs?

1	2	3	4	5
We get name, address, and serial number, but nothing else.	We gather enough info on our customers to make our database attractive to other people	We're very leery of asking for too much information. What we gather we use strictly for customer-tailored offerings.	We gather a lot of info, but we keep it confidential. We use it to make very tailored offerings to those customers.	We ask our customers for a lot of information, and we use it to custom-tailor our communications and offerings. Our system can ID customers when they sign on, and we use that info to tailor their visit. And we never, never let anyone else at the data.

E-COMMERCE IS GROWING UP: DON'T BE THE PERPETUAL TEENAGER

E-commerce is still in its sullen teenage years. Consumers, even B2B associates understand this and expect shopping online to be occasionally difficult to deal with, awkward, and constantly changing. But its adolescent years are fast coming to an end, and soon that awkward teen who everyone was willing to excuse due to growing pains will be an adult who will be expected to perform accordingly and earn his or her own way.

Consider this chapter part of your graduation requirements. Consider the assessment an early SAT. Use it to learn as much as you can about what you are and what the possibilities are for the future. Go ahead. Live up to your potential. We dare you!

HOW'D YA DO?

Go back through the ten questions in this chapter, add up your score (the numbers you circled), and put it here:

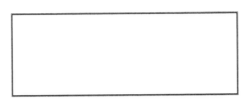

You know the routine. Following is the interpretation of your score:

10-20:   Come on! You can't be that bad, can you? You'd have to declare Chapter 11 to be this bad!

21-30:   Oh woe is you! You've really got work to do. Go back, find your lowest self-rating and get a team on that factor—yesterday.

31-40:   Well, you're not any worse than most. That's nothing to be proud of, but you're still hanging in. Look at your lowest two ratings and work at raising your sights. Right now you're just another Acme, Inc.

41-50:   Congratulations! You are a distinguished, distinctive, e-service master. A real black belt (are you sure you were absolutely, ruthlessly honest with yourself?) You oughtta write a book!

THE FUTURE OF THE NET

Take These Predictions to the Bank

CLEARLY,

the Internet will change—is changing—the way organizations interact with their customers. The Internet has already made massive changes in how time, space, and location affect customer relationships. Outside of the workplace it has produced—and will continue to produce—massive amounts of change in your life and the lives of your neighbors.

The most amazing thing about the Internet is that most of the changes it makes in our lives are still to come.

In our far from infinite wisdom, we've thrown caution to the wind and made some predictions about the ways service will be provided over the Net in the months and years to come. Some of our predictions may surprise you, some won't, and if you are in the 'way cool' technical know, you may even yawn, but then again, if you are that e-service hip, why are you reading this book?

However that ball comes to rest, we hope that at least one or two of these predictions start you thinking about your organization's e-service future. Read through them before your next neighborhood party. If there are a couple of them you particularly agree with or think are especially exciting, bring them up and see if you can impress your friends or better yet pull them into a bet about the future of the Web.

We've broken our bets into three categories: twelve months, eighteen months, and twenty-four months. In a number of the predictions, we've used the term PAD, short for Personal Access Device. That term includes an array of existing and yet-to-be-created ways of connecting to the Internet: cell phone, personal digital assistant, and hand-held computers. The boundaries between these devices are already blurring.

So get ready. The Web is going to dramatically change the way we live, think, and buy—as businesspeople and as consumers. Consider these predictions our sneak preview into your own future.

In the next twelve months you—or one of your neighbors—will:

◆ **Purchase a new suit online.** A body scanner will measure you digitally at thousands of body points. The information will then be sent via the Net to a manufacturing facility. Three days later, your suit will arrive. It will be a perfect fit (if you haven't put on ten pounds or grown a couple of inches). You'll buy a pair of shoes at the same time and in much the same manner. They also will arrive in three days. Even if one of your feet is slightly larger than the other, the shoes will still fit perfectly.

◆ **Pick out a muffler for your Harley by listening to it online.** You'll hear how it sounds and then click to access the dealer closest to you. At the Harley dealership, you'll notice that median income for Harley owners appears to be slightly higher than that of physicians. They know that as well and position their aging Boomer toys accordingly.

◆ **Call out a series of voice commands to your car regarding the cabin humidity and temperature you desire, the songs on a CD to be played, and the direct, rather than the scenic, route to your ultimate destination.** The car will respond appropriately by raising the temperature by three degrees, playing the songs in the exact sequence you requested at the preset decibel level for each song, and delivering the directions to your destination, both the complete sequence and the individual turns along the way. The directions will include a short sequence that will take you around a tie-up on I-94.

◆ **See your teenager lending money to a friend to buy a shake, burger, and fries by remote control.** The loan will be beamed from one PAD to another. The recipient of the loan will then zap it to the cashier at the burger place. You'll think that's interesting but a little weird, until you see the kid's credit card tab.

◆ **Will check on a child's homework assignments, current grades, and teacher comments on a Web site maintained by the school— and give feedback to the teacher and your offspring.**

◆ **Check the weather for your block, the route to work, the shopping center parking lot, and the golf course you are planning to play this afternoon using a PAD.** You will be able to program it to alert you if the conditions are changing—handy in this age of escalating greens fees.

◆ **Notice that all of your neighbors will have stopped using the words e-commerce, e-customer, and e-service.** We'll notice the same thing. There will just be commerce, customers, and service. Companies engaged in commerce will provide value to customers through a variety of channels—one of which will happen to be electronic. Brick and click will be an assumed blend; most pure dot-coms will be part of syndicated structures, especially those dealing in information and pure services.

In the next eighteen months you—or one of your neighbors—will:

◆ **Borrow money for dinner from someone by having the amount beamed from one PAD to another.** You'll then beam the money to the restaurant. You thought it was interesting but weird when your teenager did it. Now you think technology is really cool.

◆ **See a child married off to someone with whom they first exchanged phone numbers via a PAD—across a crowded frat party.**

◆ **Be walking down an aisle in the supermarket and will be alerted to a special sale on an item you frequently buy.** The notification will come via your PAD. It will be the only notice you receive because it will be the only item in the store with a promotion attached to it that you identified as being one you'd like to receive notices of. Forty-three percent of the items you purchase on this trip will be items you preselected by scanning the barcode of empty containers and uploading them on the Net. Sixty minutes before you left for the grocery store, you downloaded that information to the store. Those items were waiting for you when you arrived. The rest of your shopping was for fresh and impulse items.

◆ **Play "Blue Suede Shoes," "Hotel California," "Angel Is a Centerfold," and "Smells Like Teen Spirit" all on the same jukebox.** After you beam your money in from your PAD, the music will be downloaded from the Net and played. Then a clutch of teenagers will come by and play VR games on the same jukebox. They'll play against teams in four other countries. Those same teenagers will benefit from the two digital dollars you accidentally left behind to play a couple of their own songs; songs that were created on the Web by a Web group, the members of which have never met.

◆ **Be warned against taking a medication that might cause an adverse reaction with one of your allergies or that is imprudent to blend with another medication you are taking.** The warning will show up on your PAD. The voice giving you the warning will come from a health care server where you have stored your personal information, and the server will have been alerted by the code the pharmacist beamed to your PAD. The message will also suggest you pick up some extra vitamin C for your cold—and a can of chicken soup.

◆ **Order a bottle of French wine by speaking into the microphone attached to your computer.** Your voice will be digitized, translated into French, sent via the Net to Burgundy, and the confirmation will come back in English—all in less than seventeen seconds. That time lapse will seem very long to you. At the time the order is confirmed, your personal Net bank account will be debited in dollars and the account of the vineyard will be credited by a comparable amount in francs. The order will be fulfilled without anything being touched by a human hand until the package is dropped on your doorstep and the cork is popped.

◆ **Decide to take a trip to Italy and will call to make arrangements over your PAD.** You will speak in English and the call will be translated into Italian for the listener at the other end. They will speak in Italian and you will hear the translated words in English. It will be a delightful madcap trip. The ground accommodations will be perfect and the meals will be delightful. Every flight you take will be late and the airline will blame the problems on acts of God. Obviously some things will always be the same, even in a totally networked world.

   In the next twenty-four months you—or one of your neighbors—will:

◆ **Order another bottle of that French wine that you ordered a year ago.** This time you'll place the order from your car without talking to a human being or leaving anyone a voicemail. The order will be confirmed and a tentative shipping date assigned in both alpha-numeric and voice mode.

◆ **Be asked by a physician to undergo a seventy-two-hour body scan.** Smart monitors in the form of straps, rings, and bands will track all your bodily functions, some to the molecular level, for those seventy-two hours. When you walk into the office, the doctor will have already reviewed all the data and the preliminary recommendations the medical software suite derived from the readouts. Between you, the doctor, and the doctor's auto support, you develop a ninety-day diet and an exercise and self-monitoring plan. You arrange a twenty-, forty-, sixty-, eighty-, ninety-day feedback plan for monitoring your progress. You have a protracted negotiation over the use of that bottle of French wine you ordered on the way to the doctor's office.

◆ **Get your car washed at a new self-service car wash.** You will pay for the car wash of your choice by dialing a number listed on the side of the car wash. The charge will show up on your PAD cellular bill, which will be one line item on your personal bill-paying consolidation site. The bill will be paid electronically, once you've drilled down and verified the charges on the various line items.

◆ **Purchase a new house.** You will never have physically set foot in that house prior to the closing. You will have visited the house on numerous occasions by means of the Net and broadband-based virtual reality. You will also have checked out the crime statistics, the school system, and the traffic patterns for the neighborhood. You will even have hired a licensed engineer to go over the house and give you a detailed run down on code adherence and likely first year refurb and update estimate.

♦ **Prepare for a long road trip by "programming" your house.** You'll preset the temperatures you want, the times at which you want lights to go on and off, the times at which you want blinds to go up and down, and the music you want played at certain times. The same system that does that will also tape your favorite television shows—without the commercials. While you're away, you'll use your notebook computer to check the feed from the vid-cams placed around the house, send messages to your house's controller from your laptop, or PAD, via the Internet. The messages check the temperature in the house and the pool and reset the lawn sprinkler routine if the weather takes an unexpected turn or its soil moisture sensors malfunction. One of the messages will also download a series of your favorite songs from your home entertainment system to the CD in your car.

♦ **Be warned of slippery road conditions on I-93 between Somerville and Woburn just north of Boston.** You'll receive the notification because you programmed your route to Boston into your PAD and asked your personal Web site to alert you to changes in road conditions en route. The road condition notification service will know of the slippery roads because chips located in the tires of the cars traveling the roads in and around Boston will send back the information regarding road conditions to a control source that redistributes the information to subscribers.

♦ **Have a child join a virtual tour of Paris along with seven classmates.** Their hologram will enable them to interact with children from Paris as well as the other fourteen countries represented in the class. While on the virtual tour, your child will visit the Eiffel Tower; walk along the Seine; and enjoy the sights, smells, and sounds of a sidewalk café. Any questions posed in English will immediately be translated into the other languages represented in the group. The sensory gloves each student wears will enable them to hold hands and sing "happy birthday" to one of the students. The term "distance learning" will have taken on a new meaning.

◆ **Purchase a new car, selected by means of a virtual reality feed in the dealer "showroom" which you may visit in person or via your PAD or laptop.** Once you have made your make and model selection and constructed and costed your option package, your choice will be "e-mailed" to the factory. Every ninety minutes, similar e-mails from around the world will be aggregated and sorted into standard part numbers. The standard part numbers will be sent to each of the tier one suppliers who supply that particular part. They will use that information to adjust their production schedule and will, in turn, send similar information to the tier two suppliers. Somewhere along this continuous information stream, within four days of your order, your new car will be slated for assembly, you will be notified, and delivery scheduled for two days hence. Oh, and you'll be able to tap into the manufacturer's assembly line data system and 'watch' your car being built. Auto prices will drop by 20 percent and both the manufacturers and the dealers will become more profitable.

◆ **Send someone a bouquet of virtual roses.** When the roses arrive at their destination, they will carry with them the compelling scent of roses in full bloom, an aroma that will emanate from the recipient's PC. Think of it as "streaming scent," one level beyond streaming audio or streaming video. It will become an imbedded feature of all the telecasts that arrive at your PC and/or flat screen, data cable, home outlet. You program your system to automatically mute the smell-o-vision during WWF matches!

◆ ***Take another trip to Italy.*** All the arrangements will be made the same way. The flights will all still be late. Specifically, your departure to Rome will be two hours late because some maintenance needs to be done. The difference in this trip is that the mechanic working on the aircraft will have the appropriate pages from the maintenance manual appear on a translucent display screen the size of a pencil eraser. The display will be an integral part of one lens of an otherwise normal-looking pair of eyeglasses. The mechanic will have an encyclopedia of repair information available on three mini-discs that play through a pocket unit that broadcasts the pages to the mechanic's glasses-mounted view screen.

◆ ***Take a trip to Japan.*** You speak no Japanese. Your hotel will provide you with a six-ounce computer in the form of a belt and an unattached screen the approximate size and weight of a Pop-Tart™. This gives you street maps, multimedia clips in fourteen languages about historic sites, and a digital camera that both records video images and takes 35-mm photographs. You can ask questions of someone who speaks no English by talking into a microphone on the screen. A small speaker on the opposite side of the screen repeats the question in Japanese. The Japanese-speaking individual to whom you have directed the question will answer into the speaker/microphone on his or her side of the module, and you will hear the answer in English. Ditto the other fourteen languages stored in the module. If the person you are addressing is actually Serbo-Croation, not Japanese and does not speak one of the fourteen languages stored in the computer, you'll be forced to beam your English question via the Net to a satellite where it will slowly be translated over a period of eight seconds before it emerges from the speaker/microphone on the other side of your module. It will be seventeen years before the Italians adopt a similar system. The French will never adopt such a system. The French Waiters Union, on the other hand, will adopt a simplified unit that responds, "Non parlez" to all queries.

◆ **Leave your PAD in a rental car.** Luckily it can't be used by anyone but you, because it has an ID switch coded to your thumbprint. While waiting for someone to shuttle your PAD to the main terminal of the airport, you check for mail and messages on your Web site using a public access terminal, using the same ID system, your thumbprint.

◆ **Have a child come home from school with a security device that allows access to the school door.** The school will be locked to all outsiders. The device, probably a ring, will contain a password and identification signal that is connected to the school's Web site. You will receive a message on your PAD that your child has entered the school. Twelve months later, a "lost child" feature will be added to the ring, enabling you to hone in on your child's location in stores and parks.

◆ **Make yet one more commitment to get in shape and join a health club.** As usual, you start to become discouraged during the third week. As you get on the exercise bike midway through the third week, the TV hanging on the exercise room wall greets you: "Good morning, Judy, you're doing well. I notice your body-fat level is dropping and your lean muscle mass is increasing. Clearly, you're getting stronger. Here's what you should look like in 60 days (photo will appear). If you stay on your current program, I feel comfortable predicting that you'll be able to complete the 10K you're targeting in less than sixty minutes. By the way, Jerry's flight just landed at Westchester and he should be home in an hour."

◆ **Place your coffee cup—with a small chip in it—under the spout in the office coffee machine.** "Good Morning, Peg, The usual?" the machine will intone. At your "yes," your favorite concoction will fill your cup to the appropriate level. You'll think nothing of the event, it being an everyday occurrence. By mid-afternoon, your cup will be reminding you that you've been planning on cutting down on caffeine—and suggesting an alternative adult beverage.

◆ **Take your teenager to visit a college campus.** Before you leave home, the school will e-mail you an applet to download into your PAD. The schedule you prearranged through the college brokerage company will be built into the applet. As you enter the main parking garage on campus, a barcode from a positioning sticker located at the entrance to the garage will be scanned into your PAD and a map showing you how to get to the first meeting will be displayed on the screen. You can check your progress along the way by scanning in barcodes of additional positioning stickers. If you need to make changes in the schedule, an intelligent agent will negotiate with other peoples' schedules and notify you of the changes.

Skeptical? The basic technology for all of these applications already exists. In fact, some of our predictions aren't even predictions, they are already in effect in some preliminary form—Palm Pilots® beam information and phone numbers to each other from a short distance; games can be played online with competitors all over the globe; music is regularly listened to, downloaded, and sold over the Internet; and homes are digitally monitored. The neighborhood weather predictor is the product of a company about to go public.

We live in the most inventive, creative age since the onset of the industrial revolution. Yesterday's brainstorms are today's business plans and tomorrow's killer "Apps." The next great Internet idea is only as far away as the imagination—and a little funding—can see. And tomorrow's todays are only a thought away.

B R O W S E R ' S   G U I D E

CHAPTER 1

◆ The long-term winners—those firms that are still profitably standing two years from now—will be those that have done the best job of supporting their customers and delivering that value in a way that seems effortless. (page 8)

◆ Whether you're a B2B or B2C, you've got to find a point of differentiation to separate from the rest of the herd, and you've got to fight for it and maintain it. (page 9)

◆ On the Web everyone has the same location; no place and every place at once. (page 9)

◆ . . . 90 percent of online shoppers consider good customer service to be the critical factor when customers are choosing a Web merchant to give their commerce. (page 11)

◆ Few people abandon their shopping carts at the neighborhood Target and Kroger. But set them loose online and they do so with frightening regularity. (page 12)

◆ The bottom line is that companies have spent millions of dollars attracting customers to their Web site and seem oblivious to the fact that acquiring customers is not the same thing as keeping customers. (page 14)

◆ Customer loyalty on the Web is even more fleeting than land–based shopping. (page 15)

◆ As the cost of customer acquisition rises and Internet competition increases, no one can afford to lose e-shoppers after only one visit. (page 15)

◆ Customer loyalty, not technology, is going to be the factor that separates the winners from the losers. (page 18)

CHAPTER 2

◆ Most consumers will be certain they waited three minutes for a page to load when in fact it took less than thirty seconds. (page 20)

◆ Every time a customer is wowed by a site's service, or gravely disappointed, he or she makes a decision about who to return to the next time—and the time after that, and the time after that. (page 23)

◆ Each service experience, regardless of whether it's online or offline, sets the stage of expectations for future service interactions, including those on your Web site. (page 24)

If you're going to run a world-class Web site, you need to provide consumers with the same or better level of information
and service than they have access to from other sources. . . .
(page 24)

You can have a great product offering, but if you combine it with
abysmally poor service, you've got an "at-risk" customer. (page
30)

If you want to succeed on the Web, you need to consistently
manage the total customer experience in a way that draws and
holds your customers. . . . (page 31)

Dell is the industry leader in remote resolution of customer
problems, resolving 70 percent of desktop issues and 90 percent of service issues within the first fifteen minutes of contact
by a customer. (page 32)

. . . this book holds the keys to much of the wisdom you'll need
to build a phenomenally successfully Web presence. (page 33)

CHAPTER 3

Studies in retail, wholesale, and Internet environments have
shown that the relationship between customer *satisfaction* and
customer *loyalty* is nonlinear. (page 36)

Someone who gives you a five (an excellent rating) is, on average, two to six times more loyal than someone who gives you a
four. (page 38)

The number of *highly satisfied* customers is the long-term
lifeblood of an online company. (page 39)

People in too many organizations fall into the trap of thinking
that "good" and "satisfactory" ratings equate with substantial
loyalty. (page 40)

Customer satisfaction is a poor predictor of loyalty. To keep them clicking back you need to create a sense of customer delight. (page 43)

Customer loyalty measured in repeat purchases and referrals is the key driver of profitability for online businesses, even more so than for offline companies. . . . (page 47)

CHAPTER 4

Nothing in the history of business has grown with the speed of commerce on the Internet. Nothing. (page 51)

The e-service masters first and foremost have an obsession with their customers. They talk to them, study them, and learn from them. (page 53)

A site designed with the customer and brand uniqueness in mind forms an indelible, lasting impression on the customer psyche. (page 54)

Commerce in Internet space may be frictionless and remote, but it need not—should not be impersonal. (page 54)

People do business with people. Creating a sense of intimacy in the e-world is both possible and important. (page 54)

CHAPTER 5

Specifically, organizations deemed "easy-to-do-business-with" by their customers are distinguished externally by their ease of access, the transparency of their systems, and the reasonableness of their policies and procedures. (page 58)

Every dollar and hour you spend anticipating and removing

barriers to customer access, fulfillment, and support will come back tenfold. (page 59)

◆ Buyers shop online because it's advertised as being faster, cheaper, and more convenient than going to a store or calling a vendor. (page 61)

◆ No matter how attractive your graphics, long downloads annoy shoppers. (page 61)

◆ The Web is where corporate purchasers change their role from order taker to product purchase powerholder. (page 62)

◆ Putting a business online does not mean you can reduce the customer service experience. (page 63)

◆ An increase in the number of options you provide for customer communication will usually decrease the cost per transaction, but not necessarily your total customer service net. (page 63)

◆ Customers are not transactions, they are people who demand respect. If you are too busy to do business with them, surely there will be others who are not. (page 64)

◆ Every time a site makes it impossible to complete an order, especially if time has been spent shopping at the site, the consumer will leave, tell others not to go there, and, of course, mark it off their own list of go-back-to sites. (page 67)

◆ Unless your primary audience is eight year olds, get rid of anything on the site that blinks, spins, or otherwise moves erratically. (page 67)

◆ Recovery is one of the most effective ways to cement loyalty and turn a frustrated shopper into a contented one. (page 68)

◆ Unlike personal consumers, corporate buyers want a personal sales rep who knows their account and is available to help if needed. (page 69)

Your continuing quest should be to seek out ways of making it easier for your customers to do business with you tomorrow than it was for them to do business with you last year, last month, last week, and last night. (page 72)

A commitment to service quality without a commitment to standards and measurement is a dedication to lip service, not e-service. (page 79)

CHAPTER 6

. . . distinctive design is only partly about building an eye-appealing Web site, more importantly it's about building trust and loyalty and creating a unique service experience. (page 96)

Whether or not they buy on the first visit, the visit is branded in their memories, and they will return to experience it again. (page 96)

Brick and mortar companies must learn to translate their distinctive customer experience to the Web and then how to use their e-commerce offering as a means to reinforce that experience throughout the entire business system. (page 100)

If you are a pure dot-com, your Web site is your brand identity. (page 100)

The single biggest gripe about Web sites heard in our retail customer focus groups is that they don't get to the point. (page 105)

The promise of trust must be built into every link, every form, every graphic. (page 108)

Shoppers give their trust to sites that are consistent from the start. (page 112)

Consumers, even the least savvy among us, are annoyed with the little struggles that are part and parcel of doing business online. (115)

CHAPTER 7

On the Web, there is little, if any, such sense of obligation. (page 118)

Someday, someday very soon in fact, technology will allow a Web e-tailer to generate individual custom e-commerce sites for every shopper who happens by, based on the shopper's personal data, shopping history, income bracket, and buying needs. (page 118)

When corporations turn to the Web to buy, it's typically after a relationship with a vendor has already been established. (page 124)

Whether or not consumers are willing to part with their personal data depends largely on the degree of trust and comfort they have with the vendor and whether they believe that providing it will have a significant return on their investment (page 130)

Our prediction: Twenty-four-hour turnaround will soon be the embarrassment of the e-service world, perhaps by the time this book is published! (page 141)

CHAPTER 8

If it's distinctive e-service and repeat business you're after, it's important you give as much attention to this last half of the race as the first. (pages 150–151)

Data indicates e-customers like to be apprised of shipping status. Giving them a do-it-yourself option not only can improve satisfaction levels, it can decrease costly shipping-related phone or e-mail contact with your call center. (page 153)

In your customer's eyes, your chosen shipper's ability to deliver on time reflects more on your organization than theirs. (page 160)

Remember this rule of thumb and you'll likely stand apart in the congested world of e-commerce: Make your process for returning products as easy as the process for buying them. (page 167)

Nothing exasperates e-customers more—and decreases their odds of becoming repeat buyers—as return policies that don't allow return of goods purchased online at a company's brick and mortar sister store just around the corner. (page 168)

Make sure the "frustration factor" of your return authorization process doesn't undo the hard work and dollars you've sunk into drawing customers to your site by making them vow to never again darken your virtual doorway. (page 170)

Nothing can turn a potential life-time customer into a one-hit wonder faster than deluging that individual with promotional e-mail he or she doesn't want. (page 172)

CHAPTER 9

800 numbers are not enough. E-customers expect a wide variety of ways to access human help. (page 184)

Rather than phone contacts to call centers decreasing after new types of Web-based communication tools are introduced, often the calls hold steady or even increase following launch of e-commerce sites. (page 188)

◆ Customers who don't receive the human support they need when they need it . . . are not only less loyal, they're more apt to spread the word about your determined inaccessibility. (page 214)

CHAPTER 10

◆ Amazon.com, Inc., founder Jeff Bezos has long been known as a vocal advocate of the position that e-commerce will, in the long run, rise or fall on the quality of service it provides to customers. (page 219)

◆ Just as it is clear that recovery counts, it is equally clear that e-commerce companies either aren't very good at service recovery or aren't very interested in it. (page 225)

◆ Expectations are the building blocks of all customer transactions; the embodiment of all the customer's wants and needs. (page 228)

◆ Internet customers can't see you working on their behalf. You have to tell them you are trying to solve their problems or answer their query if you are to get psychological credit from the customer for your efforts. (page 229)

◆ When trust has been challenged or threatened, the bridge to recovery starts with the most fundamental component of being human . . . a pure, genuine, and considerate link. (page 231)

◆ "Planned Process" means all the things you do to make it easy for your customers to complain to and communicate with you and for your people to solve problems and dialogue with your information-hungry customers. (page 239)

CHAPTER 11

. . . as more e-businesses move into adulthood, they've begun to see the folly of strategies that are all-consuming in their pursuit of new customers—that strive to continually refill the cupboards—at the expense of efforts to keep more of the same customers around for the long haul. (page 242)

The longer you keep a customer coming back, the more profitable that customer is to your business. (page 242)

Retention isn't just a result of a user-friendly Web site. It is a function of getting service right the first time on the back end of the purchasing cycle or order fulfillment. (page 247)

Reliable order delivery isn't a given in e-business, and developing expertise in that area provides another chance for you to stand apart from the competition. (page 247)

Planning for retention means understanding all the variables and dynamics that keep customers coming back and those that send them packing. (page 258)

If you only communicate with a customer when one of you needs something, the account is continually at-risk. (page 259)

CHAPTER 13

The most amazing thing about the Internet is that the most of the changes it makes in our lives are still to come. (page 292)

The Web is going to dramatically change the way we live, think, and buy—as businesspeople and as consumers. (page 292)

◆ We live in the most inventive, creative age since the onset of the industrial revolution. (page 303)

◆ The next great Internet idea is only as far away as the imagination—and a little funding—can see. (page 303)

NOTES

CHAPTER 1

1. This historical event occurred in Holland in 1637 when there was a tremendous shortage of tulips. Tulips became such a hot commodity that people were willing to pay upwards of fifteen dollars per bulb. Approximately six weeks later, a huge surplus of bulbs resulted, with prices falling drastically; never to recover.

2. "The Demise of Dot-Com Retailers," a study conducted by Forrester Research, Cambridge, Massachusetts, April 2000.

3. "Driving Sales with Service," a study conducted by Forrester Research, Cambridge, Massachusetts, November 1999.

4. Sunnyvale, California-based eGain conducted a survey of 500 individuals at a series of Internet-focused trade shows, November 1999.

5. "Shopping the Internet Circa 1999: The Good, the Bad, and the Ugly," a study conducted by Minneapolis, Minnesota–based Performance Research Associates, Inc., February 2000.

6. "Benchmarking Study of Electronic Customer Service," a study by ICSA/ e-Satisfy.com, March 2000.

7. Andersen Consulting is a research consulting firm based in Boston, Massachusetts. The Web site address is www.andersenconsulting.com.

8. BizRate.com based in Los Angeles, California, is an evaluator of e-business sites. Their Web site address is www.bizrate.com

9. Gina Amperato, "Chat Room—New Headspace," *Net Company*, 002, Winter (Suppl. to *Fast Company*), page 80.

CHAPTER 3

1. Walid Mougayar, "Stock Shoppers Beware," *Business* 2.0, February 24, 2000.

2. "Retailing Survey," by Bain & Company/Mainspring, Boston, Massachusetts, December 1999.

CHAPTER 5

1. Sam Zuckerman, *San Francisco Chronicle*, April 29, 2000.

2. "The Need for Speed," an industry report by Zona Research, Inc., Redwood City, California, June 1999.

3. "BenchMarking Study of Electronic Customer Service," a study by ICSA/e-Satisfy.com, March 2000.

4. BizRate.com based in Los Angeles, California, is an evaluator of e-business sites. Their Web site address is www.bizrate.com.

5. Andersen Consulting is a research consulting firm based out of Boston, Massachusetts. Their Web site address is www.andersenconsulting.com.

6. "Shopping the Internet Circa 1999: The Good, the Bad, and the Ugly," a study conducted by Minneapolis, Minnesota–based Performance Research Associates, Inc., February 2000.

7. Karen Thomas, "Some E-Gifts Will Be Too Late," USA *Today*, December 23, 1999.

8. "Benchmarking Study of Electronic Customer Service," a study by ICSA/e-Satisfy.com., March 2000.

9. CIO *Magazine*, (Special Advertising Supplement) April 16, 2000.

10. International Data Corporation is a research firm based in Framingham, Massachusetts.

CHAPTER 6

1. Karen Thomas, "Some E-Gifts Will Be Too Late," USA *Today*, December 23, 1999.

2. "Shopping the Internet Circa 1999: The Good, the Bad, and the Ugly," a study conducted by Minneapolis–based Performance Research Associates, Inc., February 2000.

3. "Online Retailing Survey," by Bain & Company/Mainspring, Boston, Massachusetts, December 1999.

4. "The State of Online Retailing," Boston Consulting Group, Boston, Massachusetts, July 1999, page 19.

5. "e-Commerce Trust Study," a joint research project conducted by Baskin Research and Studio Archetype/Sapient, January 1999, Redwood Shores, California, and Cambridge, Massachusetts.

6. Ibid.

7. Ibid.

8. Ibid.

9. A few years ago, when Web shopping was a new and daring venture, the common wisdom was that land-based companies had a harder time building consumer trust than "pure virtual" companies thanks to the baggage they carried with them onto the Web. Today, as more and more potential buyers come to the Internet, there appears to be a 180-degree shift in that prevailing attitude.

10. International Data Corporation is a research firm based in Framingham, Massachusetts.

CHAPTER 7

1. "Driving Traffic to Your Web Site," a study conducted by Forrester Research, Cambridge, Massachusetts, November 1999.

2. The Aberdeen Group, based in Boston, Massachusetts, is an IT consulting and market research firm. Their Web site address is www.aberdeen.com.

3. Cookies are short pieces of data used by Web servers to help identify Web users. Cookies can also be used to customize pages for consumers based on information the customer has volunteered on previous visits to the Web site; name, address, and product preferences are among the information bits typically stored on a single consumer.

4. "Driving Traffic to Your Web Site," a study conducted by Forrester Research, Cambridge, Massachusetts, November 1999.

5. "Internet Customer Care: A SOCAP Study," prepared by Yankelovich Partners, May 2000.

6. In November 1998, a single surveyor employed by Brightware, Inc., visited the Fortune 100 Web sites based on the corporate Web site addresses listed at www.fortune.com.

7. In November 1998, Jupiter Communication, based in New York City, e-mailed questions to 125 major Web sites.

8. George Anders, "At Your Service," *Wall Street Journal*, April 17, 2000, page R12.

9. A study by C. Aldrich, " The Three E-Learning Rules that Will Bury Training," a Gartner Group Commentary, Cambridge, Massachusetts, December 1999.

CHAPTER 8

1. Andersen Consulting is a research consulting firm based out of Boston, Massachusetts. Their Web site is www.andersenconsulting.com.

2. PriceWaterhouseCoopers surveyed 500 online shoppers in December 1999. Results were published in a January 24, 2000 news release entitled, "Convenience is King: Ease of Use and Accuracy—Not Price—Dictated Consumers' 1999 Holiday Shopping Behavior."

3. "Shopping the Internet Circa 1999: The Good, the Bad, and the Ugly," a study conducted by Minneapolis, Minnesota–based Performance Research Associates, Inc., February 2000.

4. "Driving Traffic to Your Web Site," a study conducted by Forrester Research, Cambridge, Massachusetts, November 1999.

5. "The State of Online Retailing," a study conducted by Boston Consulting Group, Boston, Massachusetts, July 1999.

6. "The State of Online Retailing, a study conducted by Boston Consulting Group, Boston, Massachusetts, July 1999.

7. *The McKinsey Quarterly*, 2 2000, pages 32–41.

8. Jodi Mardesich, "The Web Is No Shopper's Paradise," *Fortune*, November 8, 1999, page 188.

CHAPTER 9

1."Internet Customer Care: A SOCAP Study," prepared by Yankelovich Partners, May 2000.

2. "BenchMarking Study of Electronic Customer Service," a study by ICSA/e-Satisfy.com, March 2000.

3. *The Bloomberg News*, March 26, 2000.

4. "Driving Traffic to Your Web Site," a study conducted by Forrester Research, Cambridge, Massachusetts, November, 1999.

5. Matt Hicks,"Call Centers 2.0" PC *Week Online*, March 13, 2000.

6. "BenchMarking Study of Electronic Customer Service," a study by ICSA/e-Satisfy.com, March 2000.

7. "The State of Online Retailing," Boston Consulting Group, Boston, Massachusetts, July, 1999.

8. "BenchMarking Study of Electronic Customer Service," a study by ICSA/e-Satisfy.com, March 2000.

9. George Anders, "At Your Service," *Wall Street Journal*, April 17, 2000, page R 12.

10. "BenchMarking Study of Electronic Customer Service," a study by ICSA/e-Satisfy.com, March 2000.

11."Internet Customer Care: A SOCAP Study," prepared by Yankelovich Partners, May 2000.

12. "BenchMarking Study of Electronic Customer Service," a study by ICSA/e-Satisfy.com, March 2000.

13."Shopping the Internet Circa 1999: The Good, the Bad, and the Ugly," a study conducted by Minneapolis, Minnesota–based Performance Research Associates, Inc., February 2000.

14. "Web-Integrated Call Centers: Filling Up the Shopping Cart," by Datamonitor, November 1999, www.datamonitor.com.

15. Louis Trager, "E-tailers Display Customer Service Tools," *Inter@ctive Week*, March 23, 2000, page 26.

16. "BenchMarking Study of Electronic Customer Service," a study by ICSA/e-Satisfy.com, March 2000.

CHAPTER 10

1. Our "Shopping the Internet Circa 1999: the Good, the Bad, and the Ugly" study found customers somewhat less likely to do a return or demand their money back from an online merchant than from a brick and mortar merchant. When probed, the rationale was, "I knew it was a risk." It is an attitude that doesn't bode well for online merchants.

2. John Goodman, "Don't Fix the Product, Fix the Customer," *Quality Review*, Fall 1988, pages 8–11.

3. "Internet Customer Care: A SOCAP Study," prepared by Yankelovich Partners, May 2000.

4. Edward Baig, "Appreciating the Value of a Fine Whine," USA *Today*, April 26, 2000, page 3D.

5. Oddly enough 37 percent of company "hate board" visitors believe the postings on the site had a positive influence on their buying decision. Go figure!

6. Frederick Reichheld and W. Earl Sasser, "Zero Defections: Quality Comes to Services," *Harvard Business Review*, September-October 1990, page 105.

7. "Resource E-Commerce Watch," a study by Resource Marketing, Columbus, Ohio, January 2000.

8. "Customer Service E-Mail Response Time," a Web survey conducted by New York–based Jupiter Communications, March 1999.

9. "BenchMarking Study of Electronic Customer Service," a study by ICSA/e-Satisfy.com, March 2000.

10. "The State of Online Retailing," a study by Boston Consulting Group, Boston, Massachusetts, July 1999.

11. "BenchMarking Study of Electronic Customer Service," a study by ICSA/e-Satisfy.com, March 2000.

12. Leonard Berry, Valarie Zeithaml, and A. Parasuraman, "Five Imperatives for Improving Service Quality," *Sloan Management Review*, Summer 1990, pages 29–38.

13. Kathleen Seiders and Leonard Berry, "Service Fairness: What It Is and Why It Matters," *Academy of Management Executive*, 12(2) 1998, pages 8–20.

14. George Anders, "At Your Service," *Wall Street Journal*, April 17, 2000, page R12.

CHAPTER 11

1. Frederick Reichheld and W. Earl Sasser, "Zero Defections: Quality Comes to Services," *Harvard Business Review*, September-October 1990, pages 105–111.

2. "The State of Online Retailing," Boston Consulting Group, Boston, Massachusetts, July 1999.

3. "Online Retailing Survey," by Bain & Company/Mainspring, Boston, Massachusetts, December 1999.

4. "The State of Online Retailing," a study by Boston Consulting Group, Boston, Massachusetts, July 1999.

5. "Shopping the Internet Circa 1999: The Good, the Bad, and the Ugly," a study conducted by Minneapolis, Minnesota–based Performance Research Associates, Inc., February 2000.

6. Ron Zemke and Chip R. Bell, *Knock Your Socks Off Service Recovery*, New York: AMACOM Books, 2000. Based on models created by Dr. Jeff McLeod of ParaMetrica, Inc., Woodbury, Minnesota.

7. Frederick Reichheld and W. Earl Sasser, "Zero Defections: Quality Comes to Services," *Harvard Business Review*, September-October 1990, pages 105–111.

8. *Wall Street Journal*, May 4, 2000.

ADDITIONAL
RESOURCES

Amor, Daniel. *The E-Business® Evolution: Living and Working in an Interconnected World*. Saddle River, NJ: Prentice Hall, 2000.

Anderson, Kristin, and Ron Zemke. *Delivering Knock Your Socks Off Service, 2nd Edition*. New York: AMACOM, 1997

Aspatore, Jonathan R. *Digital Rush: Nine Internet Start-Ups in the Race for Dot-Com Riches*. New York: AMACOM, 2001.

Bell, Chip R., and Ron Zemke. *Managing Knock Your Socks Off Service*. New York: AMACOM, 1992.

Brand, Stewart. *The Media Lab: Inventing the Future at M.I.T.* New York: Penguin Books, 1987.

Christensen, Clayton M. *The Innovator's Dilemma: When New Technologies Cause Great Firms to Fail*. Boston: HBS Press, 1997.

Clark, Peter, and Stephen Neill. *Net Value: Valuing Dot-Com Companies—Uncovering the Reality Behind the Hype.* New York: AMACOM, 2001.

Connellan, Thomas K. *Inside the Magic Kingdom: Seven Keys to Disney's Success.* Austin, TX: Bard Press, 1997.

Connellan, Thomas K., and Ron Zemke. *Sustaining Knock Your Socks Off Service.* New York: AMACOM, 1993.

Dell, Michael. *Direct from Dell: Strategies that Revolutionized an Industry.* New York: HarperCollins, 1999

Focazio, Martin T. *The E-Factor: Building a 24/7, Customer-Centric, Electronic Business for the Internet Age.* New York: AMACOM, 2001.

Gutzman, Alexis D. *The E-Commerce Arsenal: 12 Technologies You Need to Prevail in the Digital Arena.* New York: AMACOM, 2001.

Holtz, Shel. *Public Relations on The Net: Winning Strategies to Inform and Influence the Media, the Investment Community, the Government, the Public, and More!* New York: AMACOM, 1999.

Levine, Rick, Christophe Locke, Doc Searls, and David Weinberger. *The Cluetrain Manifesto.* Cambridge, MA: Perseus Books, 1999.

Maddox, Kate, and Dana Blankenhorn. *Web Commerce: Building a Digital Business.* New York: John Wiley & Sons, Inc., 1997.

Martin, Chuck. *Net Future: The 7 Cybertrends that Will Drive Your Business, Create New Wealth, and Define Your Future.* New York: McGraw-Hill, 1999.

Newell, Frederick. *Loyalty.com: Customer Relationship Management in the New Era of Internet Marketing.* New York, McGraw-Hill, 2000.

Rosenoer, Jonathan, Douglas Armstrong, and J. Russell Gastes. *The Clickable Corporation: Successful Strategies for Capturing the Internet Advantage.* New York: The Free Press, 1999.

Schwartz, Evan I. *Digital Darwinism: 7 Breakthrough Business Strategies for Surviving in the Cutthroat Web Economy.* New York: Broadway Books, 1999.

Seybold, Patricia B. *Customers.com: How to Create a Profitable Business Strategy for the Internet and Beyond.* New York: Times Business, 1998.

Southwick, Karen. *Silicon Gold Rush: The Next Generation of High-Tech Stars Rewrites the Rules of Business.* New York: John Wiley & Sons, Inc., 1999.

Spector, Robert. *AMAZON.com: Get Big Fast.* New York: HarperBusiness, 2000.

Sterne, Jim. *Customer Service on the Internet: Building Relationships, Increasing Loyalty, and Staying Competitive.* New York: John Wiley & Sons, Inc., 1996.

Sterne, Jim. *Advertising on the Web: What Makes People Click.* Indianapolis: Que Corporation, 1997.

Sterne, Jim. *World Wide Web Marketing: Integrating the Internet into Your Marketing Strategy.* New York: John Wiley & Sons, Inc., 1995.

Vandermerwe, Sandra. *Customer Capitalism: Increasing Returns in New Market Space.* London: Nicholas Brealey Publishing, 1999.

Woods, John, and Ron Zemke. *Best Practices in Customer Service.* New York: AMACOM 1998.

Zemke, Ron, and Chip R. Bell. *Knock Your Socks Off Service Recovery.* New York: AMACOM, 2000.

I N D E X

Note: page number followed by *f* indicates a figure.

Aboud, John, 52
accessibility
    customer friendly, 77
    of shopping cart, 62
    on Web site, 61, 104–106
accuracy of information, 77
advertising messages, 15, 190
advisory panels, 89, 90–91
advocate customers, 31–32,
    44–46, 223
Allen, Penne, Dell Computer, 155,
    174, 209
allergies, Gazoontite.com, 24, 26

Amazon.com
    automated acknowledgment,
        194–195
    check-out process, 66
    customer recovery, 17, 239–240
    customer trust, 111, 113
    distribution centers, 164–165
    download time, 20
    e-mail responses, 76, 137
    employee skills, 198
    quality of service, 218–219
    recommended lists, 122
    return policies, 169

service representatives, 59, 79
Web-based sales, 4
American Express, 111
America Online (AOL), 4, 176
Andersen Consulting, 16, 66–67, 157
antiqueguns.com, 194
Appelbaum, Kevin, 165
ArchieMcPhee.com, 106
Ask Jeeves, 210–211
asthma, Gazoontite.com, 24, 26
at-risk customers
    experience grid, 29–32
    retention strategy, 255–257
    satisfaction of, 40, 44–45
automation
    call distributors, 185
    e-mail acknowledgment, 193
    telephone contact, 187
Avon.com, 122

backorder notices, 156
Bain & Company/Mainspring
    customer loyalty, 47, 243–244
    retention strategy, 247, 261
Barnes and Noble.com, 112, 165
Bass, Bill, LandsEnd.com, 142
BBBonline, 111
Beauty.com, 130
benchmarking, 92–93
Bezos, Jeff, 61, 219
bill payment, electronic, 166–167
BizRate.com, 16, 66
Blockbuster Video, 111
Bluefly.com, 165
Borders, customer trust, 111
Boston Consulting Group
    automated response, 195–196
    customer recovery, 227

outsourcing, 162
    retention strategy, 243, 246
Branders.com, 42, 252–253
brand identity, 97–101, 110
Brightware, Inc. 133
browsing vs. buying, 109
bulletin boards
    complaints, 224
    REI.com, 147
    self-service tools, 211–212
business-to-business (B2B), 3–4
    customer contact, 185–189
    customized service, 68–69, 106,
        119, 122, 124–128
    data sharing, 254–255
    differentiation, 9
    e-mail order reminders, 69
    ETDBW site, 68–70
    extranets, 174
    order confirmation, 152
    reorder options, 69
    sales reps, 69
    self-service policies, 69–70
business-to-consumer (B2C), 3–4
    check-out process, 66–67
    differentiation, 9

callback systems, 203–205
call centers, Web-enabling, 185
Cameraworld.com
    automated acknowledgment,
        194
    back-end expertise, 158–159
    employee skills, 200
    incentives, 250
    order confirmation, 154
    self-service, 210

Cancerfacts.com, 90–91
Carlson Marketing Group, 249
CarsDirect.com, 4
Case, Steve, 61
catalogs, 47–48, 113–115
CDNow.com, 113
Cheskin Research and Studio
    Archetype/Sapient, 109,
    110–111
Chubb Organization self-service,
    69–70
Cisco systems, 4
Clinique.com
    Color Consultation, 123
    Express Shopping, 105
    LooksMaker tool, 114, 141
    navigation ease, 65
    Personal Color Consultation,
        141
    shopping cart accessibility, 62
cobrowsing, 203–205
Coca-Cola, 41
Colonel Sanders, 61
Colton, Michael, 52
community centers, 146–148
competition, 19–33
    customer experience grid,
        27–33, 28f
    impressionistic expectations,
        20–22
    online vs. offline, 23–27
    site-to-site comparisons, 22–23
complaints, 223–226
CompUSA, online vs. offline
    comparison, 25–26
confidential information, 108–110
consultants, 78

contact information, 63–64
conversion rates, 244
cookies, 128–129
Coopersnuthouse.com, 79
CornerHardware.com, 124,
    140–141, 144–145
corporate buyers, see business-to-
    business (B2B)
costs of corporate orders, 125–126
Crawford, Andy, 6–7
credit applications, 166
customers
    acquisition of, 10–11
    advisory panels, 89
    advocacy groups, 223
    communication with, 63
    download time, 20
    ETDBW thinking, see easy-to-do-
        business with
    experience grid, 27–33, 28f
    feedback from, 175–176
    life-time value of, 40–41
    loyalty of, see loyalty of
        customers
    online service, 14–16, 23–27
    perception of delivery time,
        80–81
    pleasing of, 51–56
    queries, 59, 64
    recovery of, 228–240
    site-to-site comparisons,
        20–22
    surveys, 87
    user groups, 89
customer service representatives,
    see service representatives
Cybermanagement Inc., 39

DeChambeau, Mark, 154, 163–164, 170, 199
delivery systems, 149–180
  accessibility to, 152–156
  back-end expertise, 158–159
  competitors, 10
  complaints, 157f
  customer feedback, 175–176
  efficiency, 158–161
  employee roles, 72–74
  free shipping, 165–166
  guarantees, 16, 67
  innovations, 85–86
  online bill payment, 166–167
  order confirmation, 151–152, 153f
  outsourcing, 162–165
  permission marketing, 171–172
  problem solving, 77–79
  product delivery chains, 156–157
  quality measurement, 81–84
  reliability, 22, 110
  return policies, 167–171
  self-help areas, 172–175, 177–180
  visibility of, 71–72
Dell, Michael, 61
Dell.com
  customer needs, 17
  extranets, 175
  online vs. offline comparison, 25–26
  system service tag, 173–174
Dell Computer
  Customer Experience Council, 32

customer trust, 111
education of customer, 123
natural language search engine, 53, 211
online training, 143, 145
order confirmation, 154–155
self-help options, 173
service code, 119
design of Web page, 95–115
  accessibility, 61, 104–106
  brand identity, 97–101
  business-to-consumer space, 66–67
  confidential information, 108–110
  contact options, 63–64
  delivery of products, 67
  download speed, 61–62
  e-mail answers, 64
  emotional factor, 101–103
  hyperlog vs. cyberstore, 113–115
  navigation of, 64–65
  prices, 65
  registration process, 65
  return of items, 66
  search options, 62–63
  shipping costs, 65–66
  shopping cart accessibility, 62
  simplification, 62
  splash page, 67
  time considerations, 61, 64
  trustworthiness, 106–108, 110–113
Disney, Walt, 61
DisneyStore.com, 136

distribution centers, 159, 161, 164–165
Doubletree Inn, 84–85
download times, 13, 20, 61–62, 105
DrugEmporium.com, 211
Dutch tulip mania, 5

eAdvocate, customer loyalty, 42
Eastman Chemical Co., 167
easy-to-do-business with (EDTBW), 54, 57–93
  business-to-business rules, 68–70
  changes, 78–79
  customer focus, 79–84
  delivery, 70–71
  design basics, 60–68
  employees, 58–59, 72–74
  human factor, 74
  information sources, 86–93
  innovations, 85–86
  law of rules, 74–77
  service factors, 71–72, 245
  service representatives, 59
  system solutions, 77–78
Ebay.com, 4, 52, 79
E-buyersguide.com, 130
EddieBauer.com, 204
education of customers
  free training, 143–146
  online vs. offline comparison, 24
  permission marketing, 171–172
  self-service tool, 208–210
E-Gain service analysis, 12
e-mail
  answering customers, 63–64
  automated responses, 134–135, 193
  company answers, 13, 14
  order reminders, 69
  personalization of, 76, 132–138
  routing and prioritization, 196
  vs. telephone, 177–180, 184–186
emotional factors, 101–103, 230–232
employees
  accessibility, 63
  accommodation to, 58–59
  surveillance of, 83–84, 87–88
  surveys, 89
  telephone skills, 197–200
Ernst and Young online inquiries, 153
e-Satisfy.com
  customer loyalty, 220–222
  human support, 214
  measurements, 86
  online service, 14, 189
e-service improvement lessons, 263–269
  CSR empowerment, 268–269
  design of site, 270–273
  e-mail system, 274–276
  end-to-end service, 278–279
  ETDBW quotient, 266–267
  FAQs, 280–282
  human factors, 276–277
  personalization, 273–276
  recovery, 282–284
  research competition, 265–266
  retention of customers, 285–287
eToys.com, 98

E-Trade Group, 59–60
Excite, customer trust, 111
experience grid, 27–33, 28*f*
extranets, 174

FactoryOutlook, 35–36, 37*f*
fairness failures, 237–238
FAQs (frequently asked questions)
    automated response, 196
    customer loss, 14
    vs. e-mail response, 132
    personalization, 114
    quality measurement, 83
    self-service tool, 208–210
Fast Company, 16–17
Federal Express
    delivery systems, 161, 232
    online vs. offline comparison,
        26, 27
    order confirmation, 152, 153*f*
Federal Trade Commission, 226
feedback, 76, 175–176
Fidelity Investments, 59–60
Fields, Debbie, 61
FindMRO.com, 121
Fingerhut.com, 162, 251
focus groups, 87, 109, 156
Focus Health, 41
Fogdog.com
    customer needs, 17
    e-mail responses, 136, 194
    employee skills, 200
    product differentiation, 9
    Search Squad, 214–216
    self-service, 210
    telephone contact, 188

Forrester Research, 11, 187
forums, customer, 211–212
Fredricks.com, 122
future of Internet, 291–303

Gap.com, 17, 112
Garden.com, 17, 260
Gates, Bill, 61
Gateway Computers, 205–206
Gazoontite.com, 21, 24, 26
General Electric, 6
General Motors, 40
glossaries, 208–210
Godiva.com
    check-out process, 66
    customer service, 99–100
    delivery system, 73
    registration offerings, 131
    Web page ambiance, 95–97, 98
Goodman, John, 220
Grasee, Mike, 127–128
Great Plains Software, 177–180,
    199
Guerra, Mike, 188, 194, 215

Harrah's Entertainment, 257–258
Herman Miller.com, 155, 169
Hewlett Packard customer forum,
    212
Hilton, Conrad, 61
Hilton Hotel incentives, 251
"Hockey-stick" loyalty, 35–50
Holiday Inn incentives, 251
HomeGrocer.com, 262
home improvement online
    service, 144–145
HoneyBaked.com, 62, 65

hotlines, toll-free, 91–92
how-to guides, 124
human contact, 181–216
    chat technology, 203–205
    customer contact, 183f
    customer retention, 183–186
    800 numbers, 186–189
    employee skills, 197–201
    in ETDBW delivery, 74
    expectations of, 190–193
    information to customers,
        193–196
    in-store experience, 205–207
    self-service options, 207–214
    Web and customer time,
        201–203
hyperlog vs. cyberstore, 113–115

ICSA/e-Satisfy.com study
    Benchmarking, 64, 68
    customer contact, 185, 189, 196
    customer loyalty, 222, 226
    employee skills, 199
    time factors, 201
Illuminations.com, 63, 101–102
incentives, 249–251
Influent.com, 63
information sources, 86–93
    accuracy of, 77
    advisory panels, 89
    benchmarking, 92–93
    customer surveys, 87, 89
    employee visit teams, 87–88
    focus groups, 87
    integration of, 77
    shopping services, 89–90
    toll-free hotlines, 91–92

user groups, 89
viewing room studies, 88–89
Infoseek, 111
in-house management, 74–77
in-store test drives, 205–207
instructions, customer loss, 14
International Customer Service
    Association (ICSA), 214
International Data Corporation,
    105
Internet
    predictions of, 291–303
    procurement companies,
        126–127
    stocks, lack of profit, 5
    time factors, 201–203
Internet Explorer, 111
Intuit text chat, 204
inventory, 150, 156, 159
invoices, 166–167
Ivillage.com, 131, 260

Jobs, Steve, 61
Jupiter Communications, 226
justclick delivery system, 161

Kinko's Copy Centers, 75
Kozmo.com, 161

LandsEnd.com
    comparison with other
        companies, 21
    customer needs, 17
    emotional factors, 103
    hyperlog, 114
    Saturn logo, 106, 127–128

Shop with a Friend, 142
text chat, 204
Web page ambiance, 96–97
Your Personal Model, 103, 123, 142
Levitt, Theodore, 76
LillianVernon.com, 61
  alternative sources, 76
  customer information, 130
  e-mail responses, 137
  organization of pages, 106
  personalized response, 195
Lind, Jennifer, 160
L.L. Bean, 26, 27
loyalty of customers
  at-risk customers, 31
  "hockey-stick," 35–50
  marketing programs, 248
  recovery of, 220–221
  service expectations, 15
Luminant Worldwide, 13, 218
Lure.com, 21
Lycos, 111

Magic Kingdom, 24
Mahran, Howard, 90
maintenance, repair, and
  operations (MRO) market, 120–121
Marriott Hotel, 24
McLaughlin, Jerry, 252–253
measurements, customer-
  focused, 79–84
Mezin, Danna, 42
Modern Humorist, 52
Mougayar, Walid, 39

National Consumer Advisory
  Council, 90
National Consumer's League, 225
navigation of Web
  ease of, 64–65, 104–106, 110
  logic, and customer loss, 14
Netscape, 4, 111
no-charge extras, 84–85
Nordstrom, 24
Northern Light, 210–211
Northwest Airlines (NWA.com), 171

OfficeClick.com, 23
OfficeDepot.com, 154, 166, 211
OmahaSteaks.com
  e-mail answers, 22, 202
  incentives, 251
  no-charge extras, 85
  promotional messages, 172
  retention strategy, 245
  service strategy, 75
  telephone contact, 187–188, 192
Omidyar, Pierre, 52
online vs. offline transactions, 23–27
orders
  confirmation of, 151–152
  forms, customer loss, 14
  fulfillment of, 247
outsourcing, 162–165

Parr, Barry, 105
passengerrights.com, 223
Paulson, Ron, 121

Payless.com, 166
permission marketing, 171–172
Personal Access Device (PAD),
    292–302
personalization, 117–148
    B2B buyers, 119, 122, 124–128
    communities, 146–148
    customer service
        representatives, 138–141
    customized service, 120–123
    education of customers,
        123–124
    e-mail, 132–138
    free training, 143–146
    registration, 129–132
    service codes, 119
    specialty tools, 141–143
    welcome messages, 128–129
Polaroid, 221
prices
    comparison shopping, 65
    differentiation of, 10–11
    in repurchase decisions,
        247–248
    searches, 63
principles of e-masters, 53–55
    delivery of service, 54
    design of site, 54
    easy-to-do-business with
        (EDTBW), 54
    human contact, 54
    personalization, 54
    recovery, 55
    retention strategy, 55
probability of return, 49–50, 50f
problem notification, 150

Procter & Gamble, 254
product differentiation, 9–10
profile building features, 23
Proflowers.com, 131
promotional messages, 172
psychological recovery, 234–236

Rampage.com, 204
Rayport, Jeffrey, 16–17
recovery from problems, 217–240
    assurance, 229–230
    basics of, 220–225, 221f
    benchmarks of, 218–219
    customer expectations, 228–234
    empathy, 230–232
    fairness failures, 237–238
    high-quality service, 228–240
    partnership, 236–237
    as planned process, 238–240
    psychological factors, 234–236
    reliability, 229
    responsiveness, 232–233
    state of the art, 225–227
    tangibles, 233–234
registration process, 65, 129–132
Reichheld, Frederick, 224–225,
    242, 261
REI.com
    bulletin boards, 147
    customer needs, 17
    delivery service, 160
    e-mail categories, 203
    emotional factors, 102
    employee skills, 200
    incentives, 250
    Learn and Share section, 124

price searches, 63
retention of customers, 260
self-service, 210
service hours, 191
reliability, 229
repeat business, 37, 47–49, 69
replenishment programs, 261–262
repurchase decisions, 247–248
Resource Marketing, 168, 226
retention strategy, 241–262
   at-risk customers, 255–257
   core customers, 257–258
   data sharing, 254–255
   formative visits, 246–247
   incentives, 249–251
   loyalty marketing, 248
   planning of, 242–244, 258, 262,
     243f
   price role, 247–248
   service factors, 245
Return Authorization numbers,
   169–170
return policies, 167–171
   customer loss, 14, 16
   problem notification, 150
   quality of service, 218–219
   simplicity of, 66, 82
Roxy.com, 188

sales representatives, 69
Samuelson, Michael, 91
Sasser, W. Earl, 224–225, 242, 261
Saturn, and Lands'End, 106,
   127–128
Schwab and Company
   customer contact, 185–186
   ETDBW viewpoint, 59–60

face-to-face contact, 206–207
seal of approval, 111
search engines
   customer loss, 14
   natural language, 53, 210–211
   options of, 62–63
Seattle Exposition of 1909, 2
security factors, 104–106
self-service
   bulletin boards and forums,
     211–212
   cost factors, 207
   FAQs, glossaries, and
     educational articles, 208–210
   limits of, 212–214
   natural language search
     engines, 210–211
   postsale, 172–175
service code, Dell computer, 119
service representatives, 73,
   138–140
   Amazon.com, 59
   marketing of, 140–141
   quality of service, 218–219
shipping, 152–156
shipping costs, 65–66, 82
   registration forms, 129–132
   waiver of, 165–166
shopping carts
   abandonment of, 12–13
   accessibility of, 62
   at-risk customers, 29–31
shopping services, 89–91
site-to-site comparisons, 20–23
SmarterKids.com
   customer needs, 17
   employee skills, 198–199

incentives, 249
order confirmation, 154
outsourcing, 163
return policies, 170
text chat, 204
SOCAP/Yankelovich study
    customer contact, 182, 183*f*
    customer loyalty, 222, 224
    e-mail service, 133, 134
    time factors, 201
Sony Corporation complaint
    boards, 224
speed of Web site, 104–106
splash page, 67
Staples.com, 69
storefronts, 113, 168
Streamline.com, 161
Sundheim, Doug, 13, 218–219
surveys
    of customers, 87
    of employees, 89
    real-time, 175–176

Takata, Rich, 141, 144–145
tangibles, customer recovery,
    233–234
technical quality vs. customer
    quality, 81–82
technology stocks, 5
telephone
    vs. e-mail, 177–180
    800 numbers, 186–189
    employee skills, 197–200
    text chat, 184, 203–205
    TheOnion.com, 52
third-party complaint resolution,
    163–164, 170, 223

3 Com Corp., 123
ticket ordering, 23
time factors
    customer expectations,
        190–193, 201–203
    customer-friendly, 78
    on Web site, 61
tools, personalized, 141–143
ToysRus.com
    brand identity, 98
    delivery problems, 67, 238
    download time, 20
Travelocity.com, 23
TroutRiver.com, 79, 231–232, 237
trustworthiness, 106–108, 110–113
Twain, Mark, 7

Uniglobe.com, 189
United Parcel Service (UPS), 161,
    167
USA *Today*, 111
user groups, 89, 90–91
U.S. Postal Service (USPS), 161, 170

Veno, Dale, 42
venture capitalists, 4
verification processes, 68–69
viewing room studies, 88–89
Villagehatshop.com, 147
Visa seal of approval, 111

Wal-Mart
    customer trust, 111
    data sharing, 254
    market share, 6
    outsourcing, 162
    warehouses, 156–159, 161

Web sites, 226
    design of, *see* design of Web
      page
Webvan.com, 4, 161, 262
welcome messages, 128–129
word of mouth, 223
writing skills, of employees,
    197–200

W.W. Grainger Inc., 120–121

Yahoo! customer trust, 111

Zingermans.com, 20
Zona Research, 61–62
Zuckerman, Sam, 59–60

ABOUT THE AUTHORS

Ron Zemke is a management consultant and researcher who has become one of the best-known and most widely quoted authorities on the continuing service revolution. As senior editor of TRAINING magazine and a syndicated columnist, he has covered the emergence and development of the global service economy. Ron has authored or coauthored twenty-seven books, including the eight-book **Knock Your Socks Off Service** series and **Generations At Work,** which was selected as one of the thirty best business books of 2000 by Soundview Executive Book Summaries. In 1994 he was given the MOBIUS award by the Society of Consumer Affairs Professionals, and in 1995 was named one of the New Quality Gurus by *Quality Digest Magazine.*

Ron travels the globe sharing with organizations around the world the importance of developing strong relationships with customers and the long-term value and impact retaining those customer relationships can have to the bottom-line.

Tom Connellan is a senior principal with Performance Research Associates and manages offices in Orlando Florida, and Ann Arbor, Michigan. He is a leading authority on creating exceptional customer experiences. The author of five books and numerous articles, including the best-selling, **Inside the Magic Kingdom, Seven Keys to Disney's Success** (Bard Press, 1997), he is regularly quoted in publications such as U.S. *News & World Report*, the *New York Times*, and *Boardroom Reports*.

He is a speaker, trainer, and consultant with such clients as, the National Association of Wholesaler/Distributors, the Young President's Organization, and a number of other trade and professional associations. His corporate clients include such leaders as GE, Motorola, Dell Computer, IBM, Neiman-Marcus, Glaxo Wellcome, Bayer, The Body Shoppe, Merrill Lynch, and Prudential Securities. An early-stage technology investor, Tom is on the advisory board of several e-commerce firms.

Performance Research Associates is one of North America's premier customer relationship management consulting firms, specializing in helping organizations develop a customer-centric perspective. Performance Research Associates has offices in Minneapolis, Dallas, Ann Arbor, and Orlando, providing speaking, training and consulting services to clients in North America, Europe, South America, and along the Pacific Rim. The **Knock Your Socks Off Service** series draws on the experience and work of the partners of Performance Research Associates. Readers interested in information about keynote presentations, training, consulting, or other Performance Research Associates services may contact the firm's Minneapolis office at (800) 359-2576 or e-mail them at pra@socksoff.com.